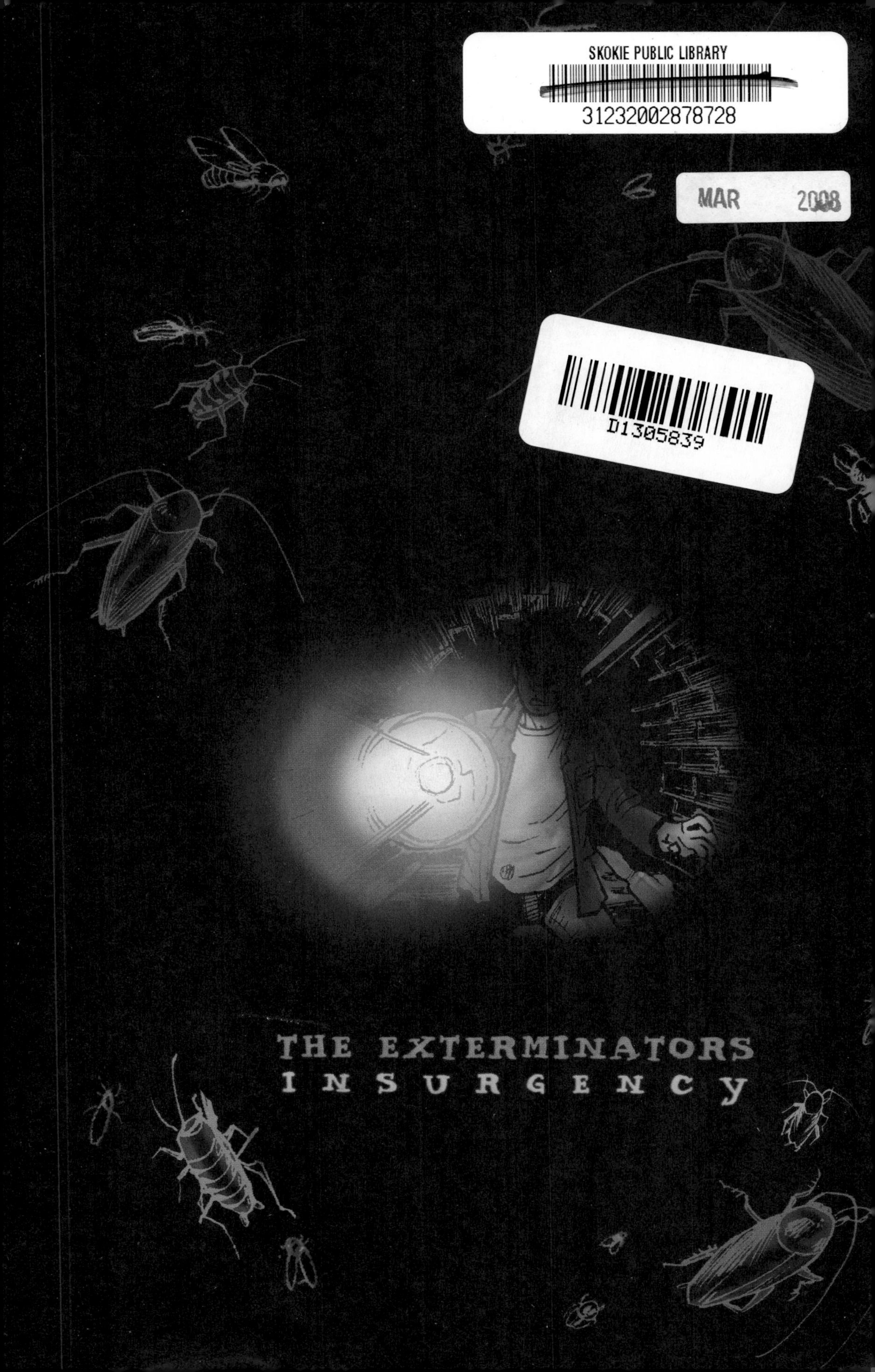
THE EXTERMINATORS
INSURGENCY

Cover illustration by Philip Bond
Publication design by Amelia Grohman
Logo design by Ken Lopez

THE EXTERMINATORS: INSURGENCY

DC Comics, 1700 Broadway, New York, NY 10019
A Warner Bros. Entertainment Company.
Printed in Canada. First Printing.
ISBN: 1-4012-1221-2
ISBN 13: 978-1-4012-1221-6

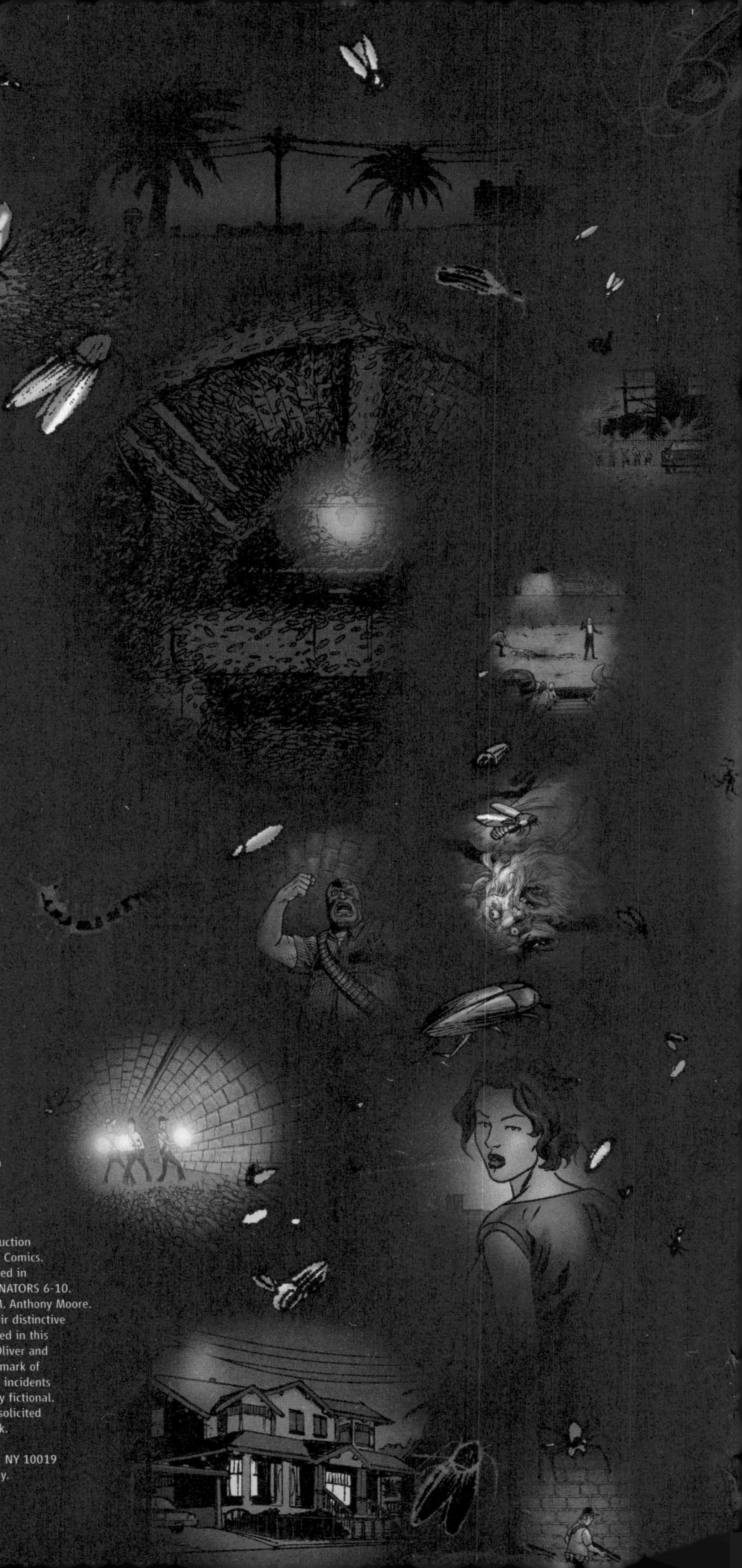

SIMON OLIVER WRITER

TONY MOORE PENCILLER CHAPTERS 1-4

CHRIS SAMNEE ART INTERLUDE

THE EXTERMINATORS
INSURGENCY

ANDE PARKS, SEAN PARSONS & TONY MOORE INKERS

BRIAN BUCCELLATO COLORIST

PAT BROSSEAU & JARED FLETCHER LETTERERS

"THE SWATTER" by SIMON OLIVER

PHILIP BOND ORIGINAL SERIES COVERS

THE EXTERMINATORS CREATED BY
SIMON OLIVER & TONY MOORE

THE SWATTER

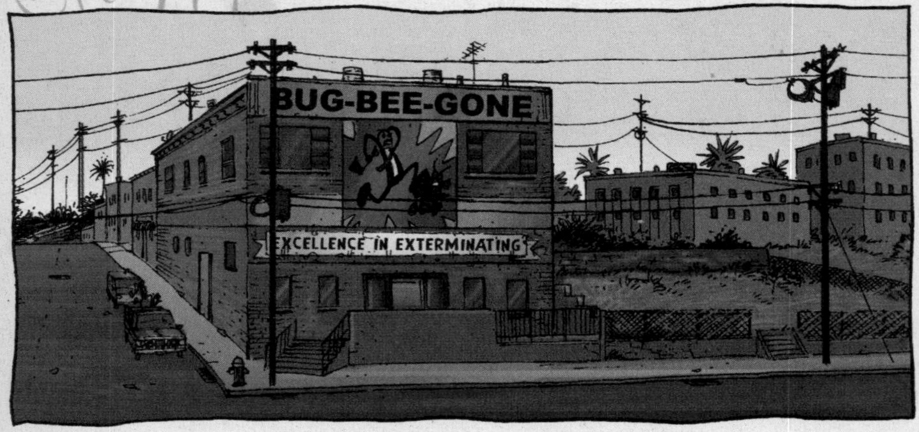
BUG-BEE-GONE
EXCELLENCE IN EXTERMINATING

So far, in my new investigative column, *The Swatter,* I've covered such hot button issues, as "the real future of fumigation" and "Is pigeon eradication the silver lining of a bird flu pandemic?"

For this month's feature, we've pulled out all the stops and blown the travel budget on a round trip Greyhound ticket to the City of Angels to meet up with the owner and staff of a Los Angeles pest control institution, Bug-Bee-Gone Co.

***The Swatter*'s mission: to find out what makes an independently owned pest control business tick in the 21st century.**

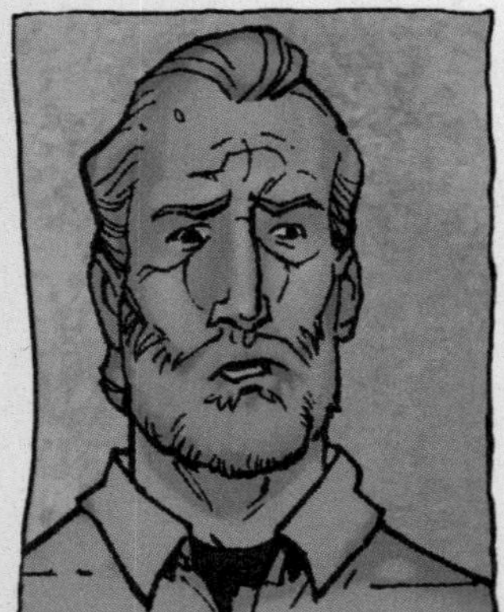

NILS

I'm standing here with Nils Petterson, current General Manager and son of Bug-Bee-Gone founder Nils Petterson Sr.

THE SWATTER: Is it true that we're actually standing in the same building that the very first BBG truck departed from nearly seven decades ago?

NILS: Yep. And I'm proud to say that we're coming up on our 70th anniversary next year.

SWAT: Quite an achievement. So, having grown up in the bosom of the pest control industry, what kind of changes really stand out for you over the past few years?

NILS: Good question. Personally I think the treatment and abatement side of the pest control business has become far more specialized. Instead of using those kill-'em-all high toxicity systems of 25 years ago, the modern pest control specialist has an entire arsenal of products for pest eradication, whether it be blowflies, fire ants or cockroaches in his cross hairs. And of course there's been the subsequent drop-off in hair-loss, infertility, and malignant metastasic tumors among the guys.

SWAT: What would you describe as the key factors of a successful family-owned and operated pest control business?

NILS: First and foremost, if you don't take care of the customer, everything else is largely irrelevant. I'd rank strong customer service as the keystone of BBG's longevity in the marketplace.

SWAT: And then?

NILS: An old Norse proverb my father was rather fond of comes to mind, roughly translated: "Keep both feet firmly in the present but one eye on the future."

SWAT: Very true. So is your son Stefan planning on continuing the family tradition at BBG?

NILS: You must be mistaken. I don't have a son. Just a stepson...

SWAT: Really? Because my research notes were very clear. Look right here, Stefan Petterson, born 12th of October, 19—

NILS: This was supposed to be about the business. Nothing personal.

SWAT: Maybe we should pick this up another time?

So with an eye firmly on the future, Bug-Bee-Gone has gone to the extraordinary lengths of establishing its very own research division in the basement of its aging headquarters: Bug-Bee-Gone Research Industries Inc.

That's The Swatter's next stop, where we encounter the company's chief scientist, Dr. Saloth Sar.

SALOTH

SWAT: Hi, Dr. Sar, I'm...

SALOTH: Who are you and how do you know my name?

SWAT: I'm from *The Journal of American Pest Abatement.* Maybe Mr. Petterson mentioned the article I'm writing?

SALOTH: I.D. Two forms. With picture.

SWAT: Well, as part of my piece I was wondering if maybe I could get a tour of the facility, a few photos and have you talk on the record?

SALOTH: This is simply not possible.

Well, I'm guessing Dan Rather and even Stone Phillips have had the occasional door closed in their faces. So I brushed myself off and decided to try my luck with the boys on the loading dock.

STRETCH

SWAT: And here I'm talking to a pest controller named...?

STRETCH: Everyone just calls me Stretch.

SWAT: So, Stretch, what kind of issues are on your mind as a pest-control specialist operating in the 21st century?

STRETCH: I guess the usual stuff. Death and the impermanence of life. The fear of being reborn into a lower realm.

SWAT: Okay. And—?

STRETCH: My daily struggle to live by the doctrines of the Eightfold Path and attain the Six Perfections.

SWAT: Right. On a technical note, I can't help but notice that Bug-Bee-Gone appears to be shunning Draxx, the industry-standard gel bait and by far the number-one seller. Why is that?

STRETCH: Certain unexpected complications.

KEVIN: Yeah. It makes the cockroaches smart as little whips and madder than hell. And it made AJ's insides explode all over the truck cab.

SWAT: Somebody exploded?

KEVIN

STRETCH: Uh, Kevin, we gotta be somewhere. Maybe the reporter can talk to our newest superstar bug killer, Mr. Henry James.

HENRY

SWAT: Interesting. Well, without wanting to court controversy, some in the industry would contend that we must maintain future revenue streams. That, as pest-control technology improves, we are actually killing our own industry.

HENRY: Do you honestly think we have that kind of luxury? That we have any real fucking choice in this?

SWAT: But wouldn't you say the latest developments have pushed us closer to the point of victory?

HENRY: Propagandist corporate bullshit. You know most days when I'm driving home and I take a look around me, I'm overwhelmed by the futility of the human condition in the face of the sheer power of nature.

But what the fuck? I know all the boys here at Bug-Bee are going to go down fighting for this city, every square inch

---

"...You know most days when I'm driving home and I take a look around me, I'm overwhelmed by the futility of the human condition in the face of the sheer power of nature."

HENRY: He is joking, of course. I'm just the new fish around here. Just started in the business.

SWAT: Welcome to *The Swatter*, Henry. So what were you up to before getting into the pest control business?

HENRY: Time off for good behavior.

SWAT: Well, er, let's get down to brass tacks here. Could you describe Bug-Bee-Gone's crewing setup for us?

HENRY: I mean, I guess we're like most companies. Call-outs we generally pair up. Basic maintenance routes we try and work alone.

SWAT: As an operator on the front lines, what do you see as the key issue facing pest-control specialists in the 21st century?

HENRY: Tough one. Well, basically, in my experience there's a fuck of a lot of bugs out there and only so many hours in the day to get out and kill them all.

of it. Just like I'm sure thousands of other Exterminators in hundreds of other cities across the country are going to as well, right up until, well...

SWAT: Until what, Henry?

HENRY: Until the end when *they've* won and *we're* gone.

SWAT: Do you really see that happening?

HENRY: You know, 6 months ago I'd have had a cold beer and laughed all this off. But, yeah, I think our time's coming and it's just around the corner.

And there we have it. Some questions answered, more are raised, but as always something to think about.

Until next time, assuming there is a next time, this is THE SWATTER signing off.

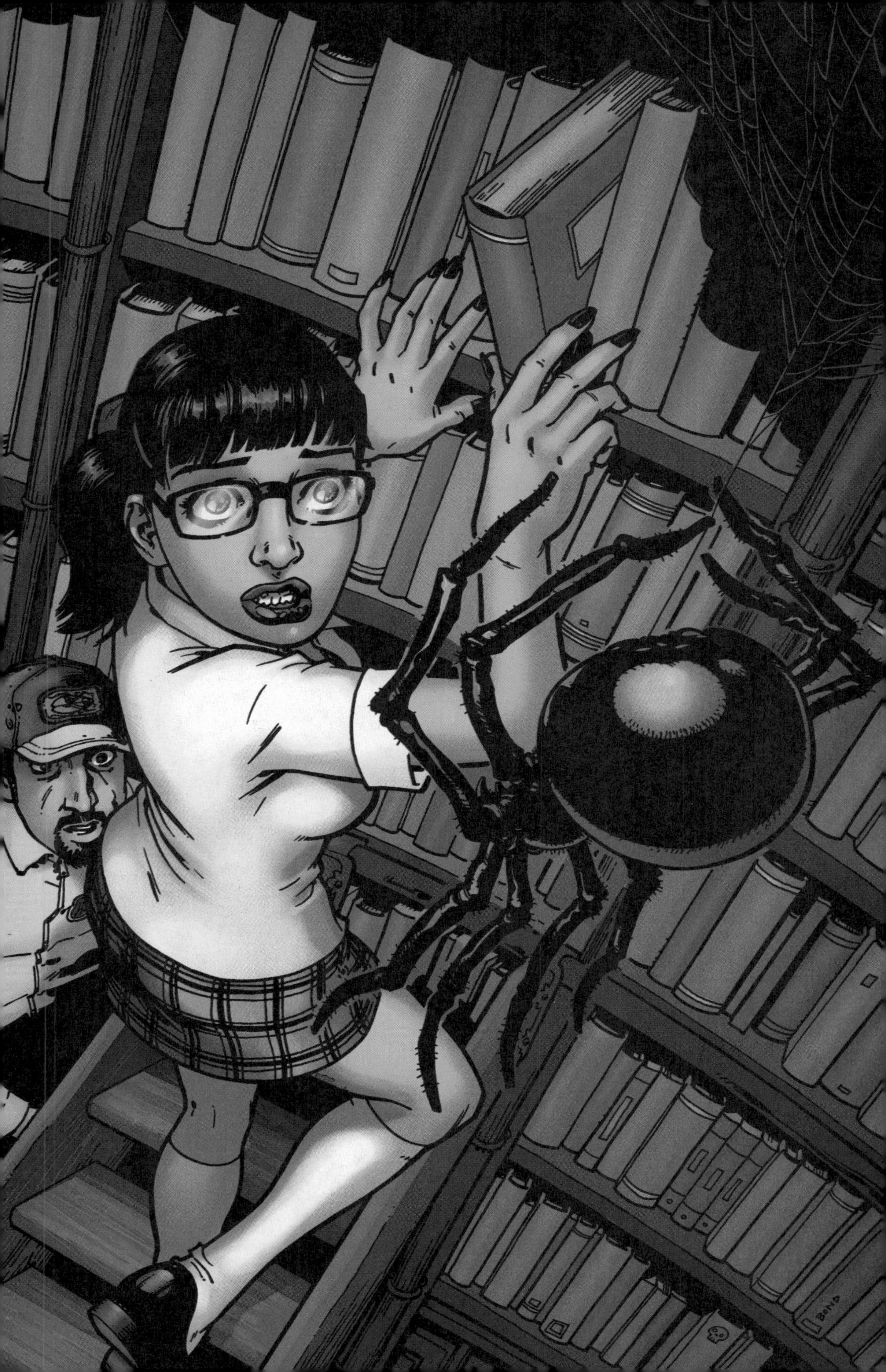

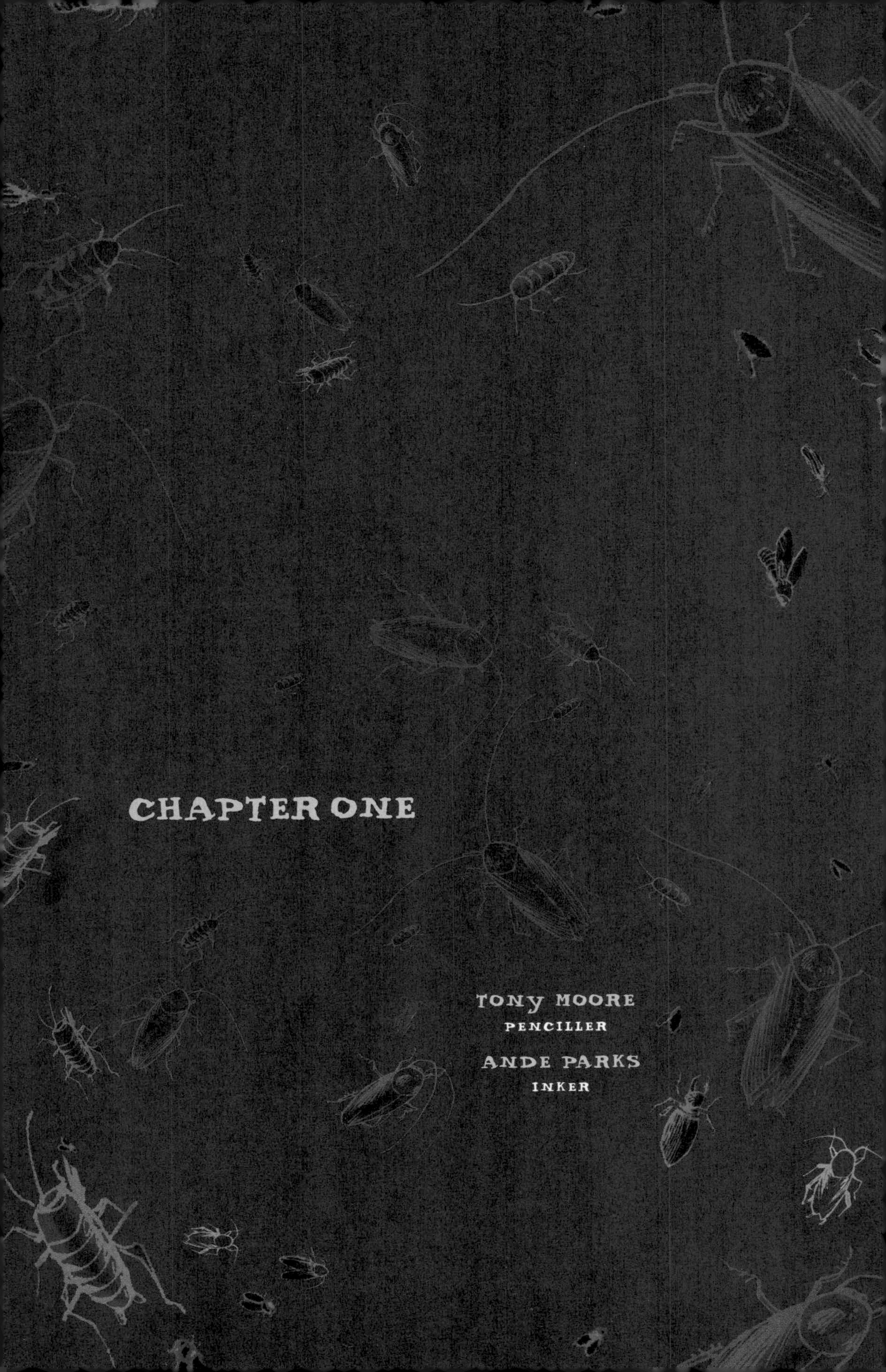

CHAPTER ONE

TONY MOORE
PENCILLER

ANDE PARKS
INKER

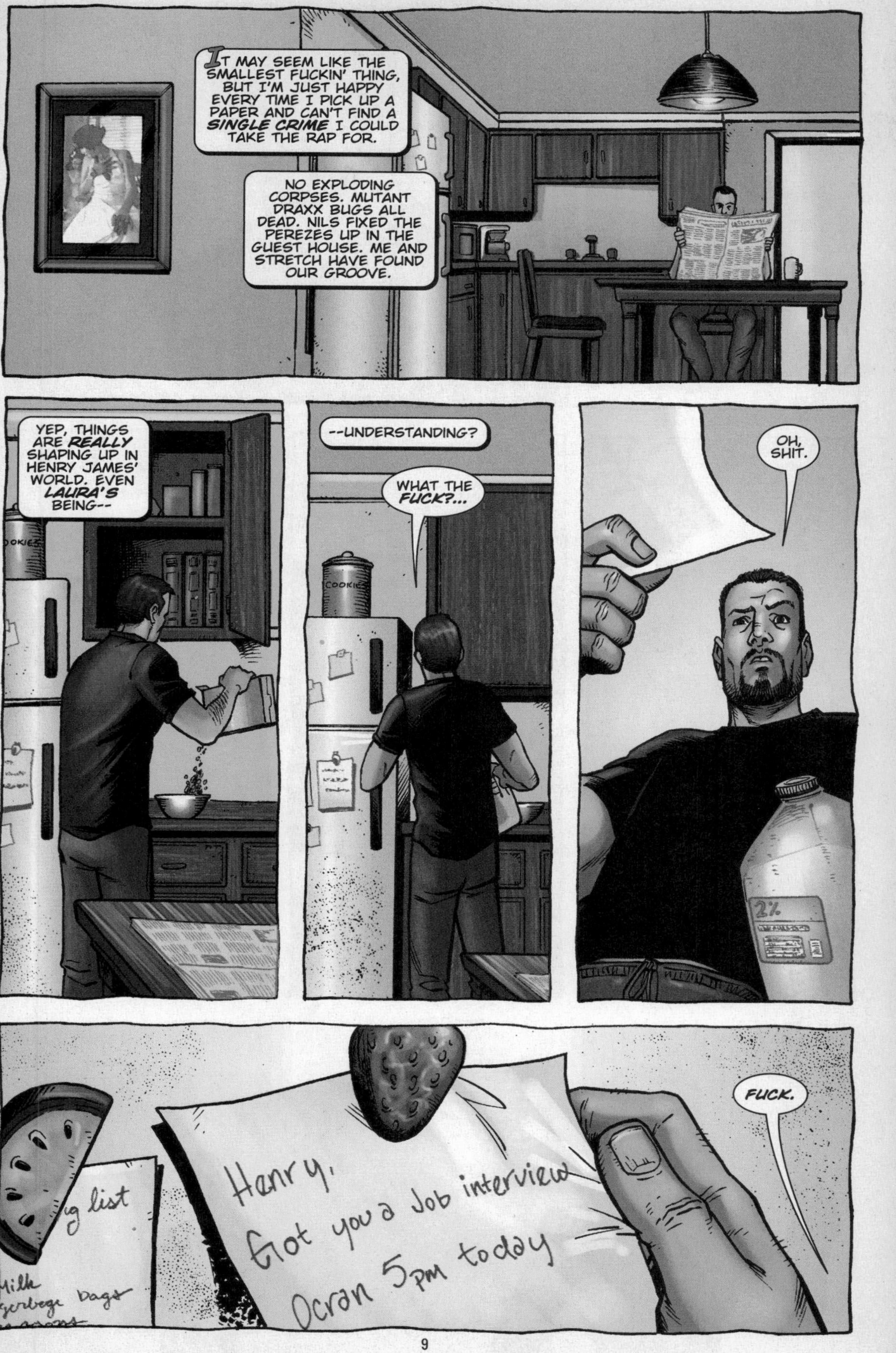
IT MAY SEEM LIKE THE SMALLEST FUCKIN' THING, BUT I'M JUST HAPPY EVERY TIME I PICK UP A PAPER AND CAN'T FIND A SINGLE CRIME I COULD TAKE THE RAP FOR.
NO EXPLODING CORPSES. MUTANT DRAXX BUGS ALL DEAD. NILS FIXED THE PEREZES UP IN THE GUEST HOUSE. ME AND STRETCH HAVE FOUND OUR GROOVE.
YEP, THINGS ARE REALLY SHAPING UP IN HENRY JAMES' WORLD. EVEN LAURA'S BEING--
--UNDERSTANDING?
WHAT THE FUCK?...
OH, SHIT.
2%
FUCK.
Henry,
Got you a Job interview
Ocran 5pm today
g list
Milk
garbage bags

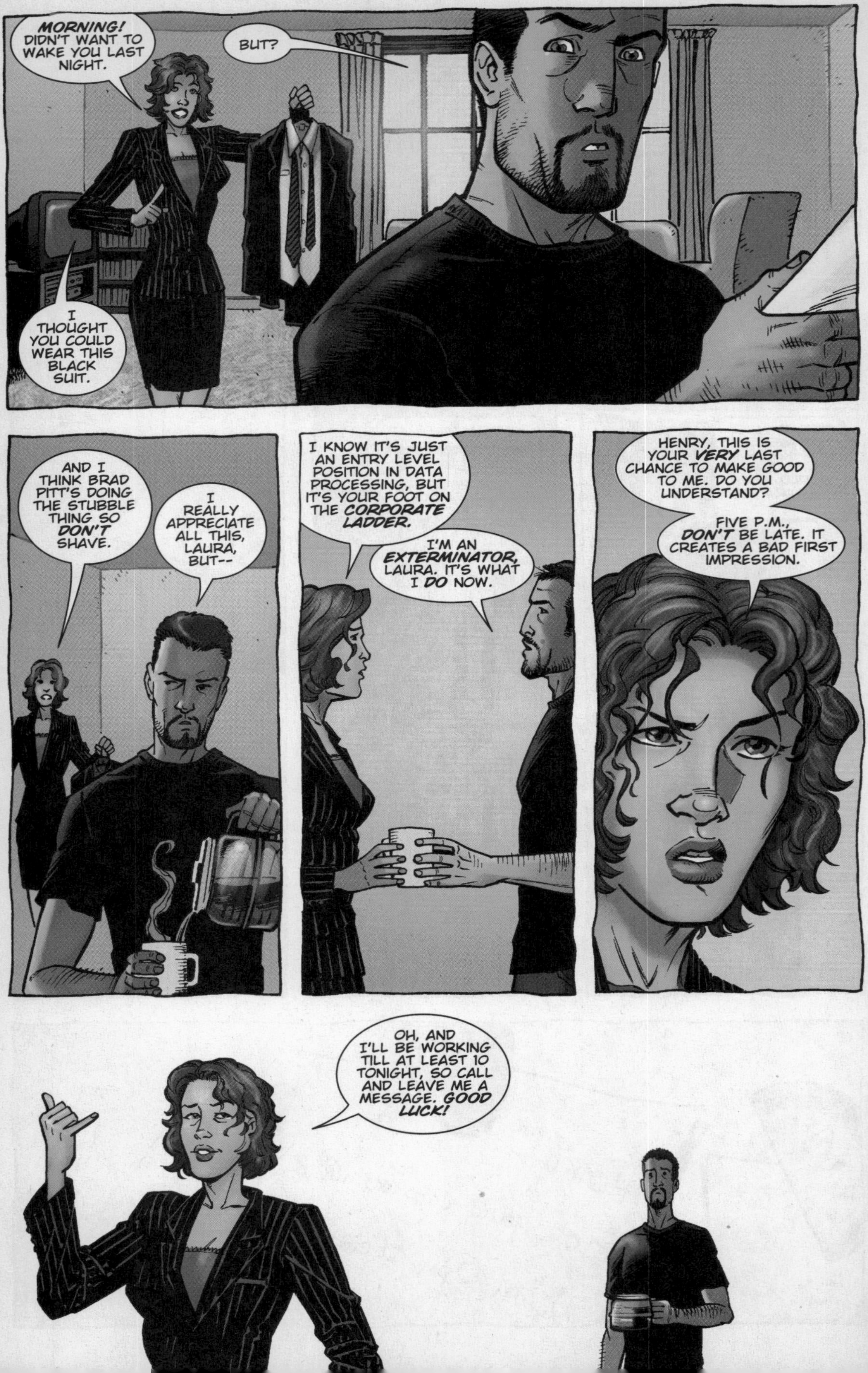
MORNING! DIDN'T WANT TO WAKE YOU LAST NIGHT.
BUT?
I THOUGHT YOU COULD WEAR THIS BLACK SUIT.
AND I THINK BRAD PITT'S DOING THE STUBBLE THING SO DON'T SHAVE.
I REALLY APPRECIATE ALL THIS, LAURA, BUT--
I KNOW IT'S JUST AN ENTRY LEVEL POSITION IN DATA PROCESSING, BUT IT'S YOUR FOOT ON THE CORPORATE LADDER.
I'M AN EXTERMINATOR, LAURA. IT'S WHAT I DO NOW.
HENRY, THIS IS YOUR VERY LAST CHANCE TO MAKE GOOD TO ME. DO YOU UNDERSTAND?
FIVE P.M., DON'T BE LATE. IT CREATES A BAD FIRST IMPRESSION.
OH, AND I'LL BE WORKING TILL AT LEAST 10 TONIGHT, SO CALL AND LEAVE ME A MESSAGE. GOOD LUCK!

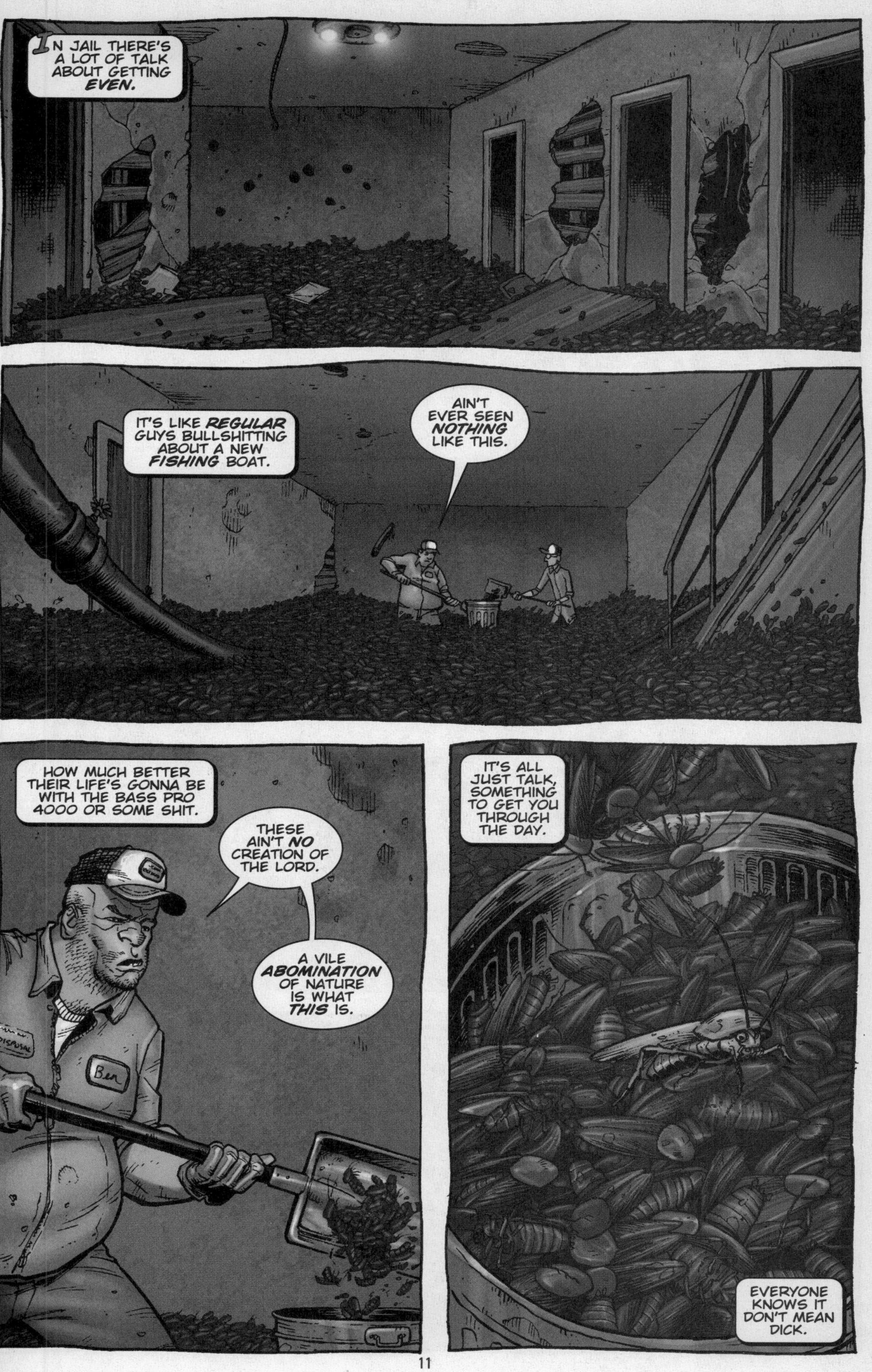
IN JAIL THERE'S A LOT OF TALK ABOUT GETTING EVEN.
IT'S LIKE REGULAR GUYS BULLSHITTING ABOUT A NEW FISHING BOAT.
AIN'T EVER SEEN NOTHING LIKE THIS.
HOW MUCH BETTER THEIR LIFE'S GONNA BE WITH THE BASS PRO 4000 OR SOME SHIT.
THESE AIN'T NO CREATION OF THE LORD.
A VILE ABOMINATION OF NATURE IS WHAT THIS IS.
Ben
IT'S ALL JUST TALK, SOMETHING TO GET YOU THROUGH THE DAY.
EVERYONE KNOWS IT DON'T MEAN DICK.

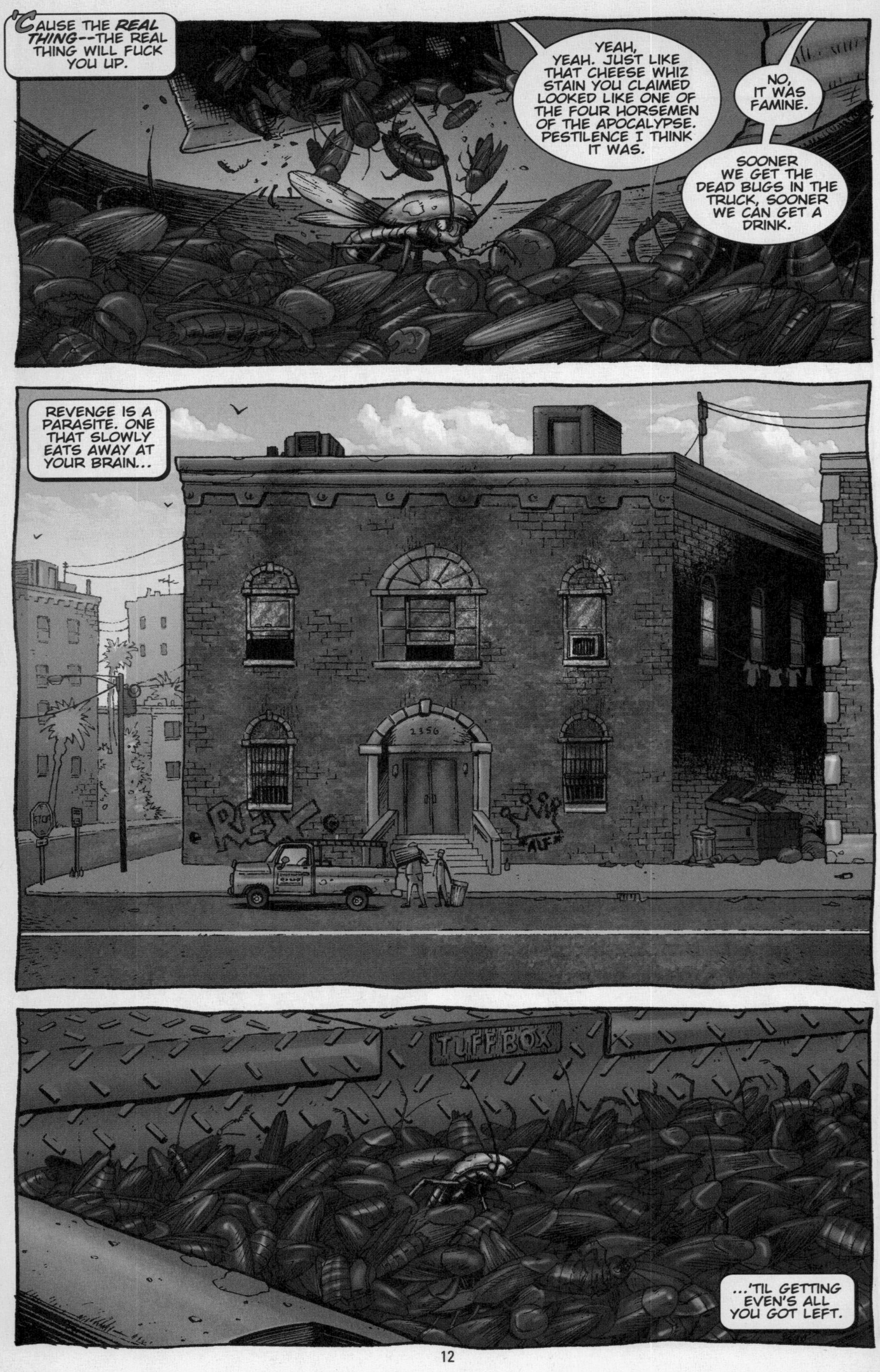
'CAUSE THE *REAL THING*--THE REAL THING WILL FUCK YOU UP.
YEAH, YEAH. JUST LIKE THAT CHEESE WHIZ STAIN YOU CLAIMED LOOKED LIKE ONE OF THE FOUR HORSEMEN OF THE APOCALYPSE. PESTILENCE I THINK IT WAS.
NO, IT WAS FAMINE.
SOONER WE GET THE DEAD BUGS IN THE TRUCK, SOONER WE CAN GET A DRINK.
REVENGE IS A PARASITE. ONE THAT SLOWLY EATS AWAY AT YOUR BRAIN...
2356
STOP
TUFF BOX
...'TIL GETTING EVEN'S ALL YOU GOT LEFT.

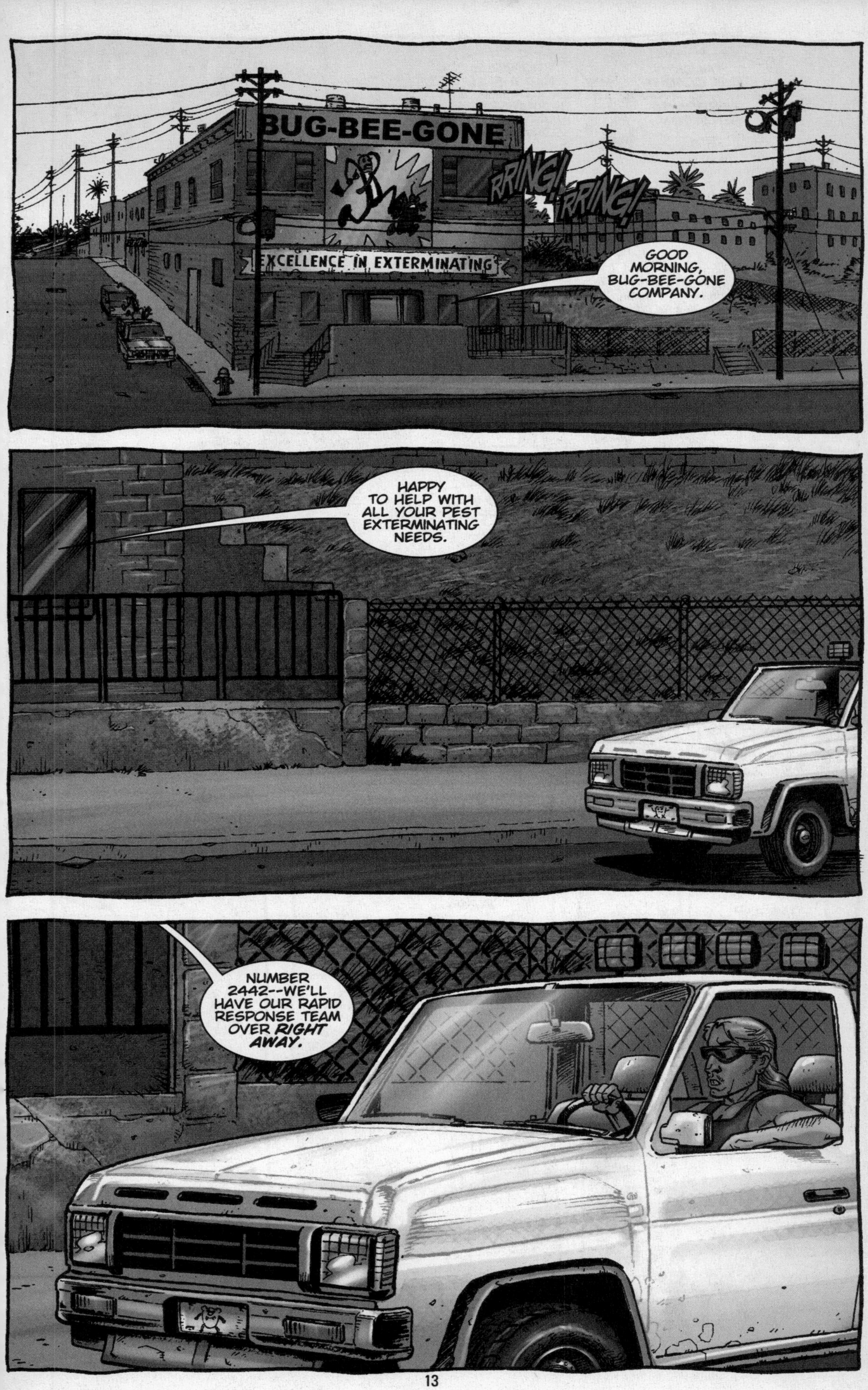
BUG-BEE-GONE
EXCELLENCE IN EXTERMINATING
RRING! RRING!
GOOD MORNING, BUG-BEE-GONE COMPANY.
HAPPY TO HELP WITH ALL YOUR PEST EXTERMINATING NEEDS.
NUMBER 2442--WE'LL HAVE OUR RAPID RESPONSE TEAM OVER *RIGHT AWAY.*

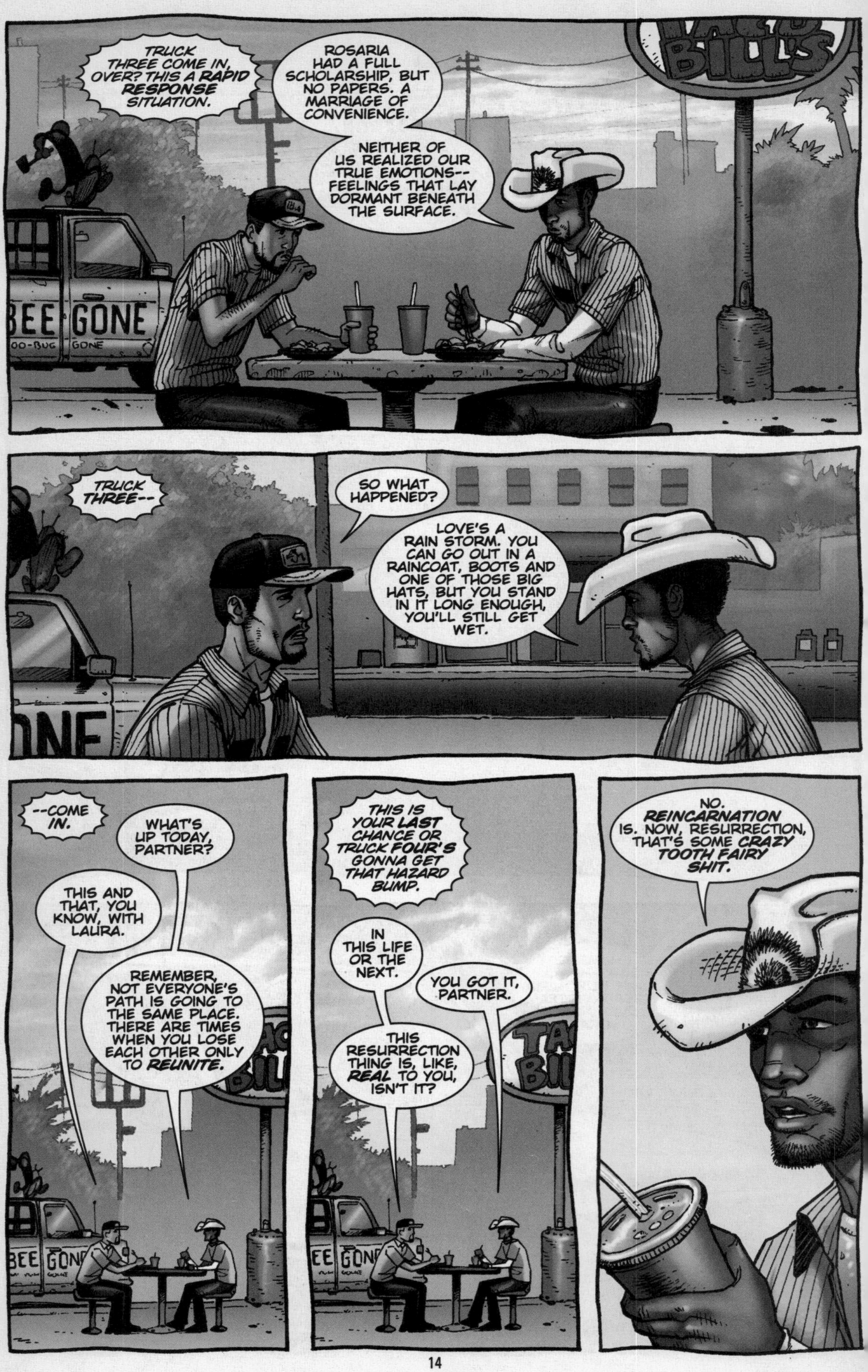
TACO BILL'S
TRUCK THREE COME IN, OVER? THIS A RAPID RESPONSE SITUATION.
ROSARIA HAD A FULL SCHOLARSHIP, BUT NO PAPERS. A MARRIAGE OF CONVENIENCE.
NEITHER OF US REALIZED OUR TRUE EMOTIONS-- FEELINGS THAT LAY DORMANT BENEATH THE SURFACE.
BEE GONE
TRUCK THREE--
SO WHAT HAPPENED?
LOVE'S A RAIN STORM. YOU CAN GO OUT IN A RAINCOAT, BOOTS AND ONE OF THOSE BIG HATS, BUT YOU STAND IN IT LONG ENOUGH, YOU'LL STILL GET WET.
--COME IN.
WHAT'S UP TODAY, PARTNER?
THIS AND THAT, YOU KNOW, WITH LAURA.
REMEMBER, NOT EVERYONE'S PATH IS GOING TO THE SAME PLACE. THERE ARE TIMES WHEN YOU LOSE EACH OTHER ONLY TO REUNITE.
THIS IS YOUR LAST CHANCE OR TRUCK FOUR'S GONNA GET THAT HAZARD BUMP.
IN THIS LIFE OR THE NEXT.
YOU GOT IT, PARTNER.
THIS RESURRECTION THING IS, LIKE, REAL TO YOU, ISN'T IT?
NO. REINCARNATION IS. NOW, RESURRECTION, THAT'S SOME CRAZY TOOTH FAIRY SHIT.

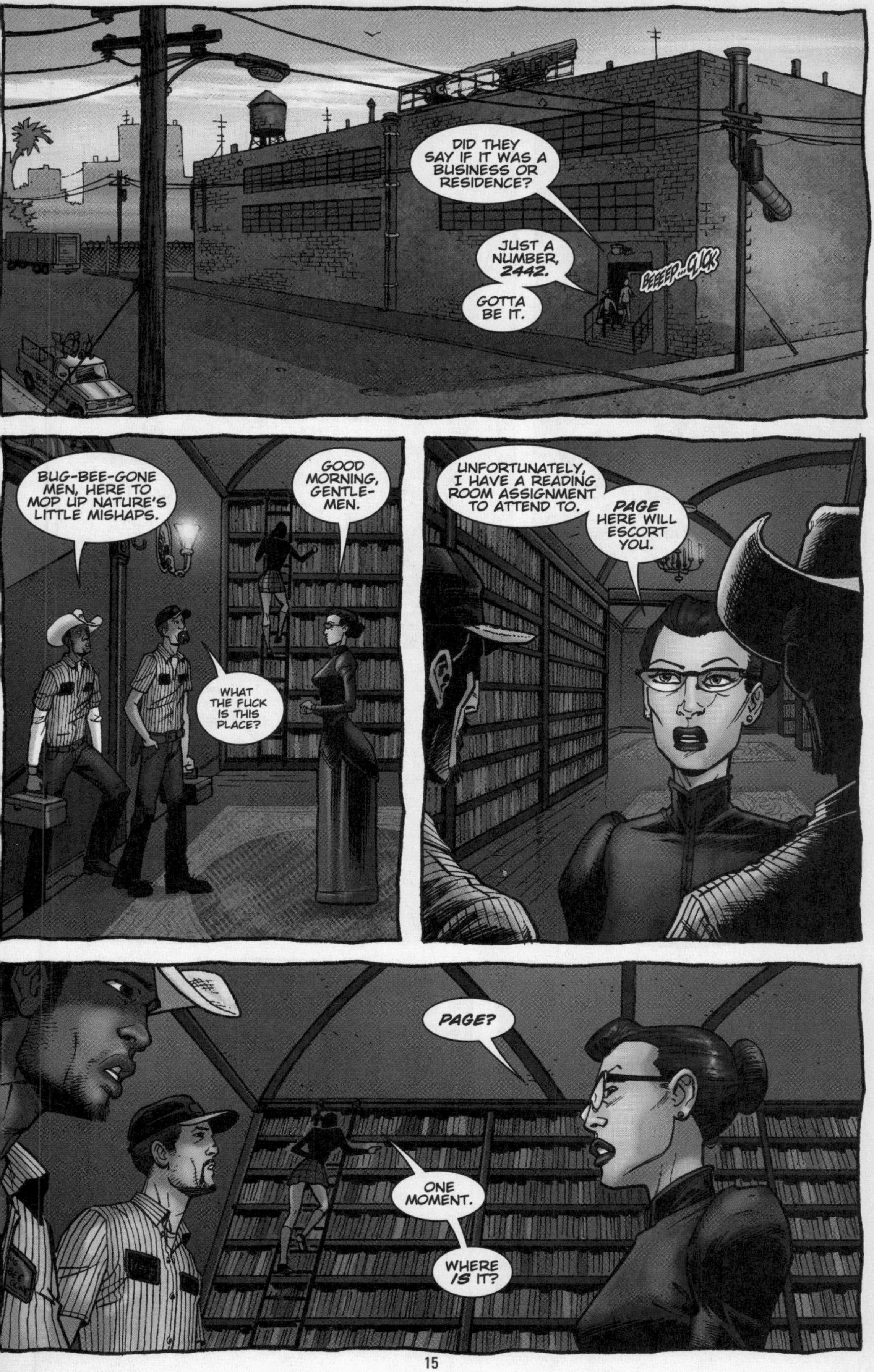
DID THEY SAY IF IT WAS A BUSINESS OR RESIDENCE?
JUST A NUMBER, 2442.
GOTTA BE IT.
BEEEEP...CLICK
BUG-BEE-GONE MEN, HERE TO MOP UP NATURE'S LITTLE MISHAPS.
GOOD MORNING, GENTLEMEN.
WHAT THE FUCK IS THIS PLACE?
UNFORTUNATELY, I HAVE A READING ROOM ASSIGNMENT TO ATTEND TO.
PAGE HERE WILL ESCORT YOU.
PAGE?
ONE MOMENT.
WHERE IS IT?

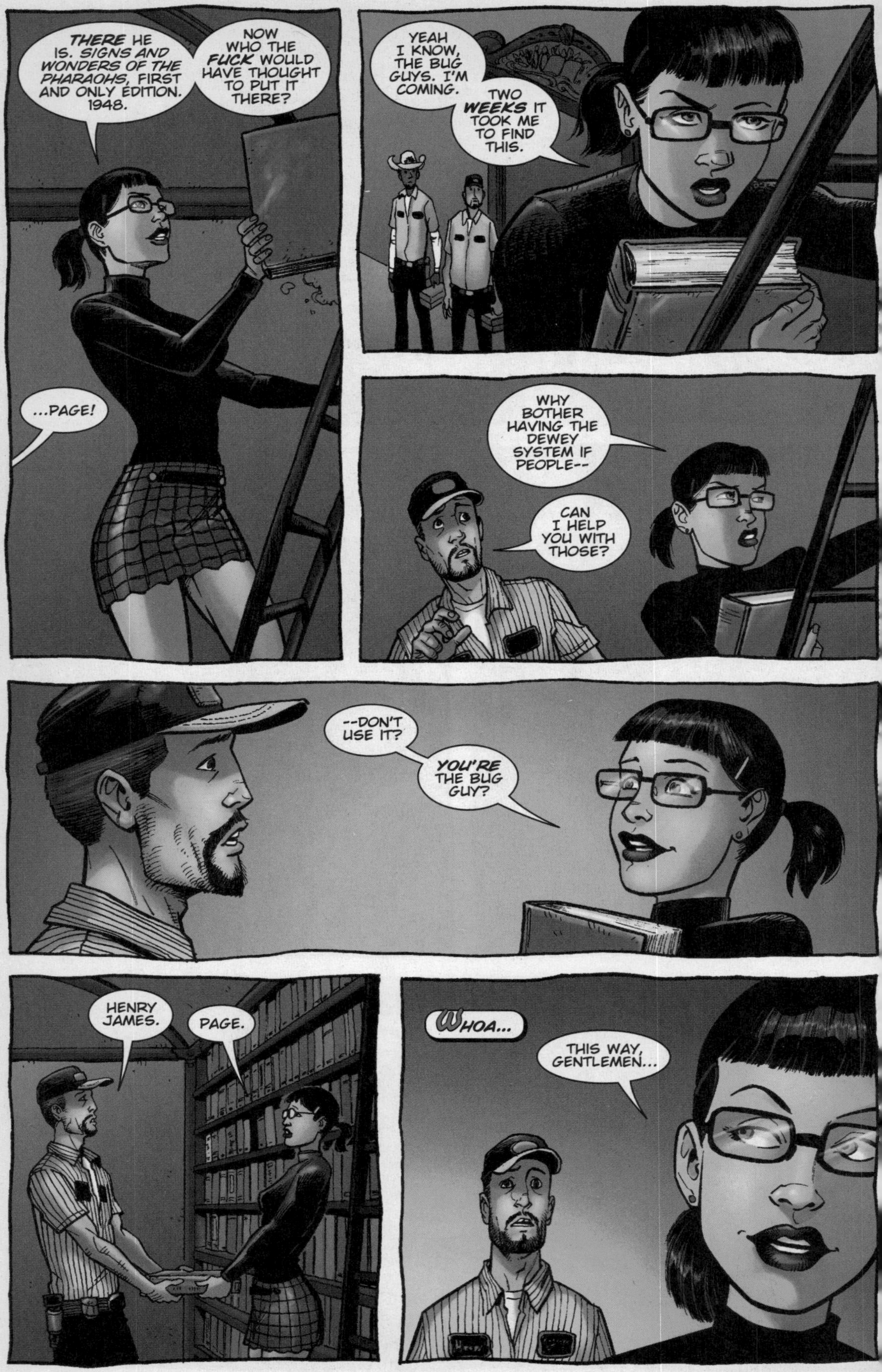
THERE HE IS. SIGNS AND WONDERS OF THE PHARAOHS, FIRST AND ONLY EDITION. 1948.
NOW WHO THE FUCK WOULD HAVE THOUGHT TO PUT IT THERE?
...PAGE!
YEAH I KNOW, THE BUG GUYS. I'M COMING.
TWO WEEKS IT TOOK ME TO FIND THIS.
WHY BOTHER HAVING THE DEWEY SYSTEM IF PEOPLE--
CAN I HELP YOU WITH THOSE?
--DON'T USE IT?
YOU'RE THE BUG GUY?
HENRY JAMES.
PAGE.
WHOA...
THIS WAY, GENTLEMEN...

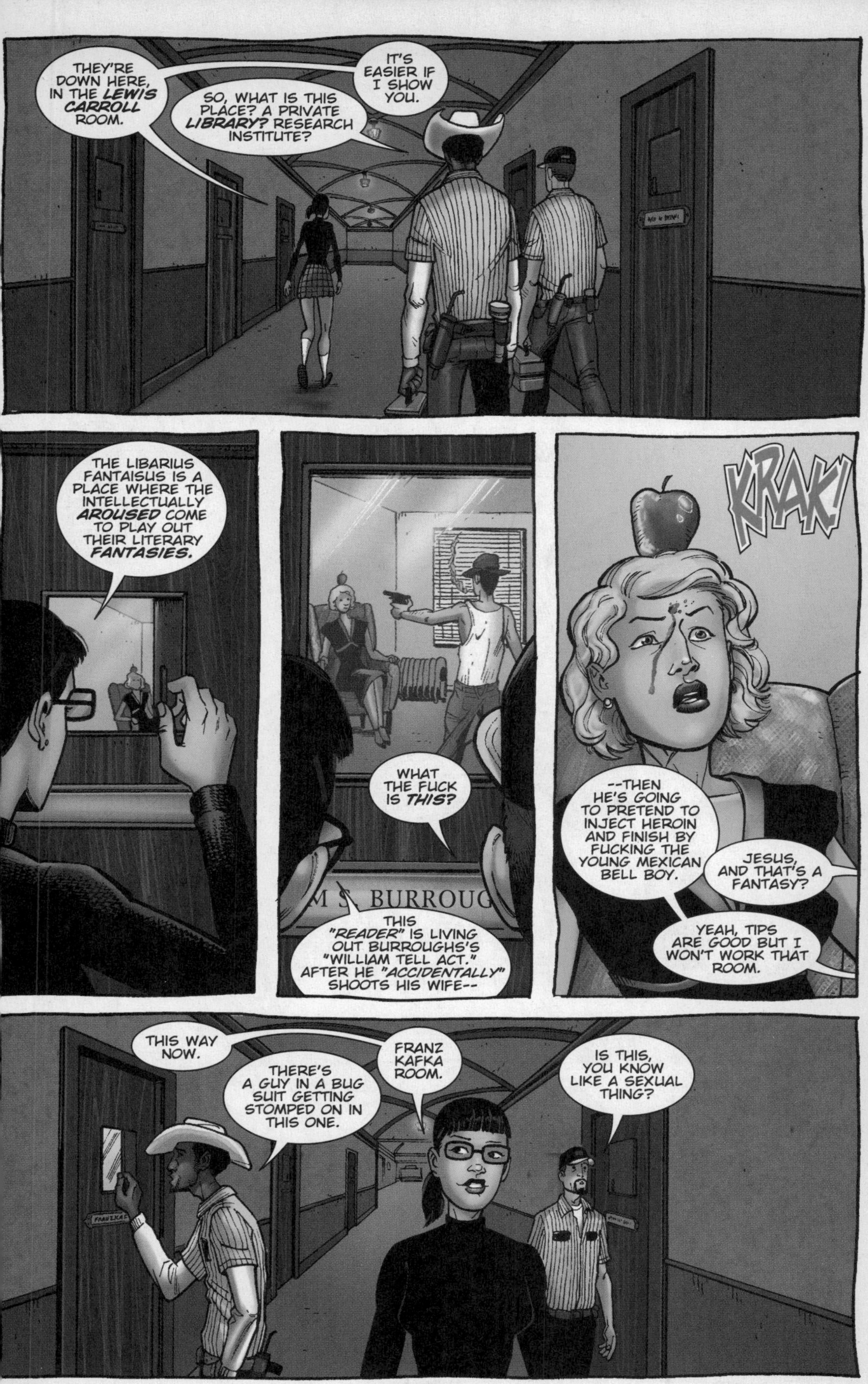
THEY'RE DOWN HERE, IN THE LEWIS CARROLL ROOM.
SO, WHAT IS THIS PLACE? A PRIVATE LIBRARY? RESEARCH INSTITUTE?
IT'S EASIER IF I SHOW YOU.
THE LIBARIUS FANTAISUS IS A PLACE WHERE THE INTELLECTUALLY AROUSED COME TO PLAY OUT THEIR LITERARY FANTASIES.
WHAT THE FUCK IS THIS?
M S. BURROUG
THIS "READER" IS LIVING OUT BURROUGHS'S "WILLIAM TELL ACT." AFTER HE "ACCIDENTALLY" SHOOTS HIS WIFE--
KRAK!
--THEN HE'S GOING TO PRETEND TO INJECT HEROIN AND FINISH BY FUCKING THE YOUNG MEXICAN BELL BOY.
JESUS, AND THAT'S A FANTASY?
YEAH, TIPS ARE GOOD BUT I WON'T WORK THAT ROOM.
THIS WAY NOW.
FRANZ KAFKA ROOM.
THERE'S A GUY IN A BUG SUIT GETTING STOMPED ON IN THIS ONE.
IS THIS, YOU KNOW LIKE A SEXUAL THING?

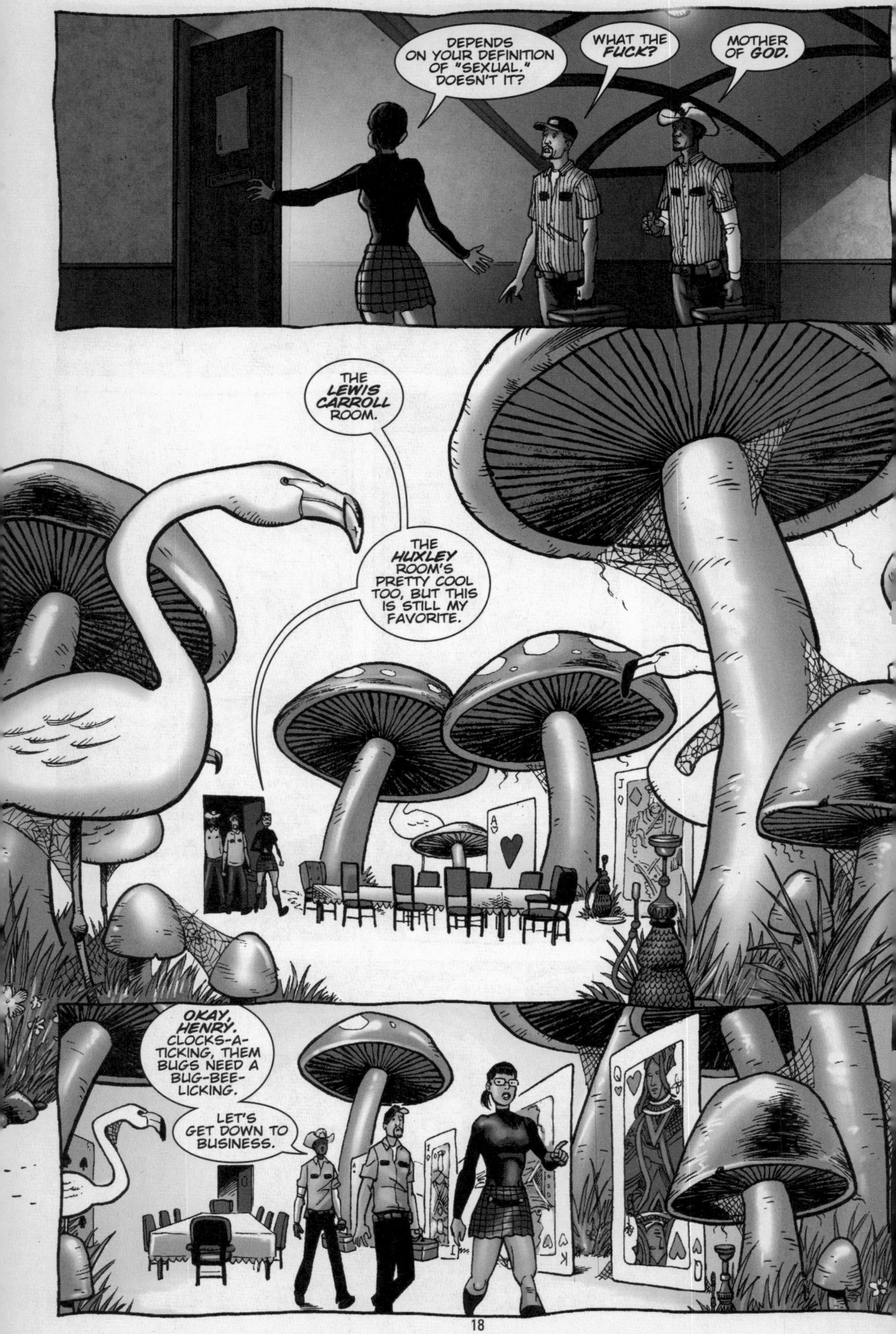
DEPENDS ON YOUR DEFINITION OF "SEXUAL." DOESN'T IT?
WHAT THE *FUCK?*
MOTHER OF *GOD.*
THE *LEWIS CARROLL* ROOM.
THE *HUXLEY* ROOM'S PRETTY COOL TOO, BUT THIS IS STILL MY FAVORITE.
OKAY, HENRY. CLOCKS-A-TICKING, THEM BUGS NEED A BUG-BEE-LICKING.
LET'S GET DOWN TO BUSINESS.

WHAT WE GOT UP THERE, BROTHER?

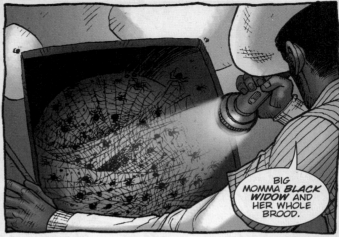

BIG MOMMA **BLACK WIDOW** AND HER WHOLE BROOD.

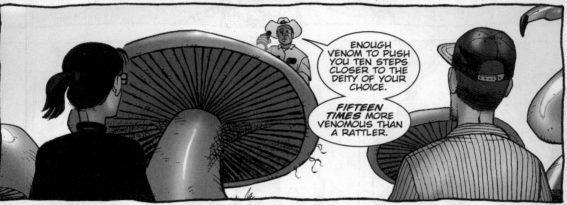

ENOUGH VENOM TO PUSH YOU TEN STEPS CLOSER TO THE DEITY OF YOUR CHOICE.

FIFTEEN TIMES MORE VENOMOUS THAN A RATTLER.

"HIS HONOR SHOULD HAVE LET ME CALL AN AMBULANCE..."

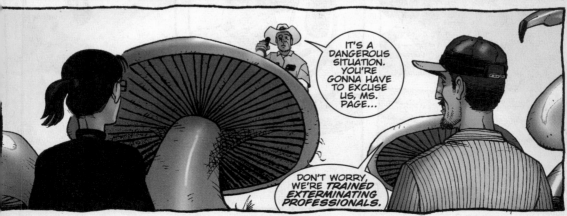

IT'S A DANGEROUS SITUATION. YOU'RE GONNA HAVE TO EXCUSE US, MS. PAGE...

DON'T WORRY, WE'RE **TRAINED EXTERMINATING PROFESSIONALS.**

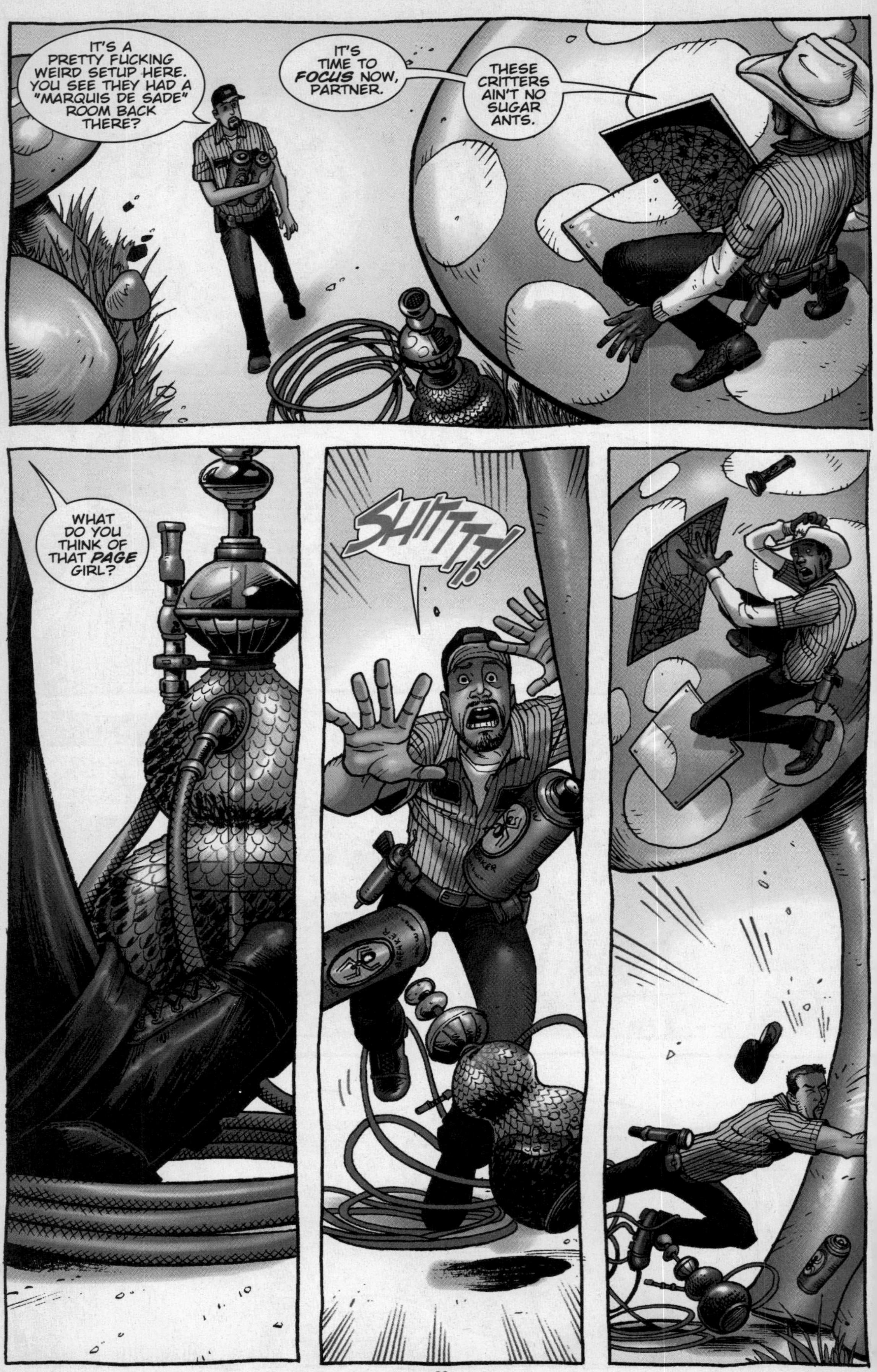

IT'S A PRETTY FUCKING WEIRD SETUP HERE. YOU SEE THEY HAD A "MARQUIS DE SADE" ROOM BACK THERE?
IT'S TIME TO FOCUS NOW, PARTNER.
THESE CRITTERS AIN'T NO SUGAR ANTS.
WHAT DO YOU THINK OF THAT PAGE GIRL?
SHITTTT!

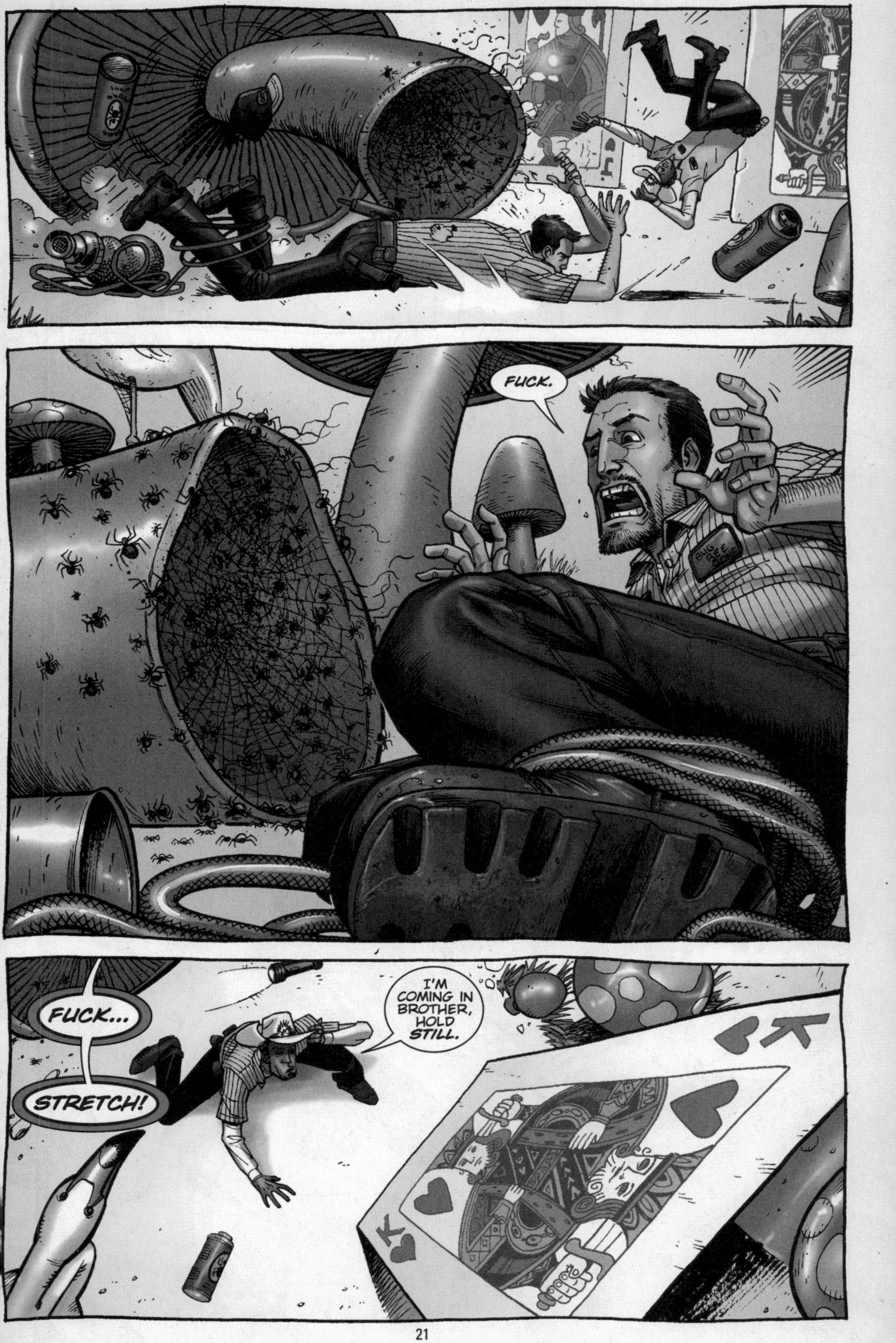
FUCK.
FUCK...
STRETCH!
I'M COMING IN BROTHER, HOLD STILL.

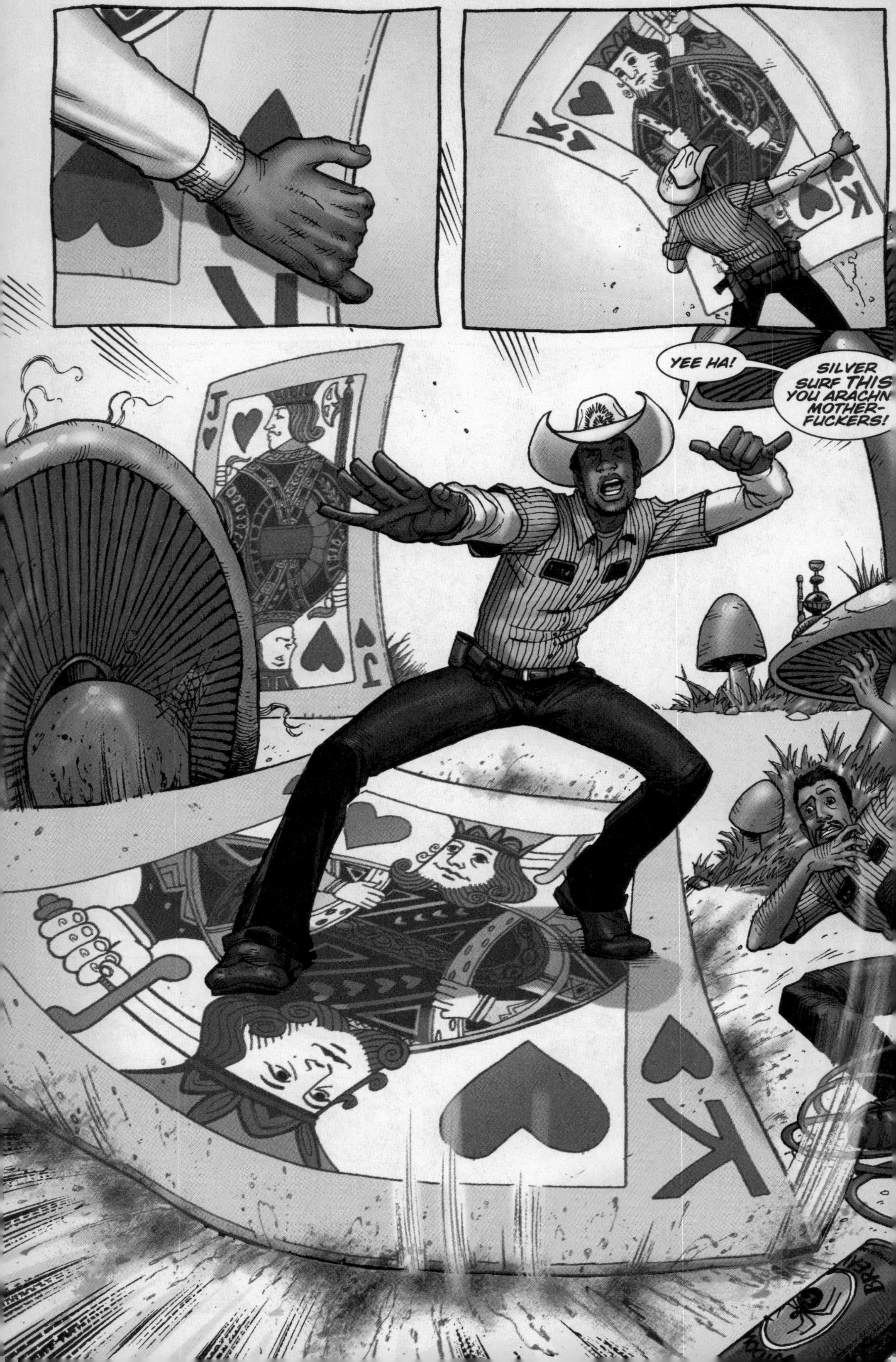
YEE HA!
SILVER SURF THIS YOU ARACHN MOTHER-FUCKERS!

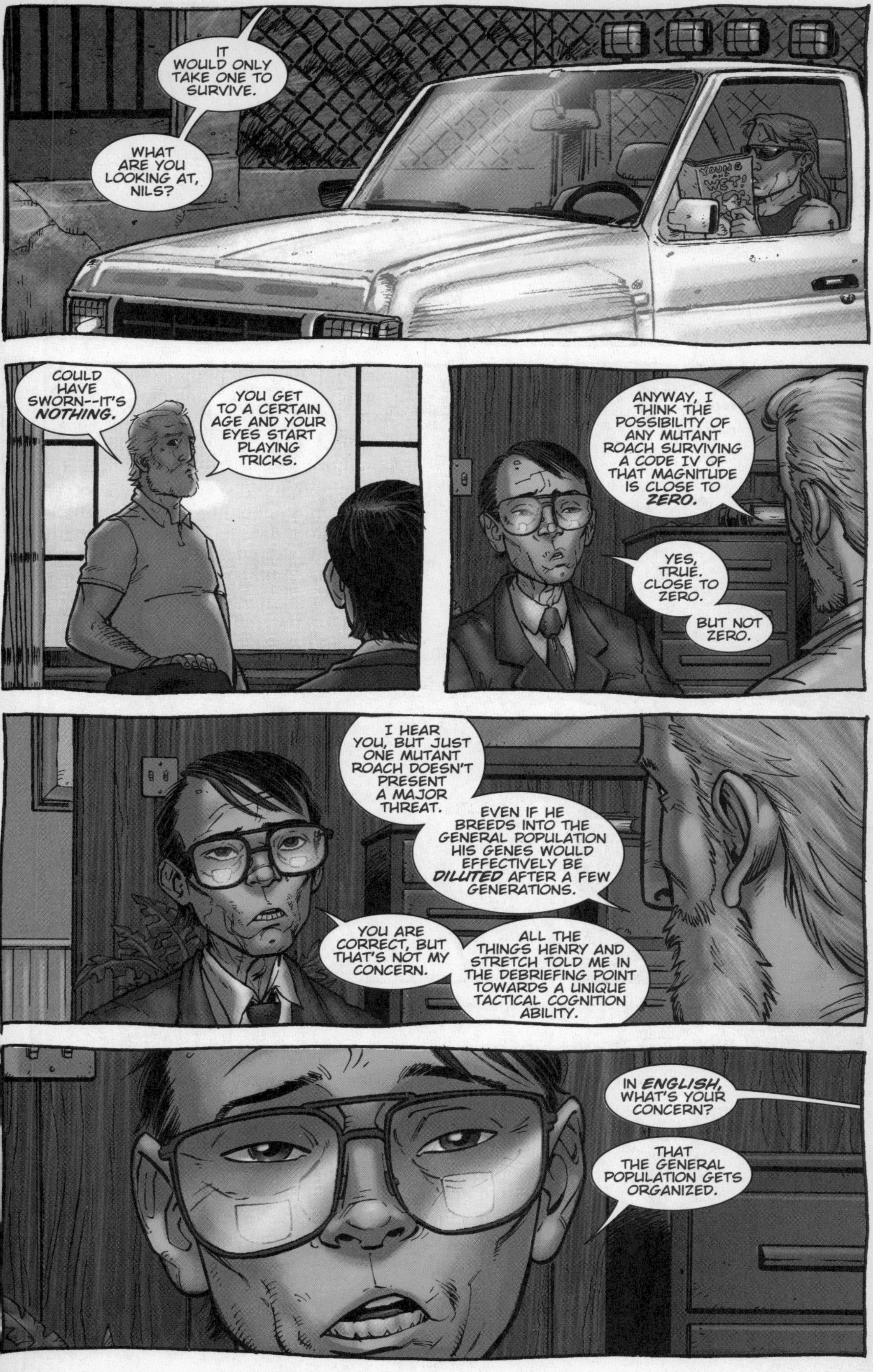
IT WOULD ONLY TAKE ONE TO SURVIVE.
WHAT ARE YOU LOOKING AT, NILS?
YOUNG AND WET!
COULD HAVE SWORN--IT'S *NOTHING.*
YOU GET TO A CERTAIN AGE AND YOUR EYES START PLAYING TRICKS.
ANYWAY, I THINK THE POSSIBILITY OF ANY MUTANT ROACH SURVIVING A CODE IV OF THAT MAGNITUDE IS CLOSE TO *ZERO.*
YES, TRUE. CLOSE TO ZERO.
BUT NOT ZERO.
I HEAR YOU, BUT JUST ONE MUTANT ROACH DOESN'T PRESENT A MAJOR THREAT.
EVEN IF HE BREEDS INTO THE GENERAL POPULATION HIS GENES WOULD EFFECTIVELY BE *DILUTED* AFTER A FEW GENERATIONS.
YOU ARE CORRECT, BUT THAT'S NOT MY CONCERN.
ALL THE THINGS HENRY AND STRETCH TOLD ME IN THE DEBRIEFING POINT TOWARDS A UNIQUE TACTICAL COGNITION ABILITY.
IN *ENGLISH,* WHAT'S YOUR CONCERN?
THAT THE GENERAL POPULATION GETS ORGANIZED.

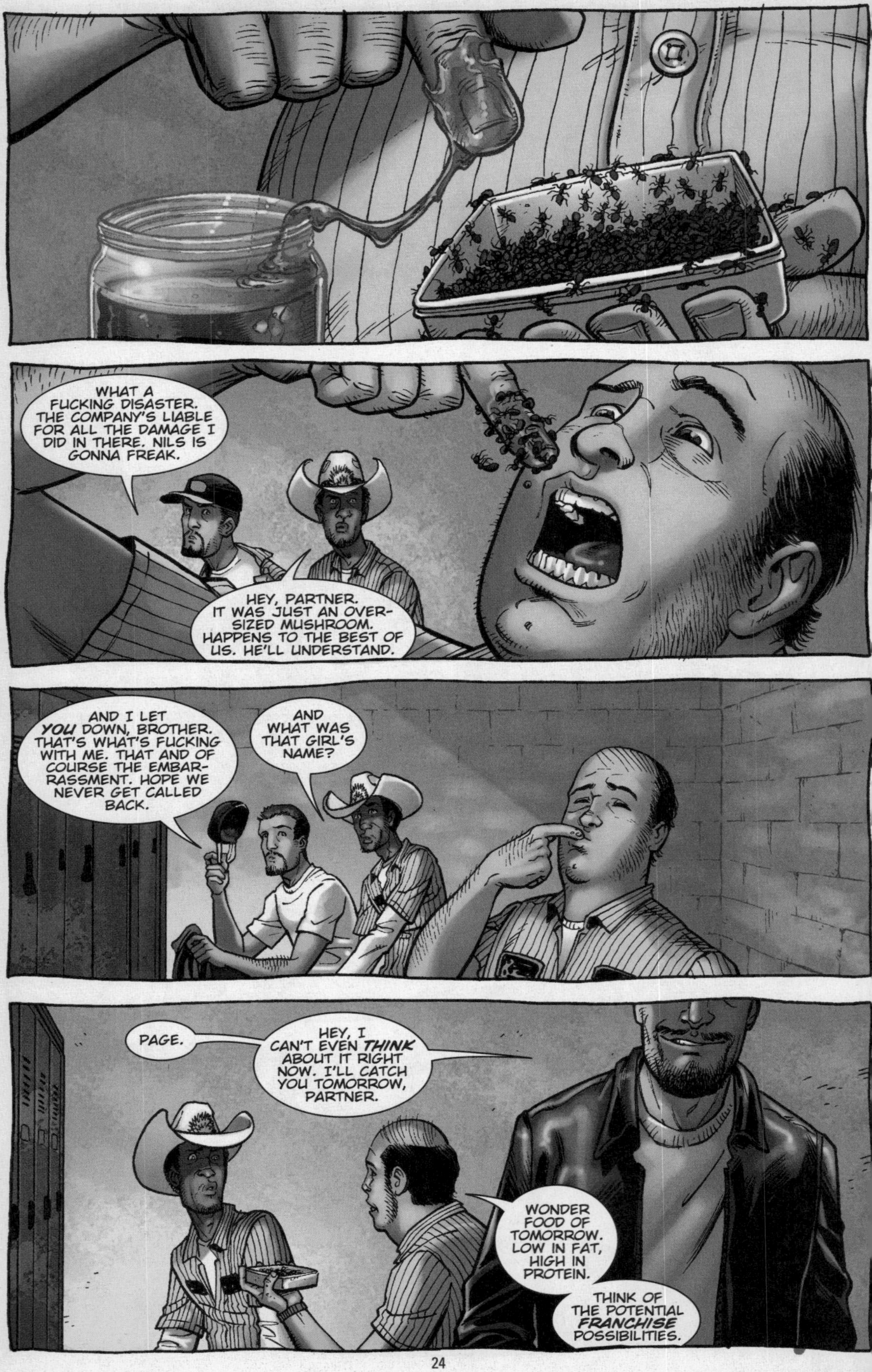
WHAT A FUCKING DISASTER. THE COMPANY'S LIABLE FOR ALL THE DAMAGE I DID IN THERE. NILS IS GONNA FREAK.
HEY, PARTNER. IT WAS JUST AN OVER-SIZED MUSHROOM. HAPPENS TO THE BEST OF US. HE'LL UNDERSTAND.
AND I LET *YOU* DOWN, BROTHER. THAT'S WHAT'S FUCKING WITH ME. THAT AND OF COURSE THE EMBAR-RASSMENT. HOPE WE NEVER GET CALLED BACK.
AND WHAT WAS THAT GIRL'S NAME?
PAGE.
HEY, I CAN'T EVEN *THINK* ABOUT IT RIGHT NOW. I'LL CATCH YOU TOMORROW, PARTNER.
WONDER FOOD OF TOMORROW. LOW IN FAT, HIGH IN PROTEIN.
THINK OF THE POTENTIAL *FRANCHISE* POSSIBILITIES.

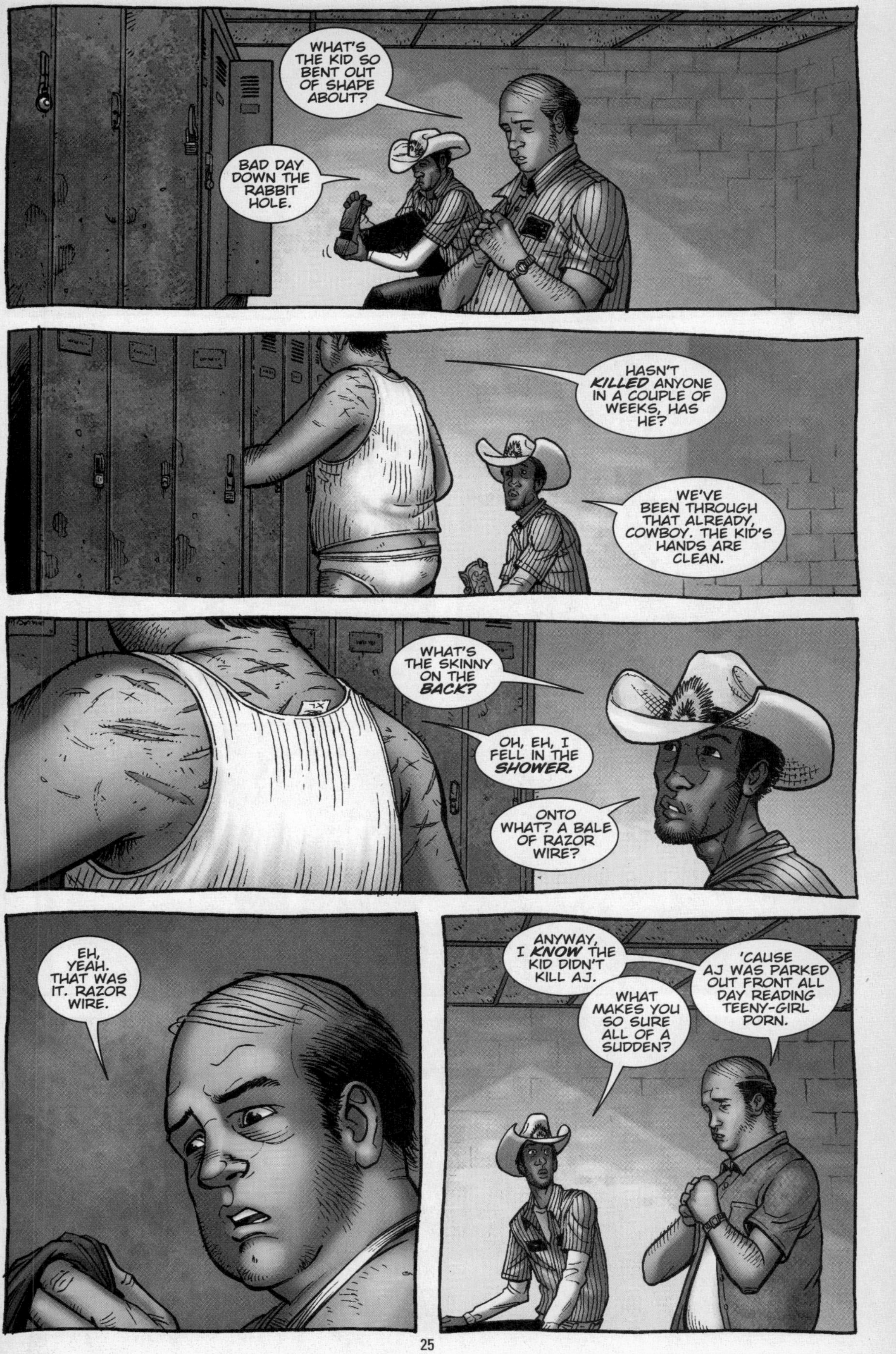
WHAT'S THE KID SO BENT OUT OF SHAPE ABOUT?
BAD DAY DOWN THE RABBIT HOLE.
HASN'T *KILLED* ANYONE IN A COUPLE OF WEEKS, HAS HE?
WE'VE BEEN THROUGH THAT ALREADY, COWBOY. THE KID'S HANDS ARE CLEAN.
WHAT'S THE SKINNY ON THE *BACK?*
OH, EH, I FELL IN THE *SHOWER.*
ONTO WHAT? A BALE OF RAZOR WIRE?
EH, YEAH. THAT WAS IT. RAZOR WIRE.
ANYWAY, I *KNOW* THE KID DIDN'T KILL AJ.
WHAT MAKES YOU SO SURE ALL OF A SUDDEN?
'CAUSE AJ WAS PARKED OUT FRONT ALL DAY READING TEENY-GIRL PORN.

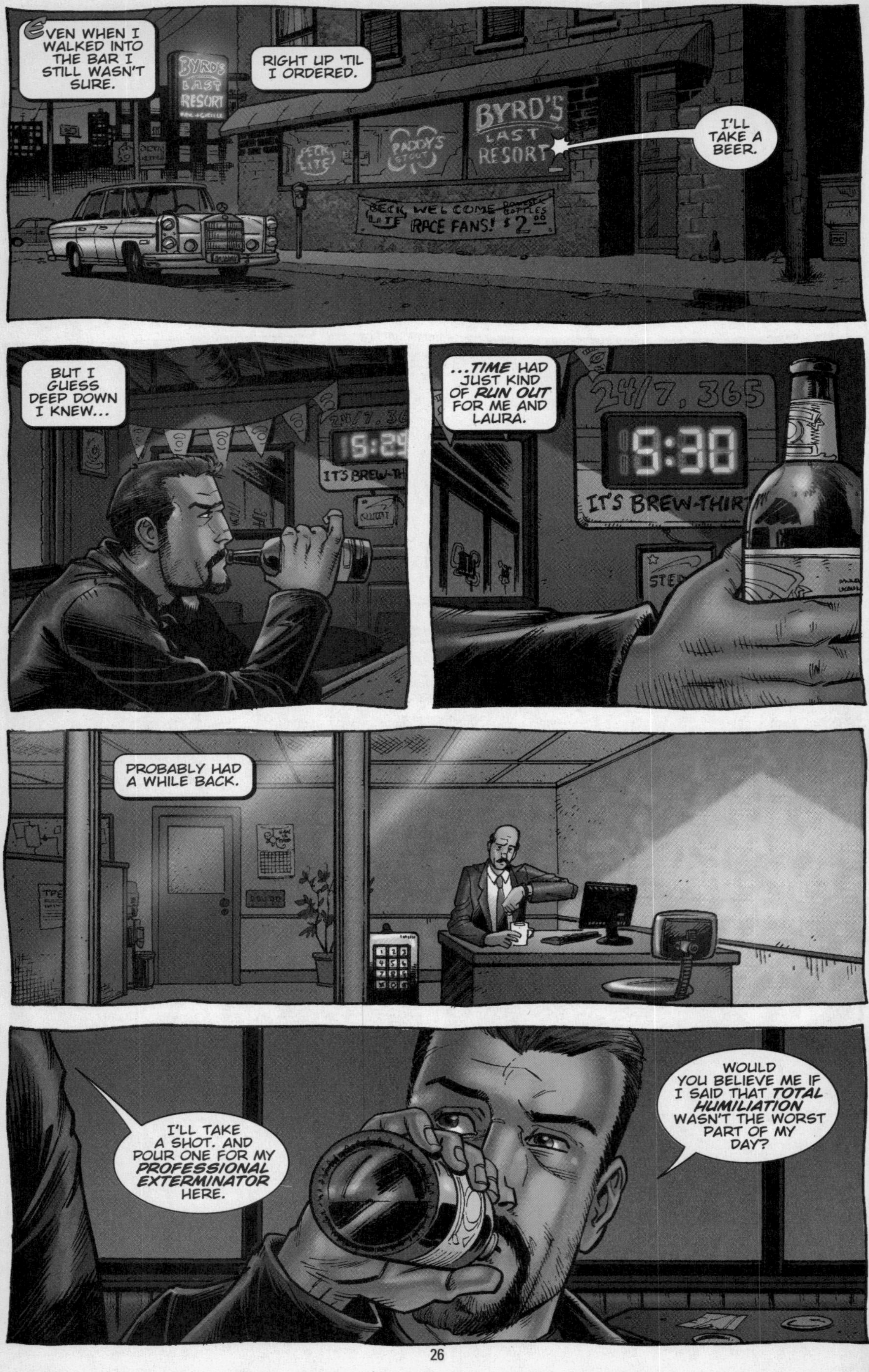
EVEN WHEN I WALKED INTO THE BAR I STILL WASN'T SURE.
RIGHT UP 'TIL I ORDERED.
BYRD'S LAST RESORT
BECK LITE
PADDY'S STOUT
BYRD'S LAST RESORT
I'LL TAKE A BEER.
BECK WELCOME RACE FANS! $2.00
BUT I GUESS DEEP DOWN I KNEW...
...TIME HAD JUST KIND OF RUN OUT FOR ME AND LAURA.
24/7.365
5:30
PROBABLY HAD A WHILE BACK.
I'LL TAKE A SHOT. AND POUR ONE FOR MY PROFESSIONAL EXTERMINATOR HERE.
WOULD YOU BELIEVE ME IF I SAID THAT TOTAL HUMILIATION WASN'T THE WORST PART OF MY DAY?

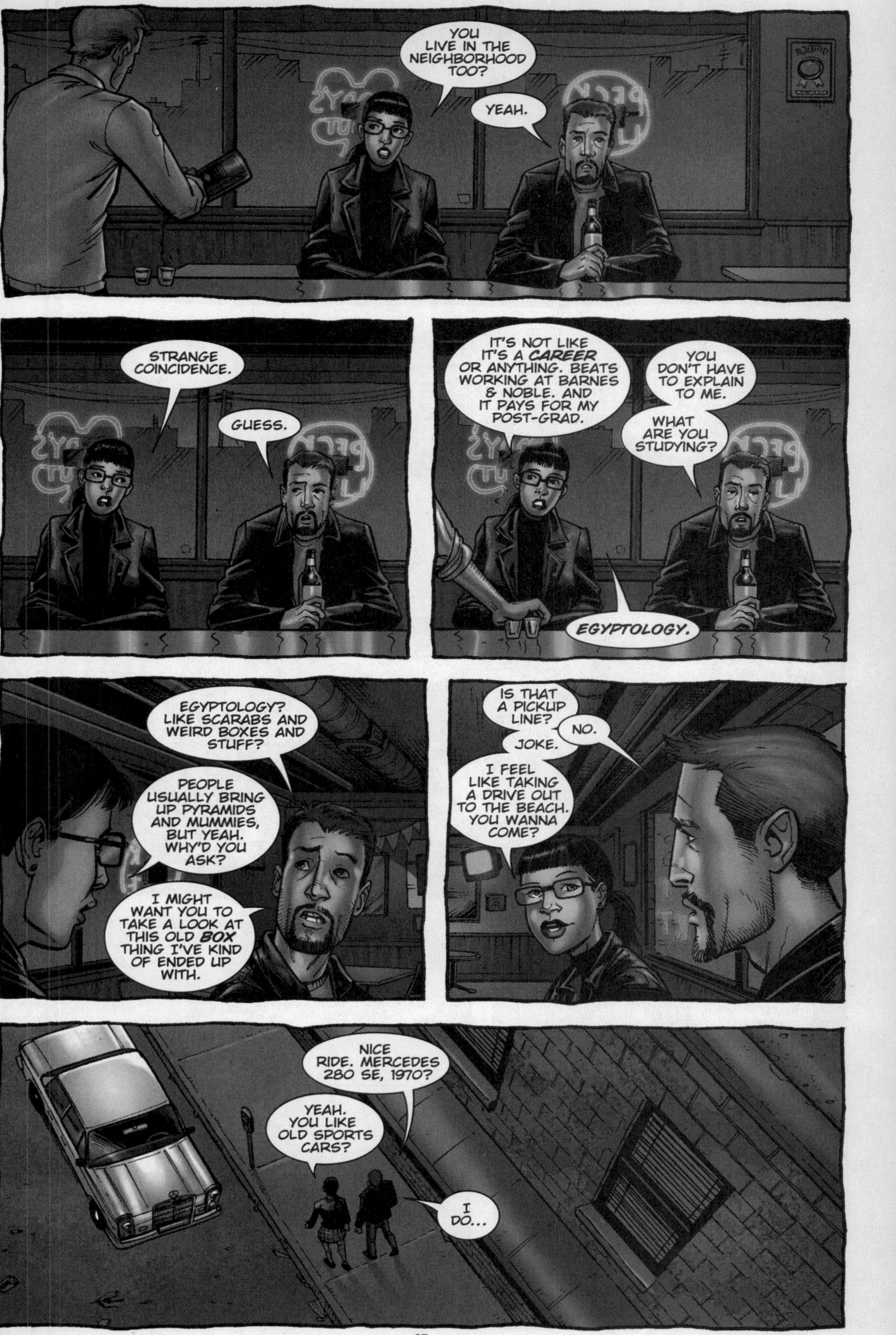
YOU LIVE IN THE NEIGHBORHOOD TOO?
YEAH.
STRANGE COINCIDENCE.
GUESS.
IT'S NOT LIKE IT'S A *CAREER* OR ANYTHING. BEATS WORKING AT BARNES & NOBLE. AND IT PAYS FOR MY POST-GRAD.
YOU DON'T HAVE TO EXPLAIN TO ME.
WHAT ARE YOU STUDYING?
EGYPTOLOGY.
EGYPTOLOGY? LIKE SCARABS AND WEIRD BOXES AND STUFF?
PEOPLE USUALLY BRING UP PYRAMIDS AND MUMMIES, BUT YEAH. WHY'D YOU ASK?
I MIGHT WANT YOU TO TAKE A LOOK AT THIS OLD *BOX* THING I'VE KIND OF ENDED UP WITH.
IS THAT A PICKUP LINE?
NO.
JOKE.
I FEEL LIKE TAKING A DRIVE OUT TO THE BEACH. YOU WANNA COME?
NICE RIDE. MERCEDES 280 SE, 1970?
YEAH. YOU LIKE OLD SPORTS CARS?
I DO...

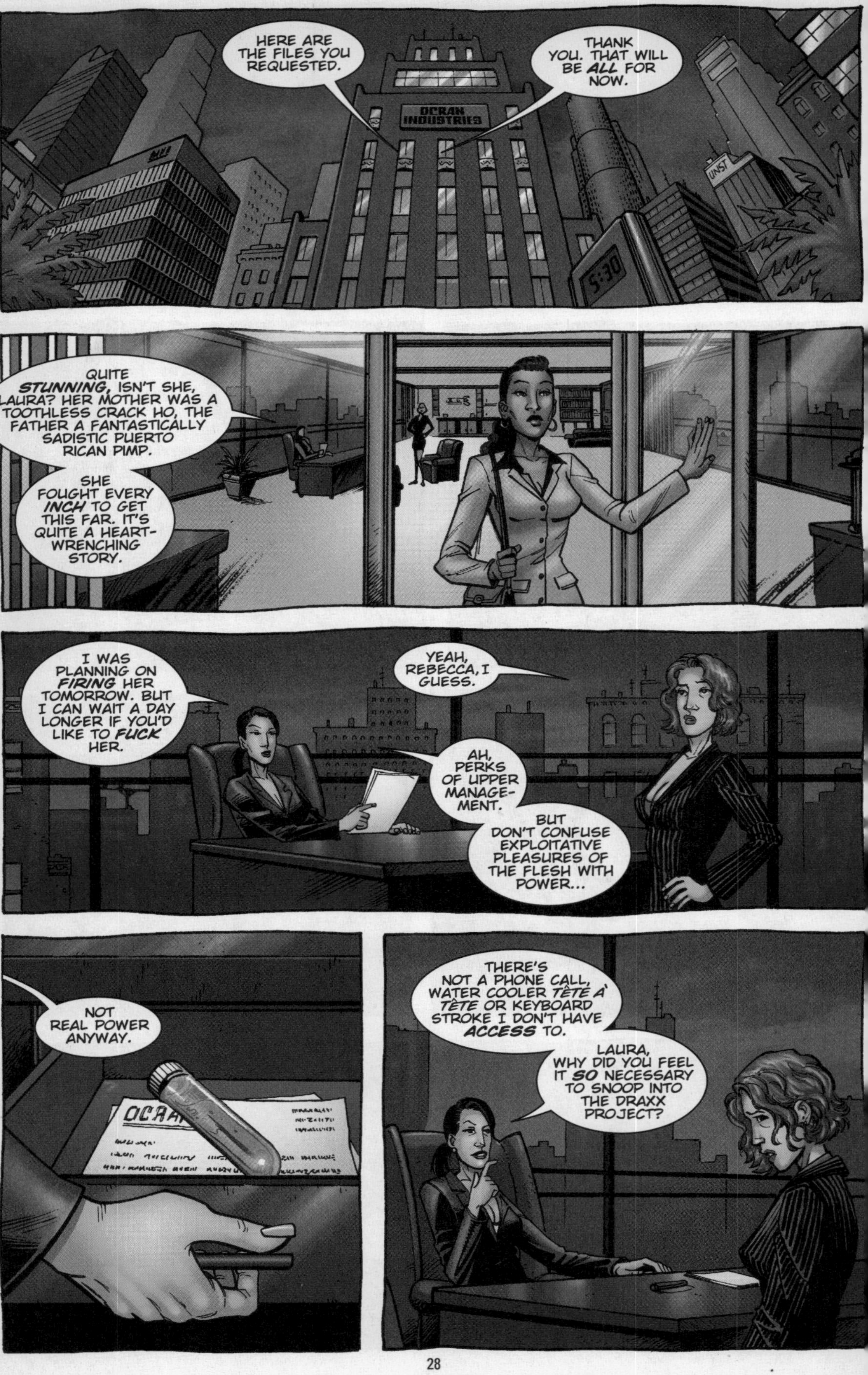
HERE ARE THE FILES YOU REQUESTED.
OCRAN INDUSTRIES
THANK YOU. THAT WILL BE ALL FOR NOW.
5:30
QUITE STUNNING, ISN'T SHE, LAURA? HER MOTHER WAS A TOOTHLESS CRACK HO, THE FATHER A FANTASTICALLY SADISTIC PUERTO RICAN PIMP.
SHE FOUGHT EVERY INCH TO GET THIS FAR. IT'S QUITE A HEART-WRENCHING STORY.
I WAS PLANNING ON FIRING HER TOMORROW. BUT I CAN WAIT A DAY LONGER IF YOU'D LIKE TO FUCK HER.
YEAH, REBECCA, I GUESS.
AH, PERKS OF UPPER MANAGE-MENT.
BUT DON'T CONFUSE EXPLOITATIVE PLEASURES OF THE FLESH WITH POWER...
NOT REAL POWER ANYWAY.
THERE'S NOT A PHONE CALL, WATER COOLER TÊTE À TÊTE OR KEYBOARD STROKE I DON'T HAVE ACCESS TO.
LAURA, WHY DID YOU FEEL IT SO NECESSARY TO SNOOP INTO THE DRAXX PROJECT?

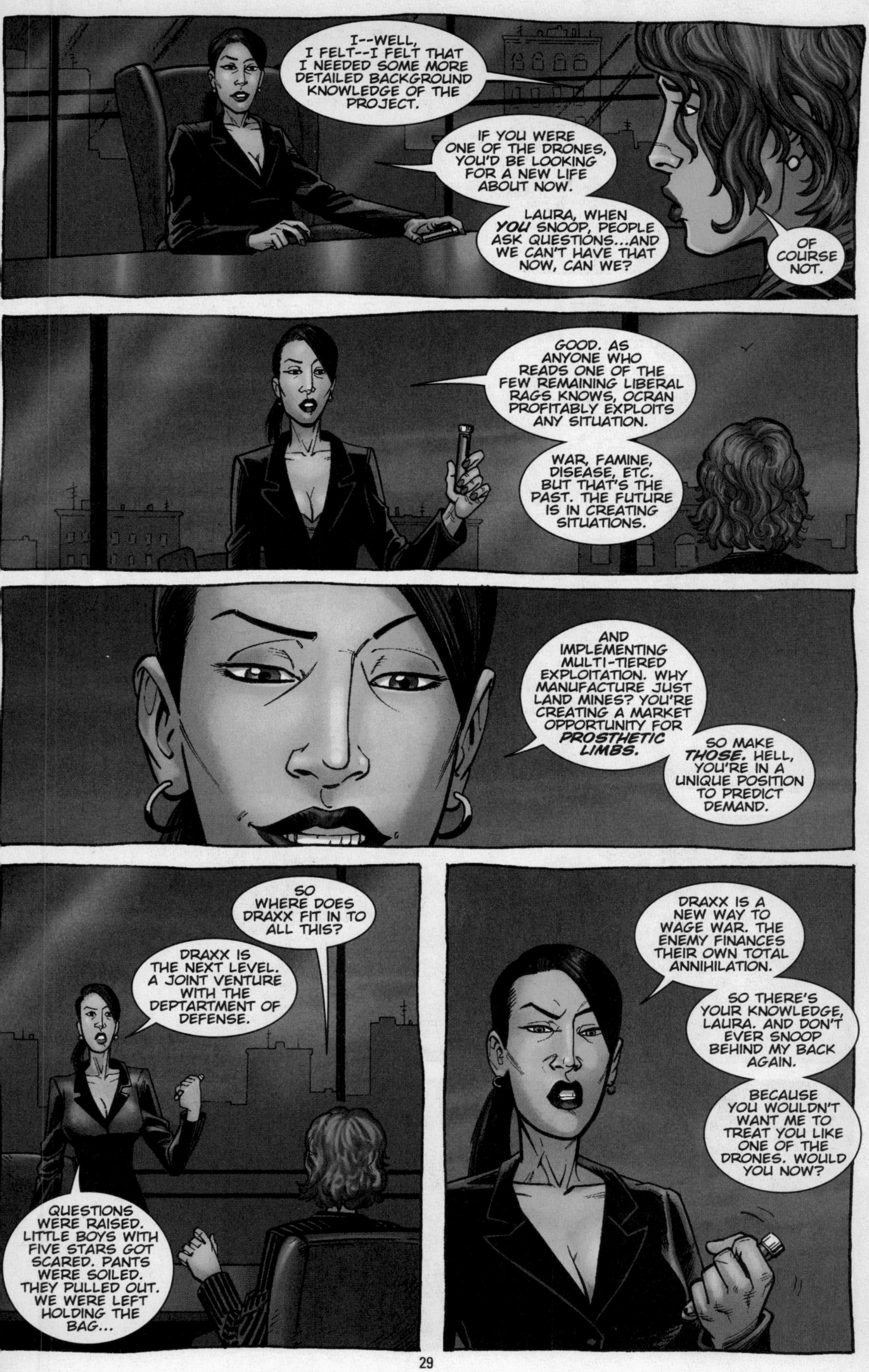
I--WELL, I FELT--I FELT THAT I NEEDED SOME MORE DETAILED BACKGROUND KNOWLEDGE OF THE PROJECT.
IF YOU WERE ONE OF THE DRONES, YOU'D BE LOOKING FOR A NEW LIFE ABOUT NOW.
LAURA, WHEN YOU SNOOP, PEOPLE ASK QUESTIONS...AND WE CAN'T HAVE THAT NOW, CAN WE?
OF COURSE NOT.
GOOD. AS ANYONE WHO READS ONE OF THE FEW REMAINING LIBERAL RAGS KNOWS, OCRAN PROFITABLY EXPLOITS ANY SITUATION.
WAR, FAMINE, DISEASE, ETC. BUT THAT'S THE PAST. THE FUTURE IS IN CREATING SITUATIONS.
AND IMPLEMENTING MULTI-TIERED EXPLOITATION. WHY MANUFACTURE JUST LAND MINES? YOU'RE CREATING A MARKET OPPORTUNITY FOR PROSTHETIC LIMBS.
SO MAKE THOSE. HELL, YOU'RE IN A UNIQUE POSITION TO PREDICT DEMAND.
SO WHERE DOES DRAXX FIT IN TO ALL THIS?
DRAXX IS THE NEXT LEVEL. A JOINT VENTURE WITH THE DEPTARTMENT OF DEFENSE.
QUESTIONS WERE RAISED. LITTLE BOYS WITH FIVE STARS GOT SCARED. PANTS WERE SOILED. THEY PULLED OUT. WE WERE LEFT HOLDING THE BAG...
DRAXX IS A NEW WAY TO WAGE WAR. THE ENEMY FINANCES THEIR OWN TOTAL ANNIHILATION.
SO THERE'S YOUR KNOWLEDGE, LAURA. AND DON'T EVER SNOOP BEHIND MY BACK AGAIN.
BECAUSE YOU WOULDN'T WANT ME TO TREAT YOU LIKE ONE OF THE DRONES. WOULD YOU NOW?

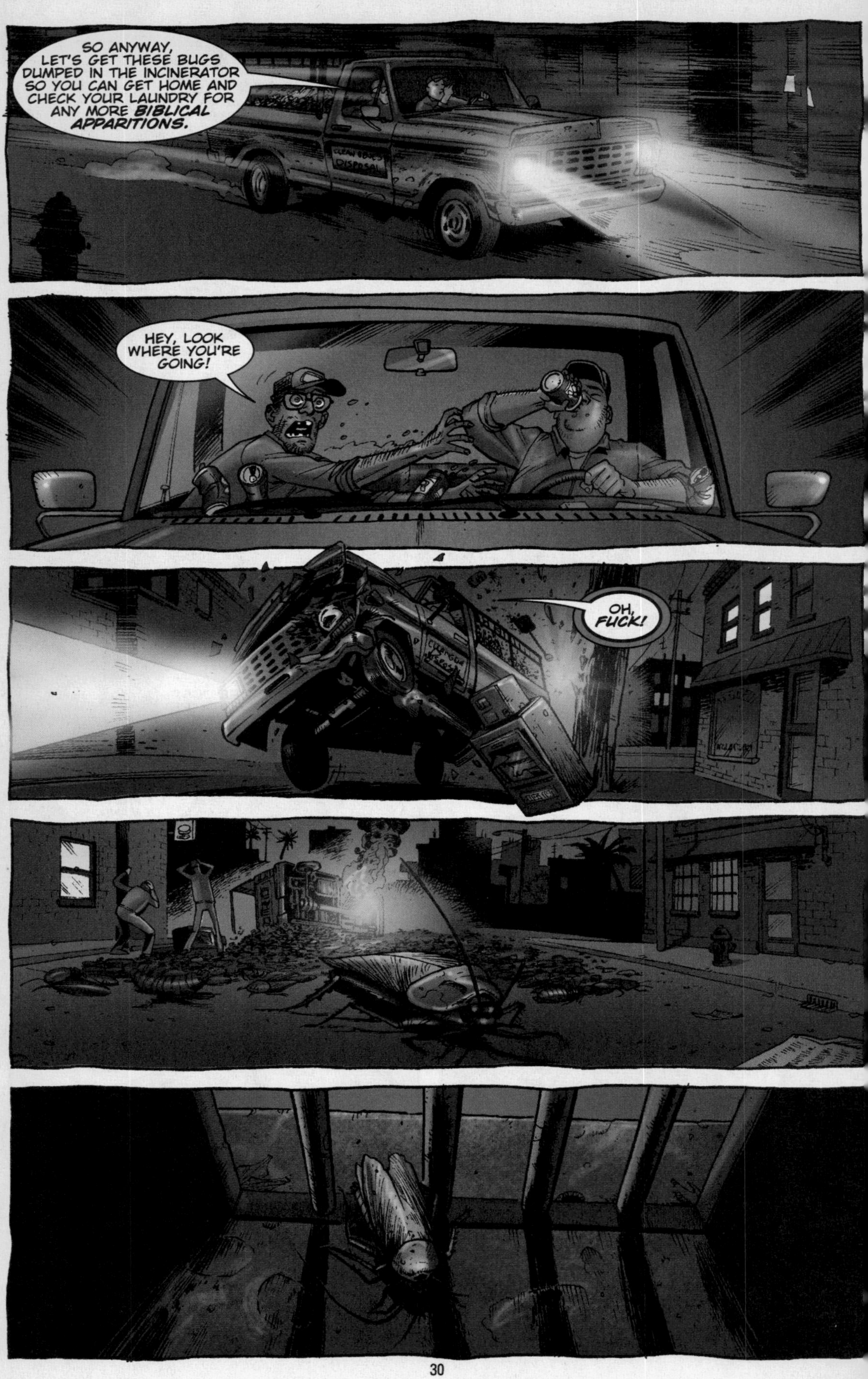
SO ANYWAY, LET'S GET THESE BUGS DUMPED IN THE INCINERATOR SO YOU CAN GET HOME AND CHECK YOUR LAUNDRY FOR ANY MORE BIBLICAL APPARITIONS.
HEY, LOOK WHERE YOU'RE GOING!
OH, FUCK!

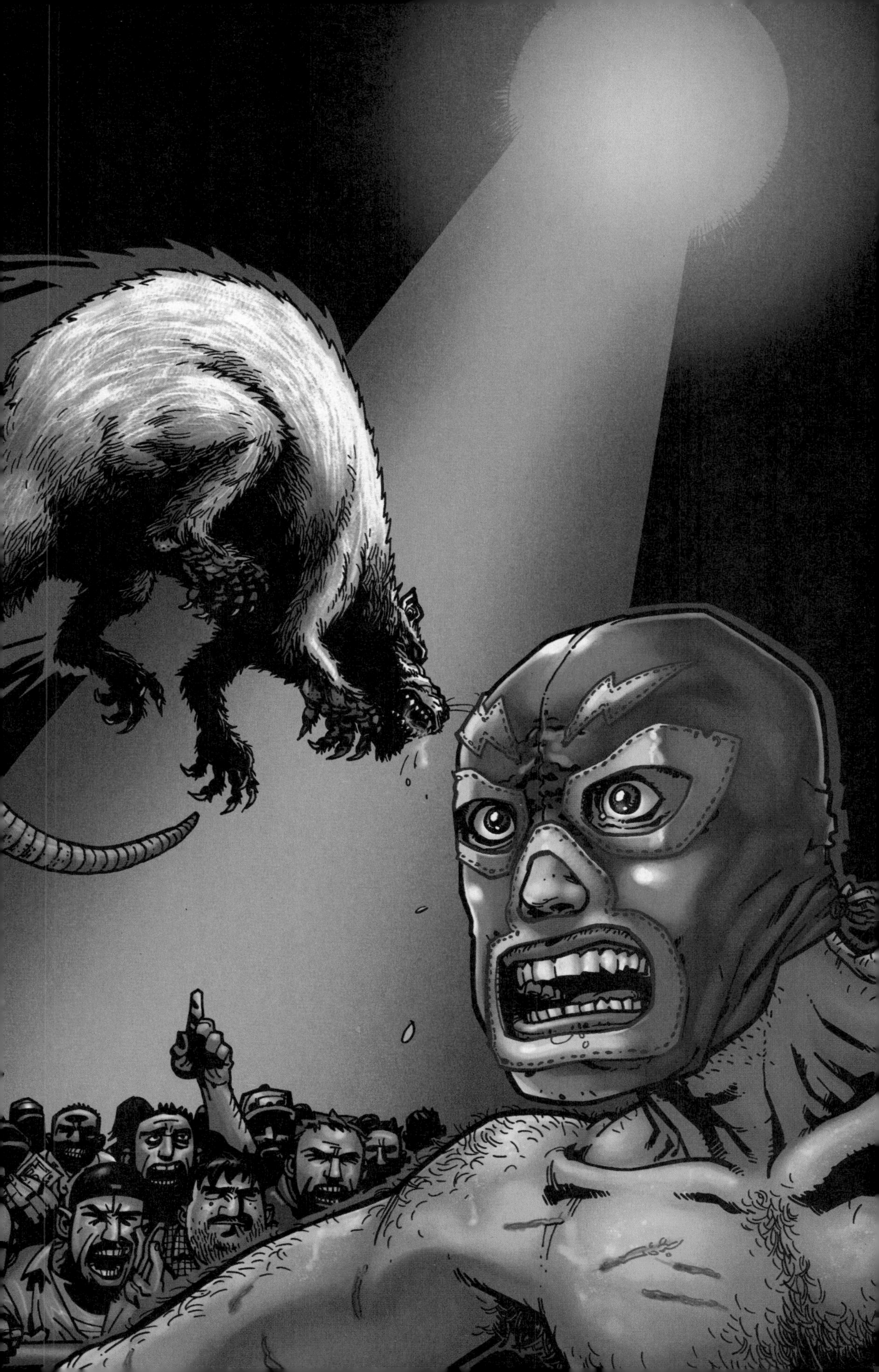

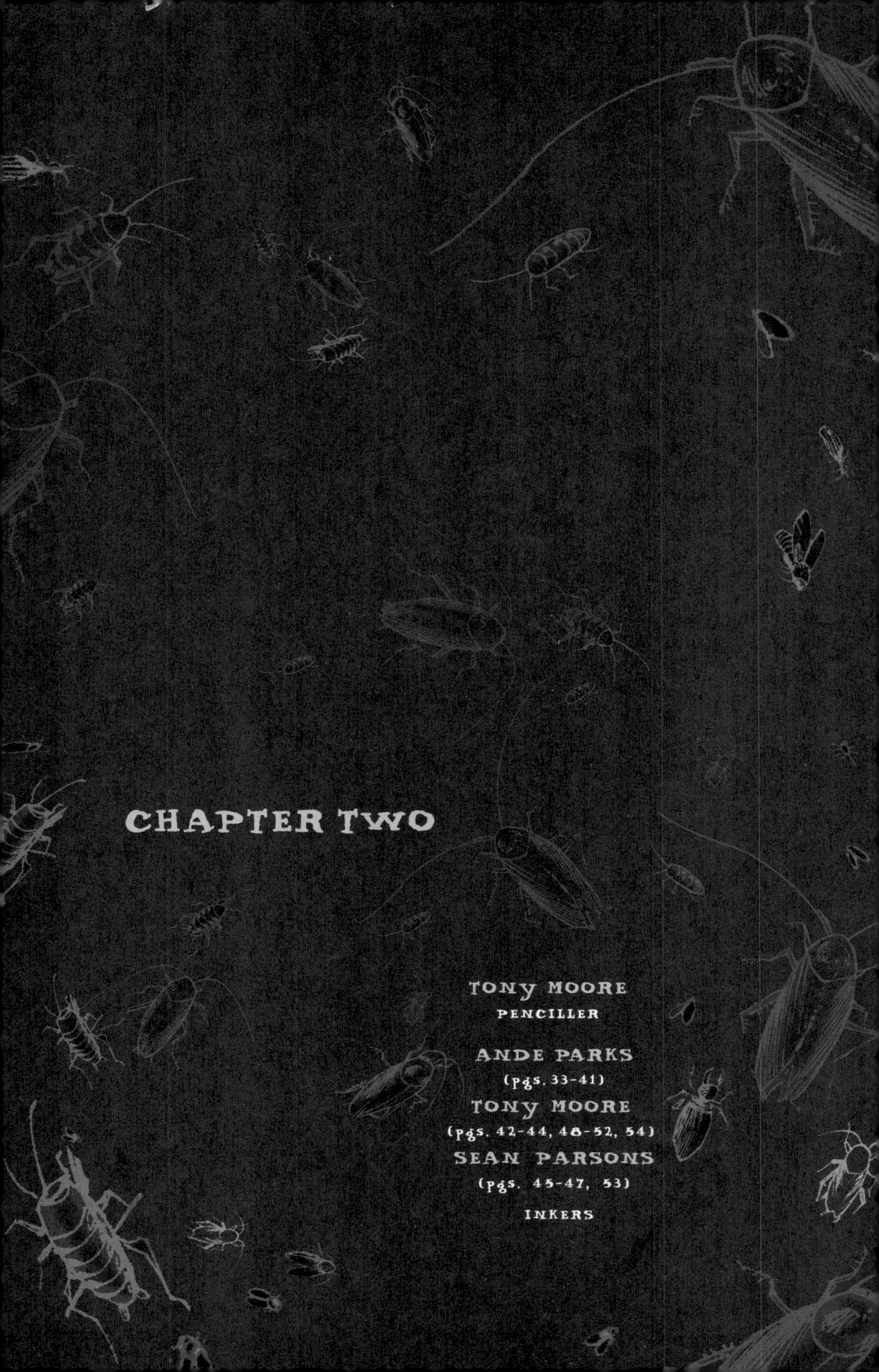

CHAPTER TWO

TONY MOORE
PENCILLER

ANDE PARKS
(pgs. 33-41)
TONY MOORE
(pgs. 42-44, 48-52, 54)
SEAN PARSONS
(pgs. 45-47, 53)
INKERS

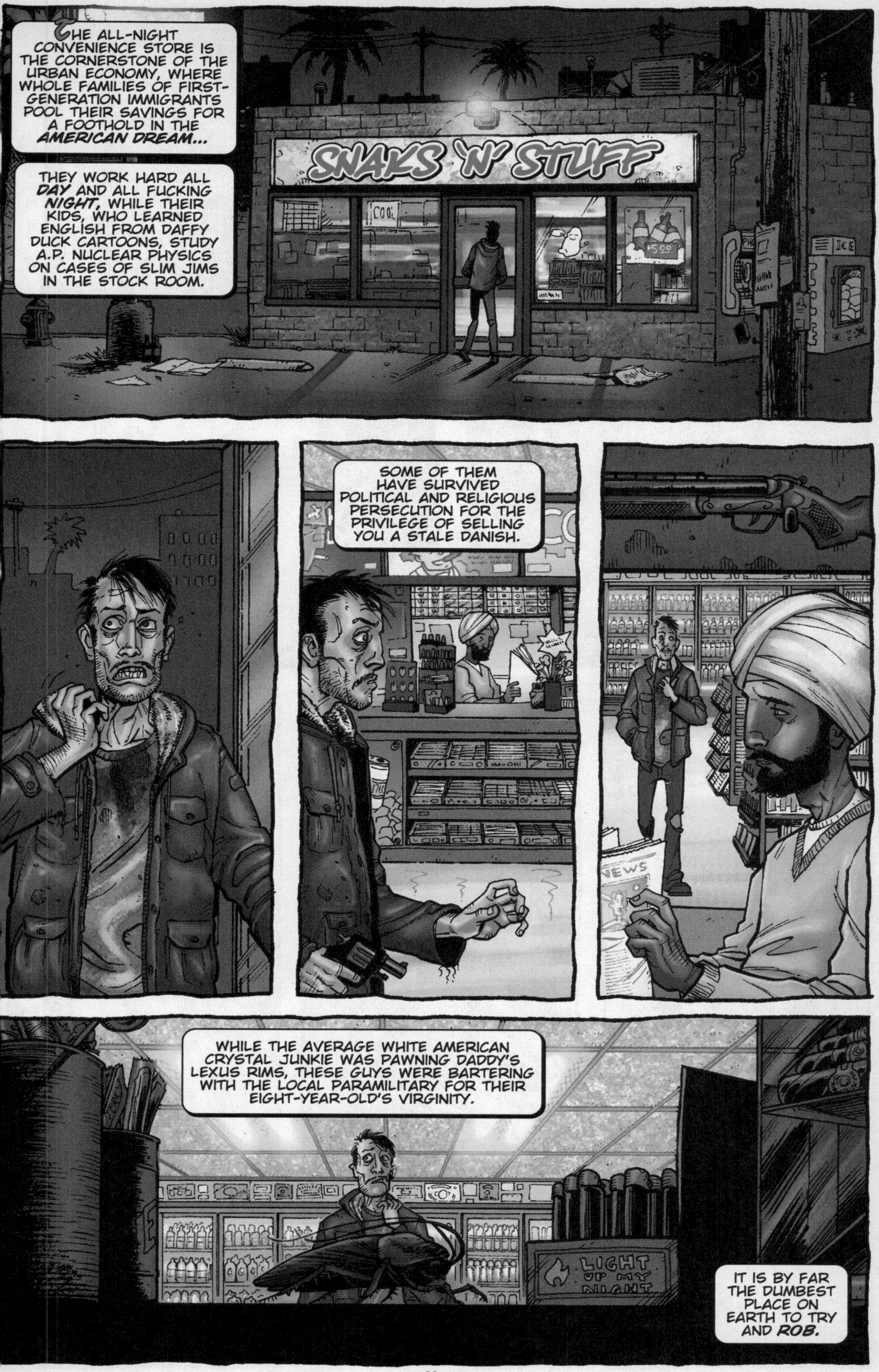
THE ALL-NIGHT CONVENIENCE STORE IS THE CORNERSTONE OF THE URBAN ECONOMY, WHERE WHOLE FAMILIES OF FIRST-GENERATION IMMIGRANTS POOL THEIR SAVINGS FOR A FOOTHOLD IN THE *AMERICAN DREAM...*
SNAKS 'N' STUFF
COOL
$5.00
THEY WORK HARD ALL *DAY* AND ALL FUCKING *NIGHT,* WHILE THEIR KIDS, WHO LEARNED ENGLISH FROM DAFFY DUCK CARTOONS, STUDY A.P. NUCLEAR PHYSICS ON CASES OF SLIM JIMS IN THE STOCK ROOM.
SOME OF THEM HAVE SURVIVED POLITICAL AND RELIGIOUS PERSECUTION FOR THE PRIVILEGE OF SELLING YOU A STALE DANISH.
NEWS
WHILE THE AVERAGE WHITE AMERICAN CRYSTAL JUNKIE WAS PAWNING DADDY'S LEXUS RIMS, THESE GUYS WERE BARTERING WITH THE LOCAL PARAMILITARY FOR THEIR EIGHT-YEAR-OLD'S VIRGINITY.
LIGHT UP MY NIGHT
IT IS BY FAR THE DUMBEST PLACE ON EARTH TO TRY AND *ROB.*

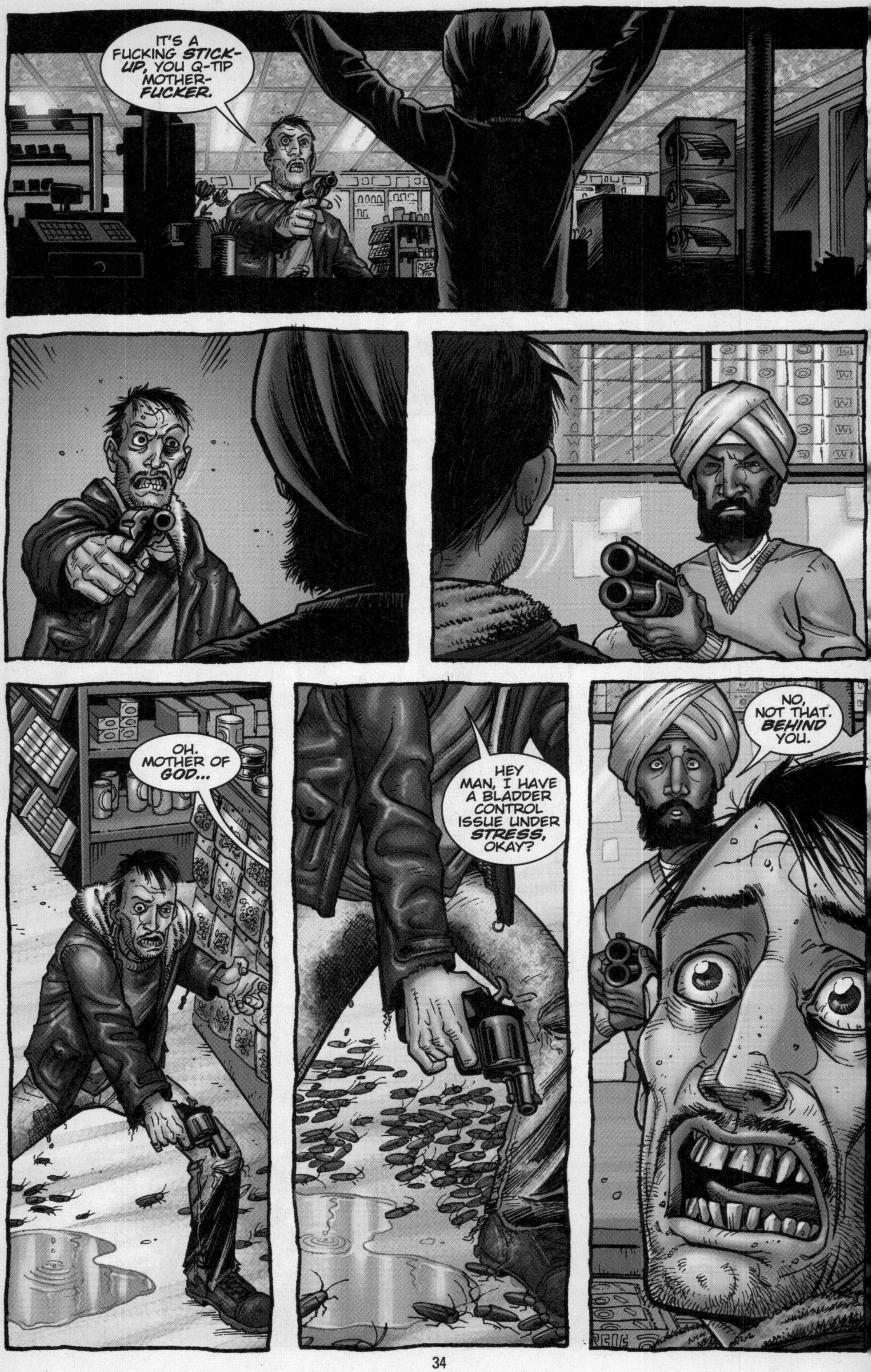
IT'S A FUCKING STICK-UP, YOU Q-TIP MOTHER-FUCKER.
OH. MOTHER OF GOD...
HEY MAN, I HAVE A BLADDER CONTROL ISSUE UNDER STRESS, OKAY?
NO, NOT THAT. BEHIND YOU.

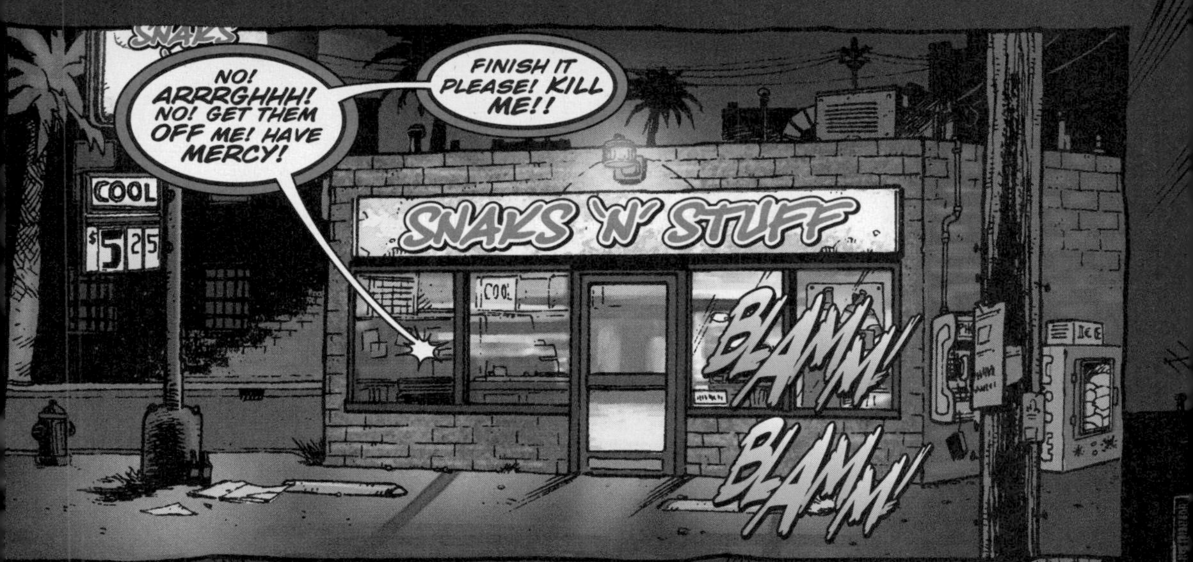
NO! ARRRGHHH! NO! GET THEM OFF ME! HAVE MERCY!
FINISH IT PLEASE! KILL ME!!
SNAKS 'N' STUFF
COOL
$5.25
BLAMM!
BLAMM!

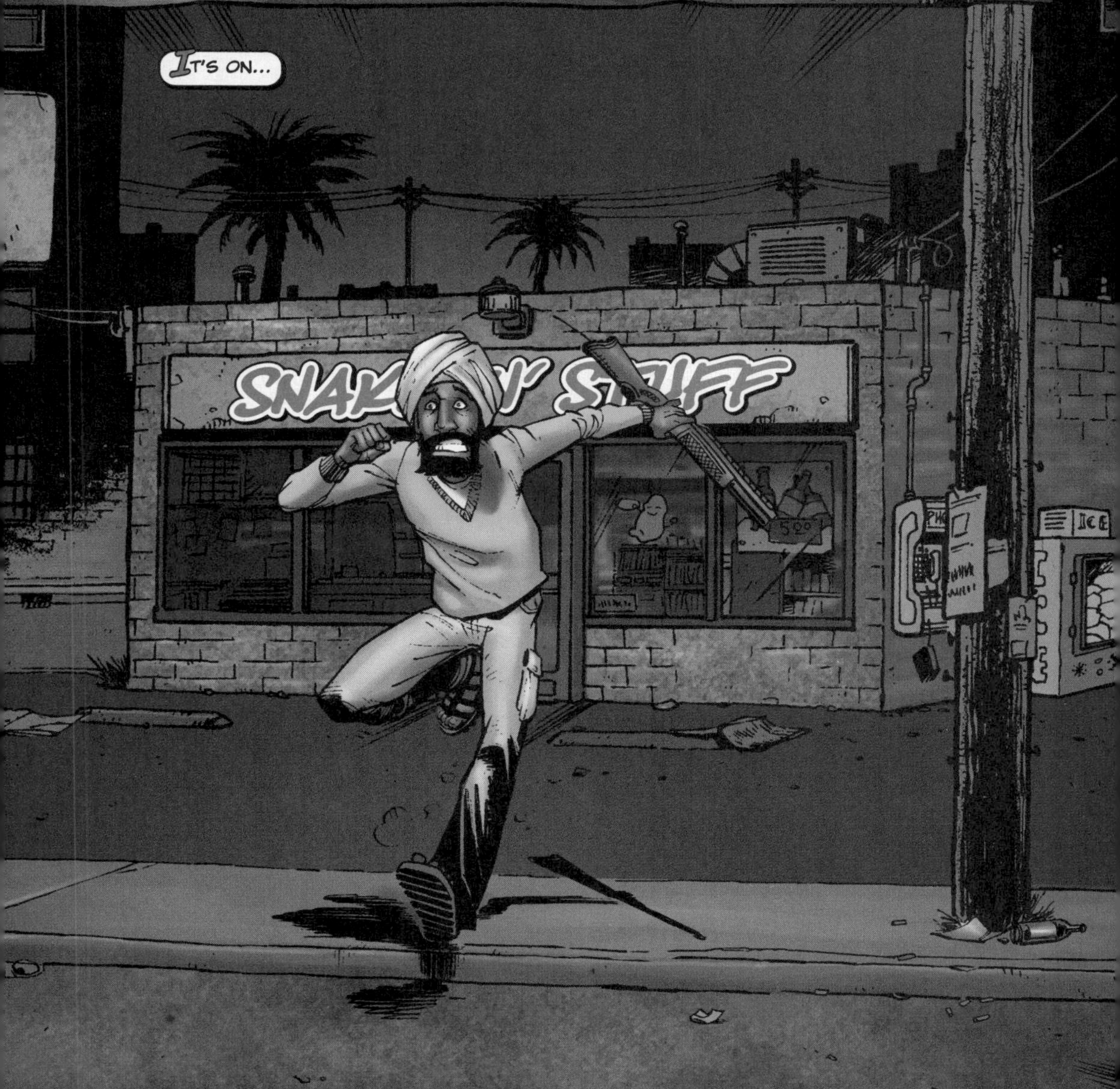
IT'S ON...
SNAKS 'N' STUFF

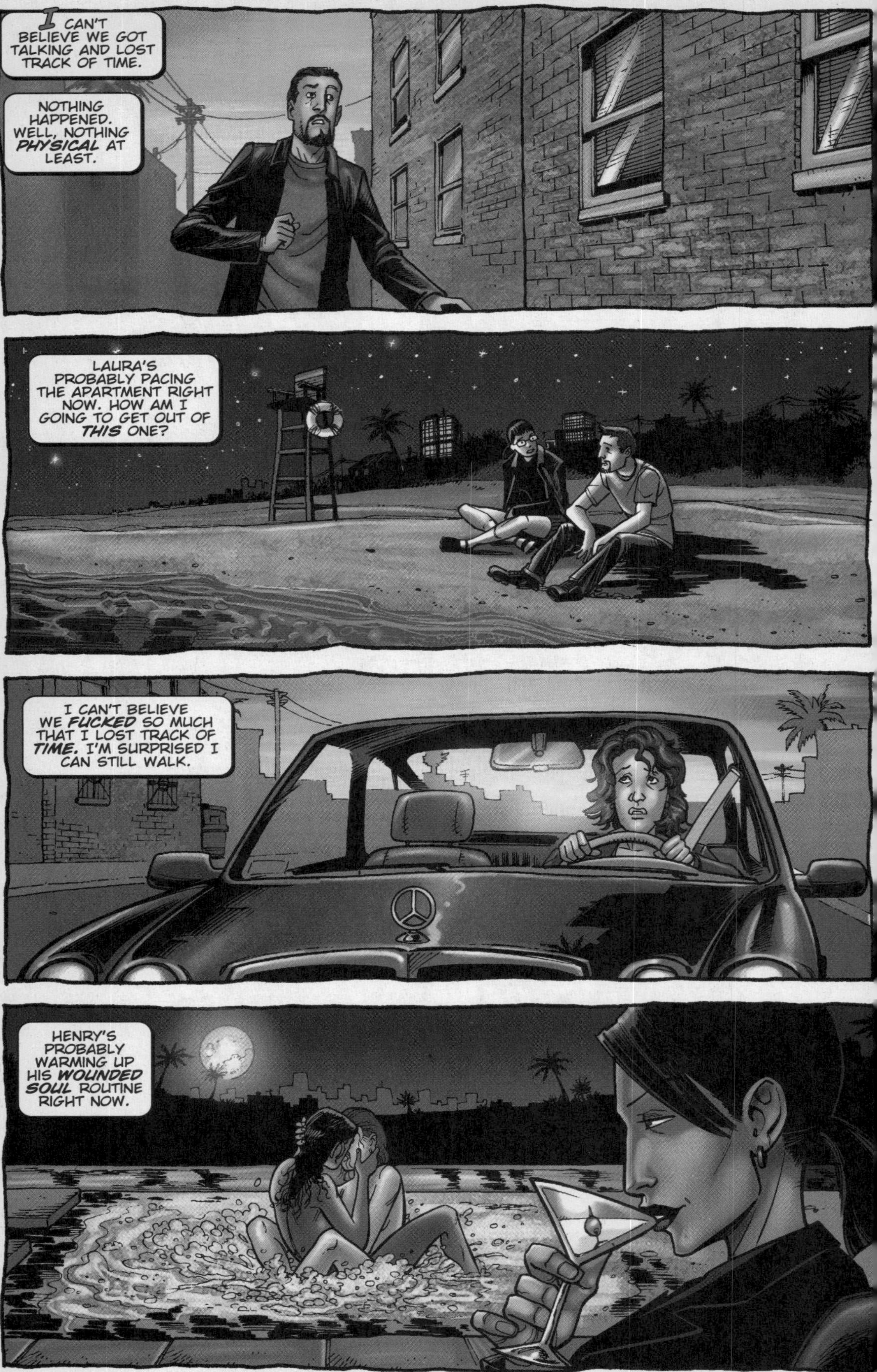
I CAN'T BELIEVE WE GOT TALKING AND LOST TRACK OF TIME.
NOTHING HAPPENED. WELL, NOTHING PHYSICAL AT LEAST.
LAURA'S PROBABLY PACING THE APARTMENT RIGHT NOW. HOW AM I GOING TO GET OUT OF THIS ONE?
I CAN'T BELIEVE WE FUCKED SO MUCH THAT I LOST TRACK OF TIME. I'M SURPRISED I CAN STILL WALK.
HENRY'S PROBABLY WARMING UP HIS WOUNDED SOUL ROUTINE RIGHT NOW.

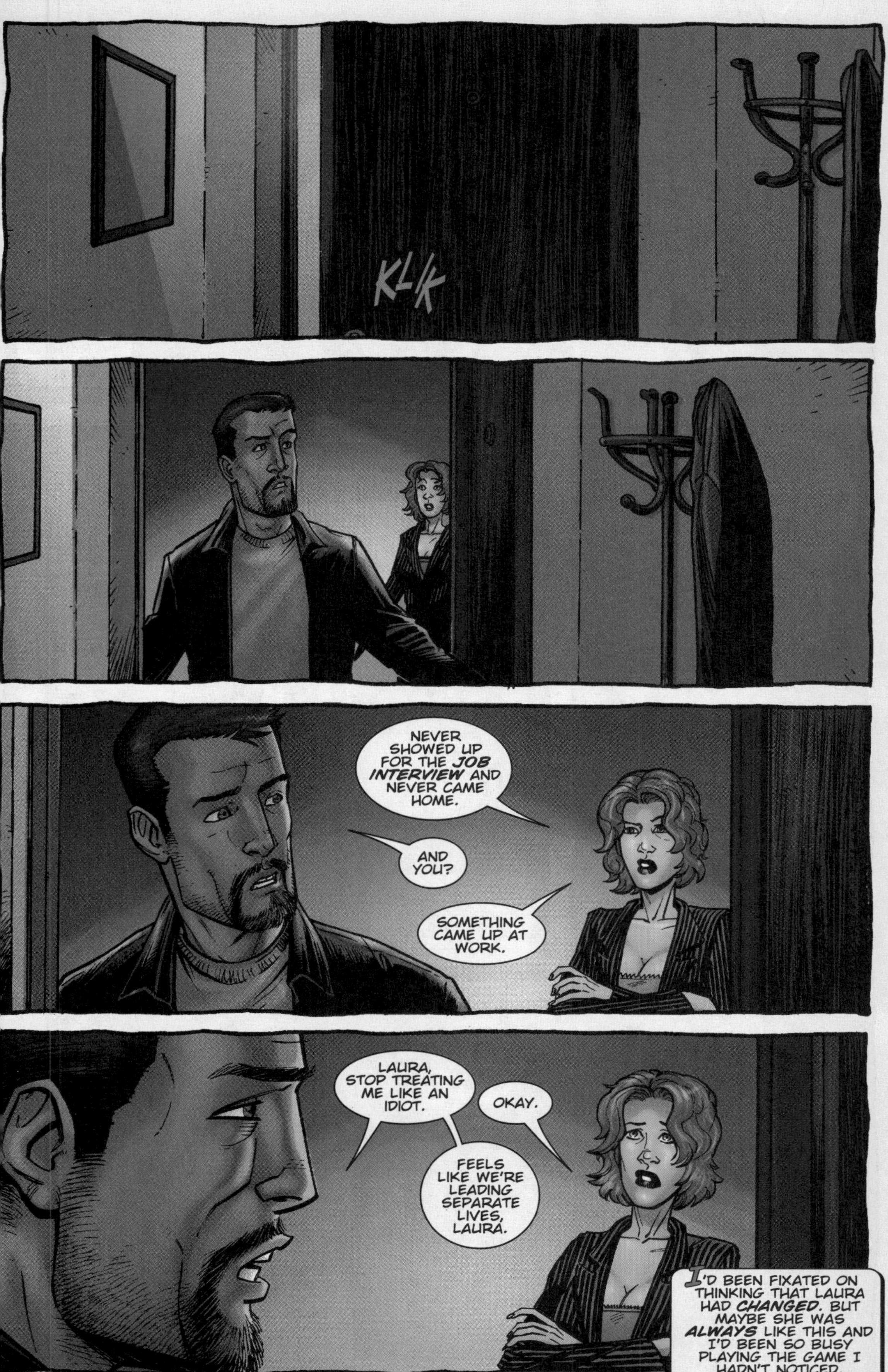
KLIK
NEVER SHOWED UP FOR THE JOB INTERVIEW AND NEVER CAME HOME.
AND YOU?
SOMETHING CAME UP AT WORK.
LAURA, STOP TREATING ME LIKE AN IDIOT.
OKAY.
FEELS LIKE WE'RE LEADING SEPARATE LIVES, LAURA.
I'D BEEN FIXATED ON THINKING THAT LAURA HAD CHANGED. BUT MAYBE SHE WAS ALWAYS LIKE THIS AND I'D BEEN SO BUSY PLAYING THE GAME I HADN'T NOTICED.

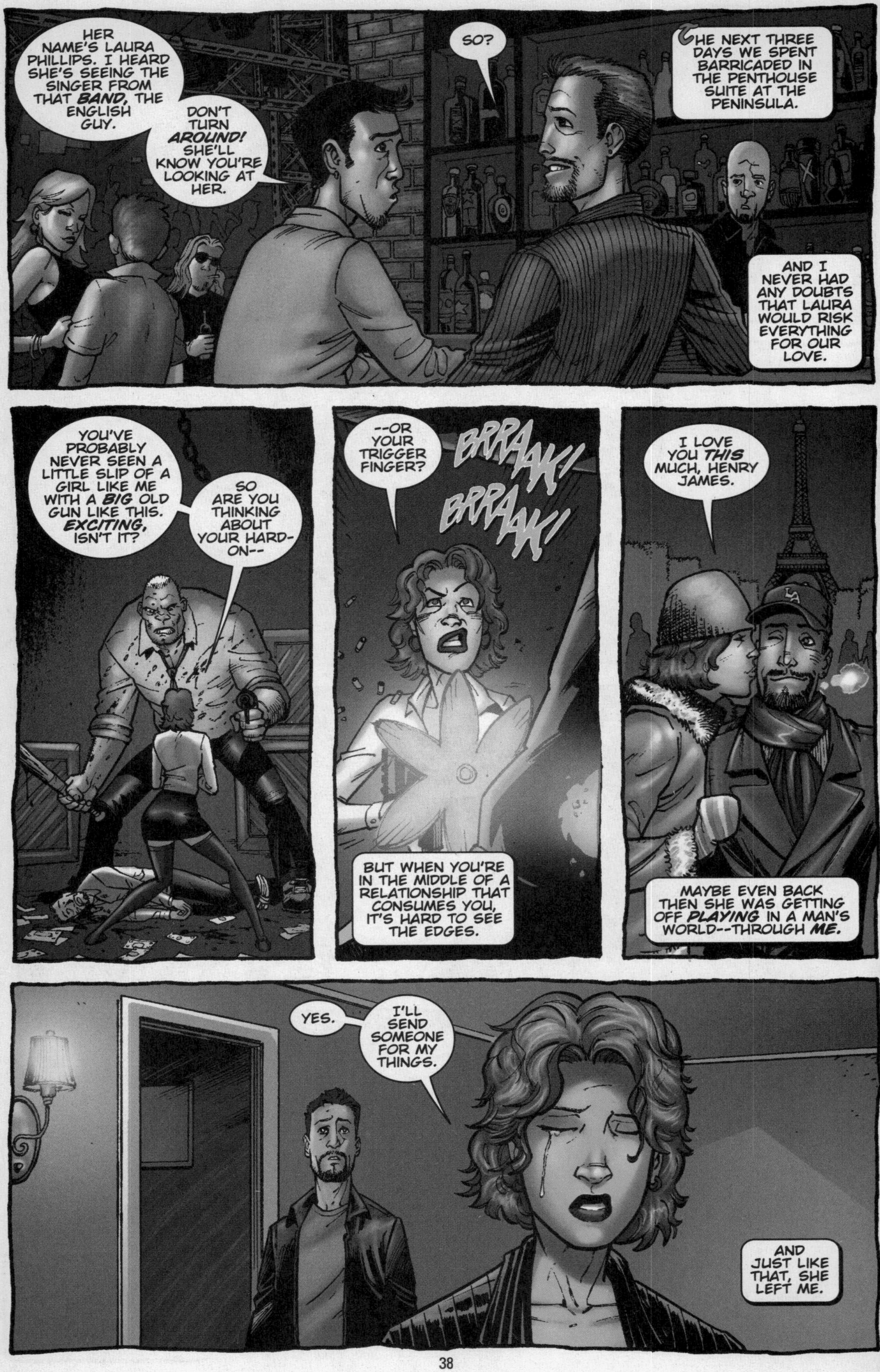
HER NAME'S LAURA PHILLIPS. I HEARD SHE'S SEEING THE SINGER FROM THAT BAND, THE ENGLISH GUY.
SO?
DON'T TURN AROUND! SHE'LL KNOW YOU'RE LOOKING AT HER.
THE NEXT THREE DAYS WE SPENT BARRICADED IN THE PENTHOUSE SUITE AT THE PENINSULA.
AND I NEVER HAD ANY DOUBTS THAT LAURA WOULD RISK EVERYTHING FOR OUR LOVE.
YOU'VE PROBABLY NEVER SEEN A LITTLE SLIP OF A GIRL LIKE ME WITH A BIG OLD GUN LIKE THIS. EXCITING, ISN'T IT?
SO ARE YOU THINKING ABOUT YOUR HARD-ON--
--OR YOUR TRIGGER FINGER?
BRRAAK!
BRRAAK!
BUT WHEN YOU'RE IN THE MIDDLE OF A RELATIONSHIP THAT CONSUMES YOU, IT'S HARD TO SEE THE EDGES.
I LOVE YOU THIS MUCH, HENRY JAMES.
MAYBE EVEN BACK THEN SHE WAS GETTING OFF PLAYING IN A MAN'S WORLD--THROUGH ME.
YES.
I'LL SEND SOMEONE FOR MY THINGS.
AND JUST LIKE THAT, SHE LEFT ME.

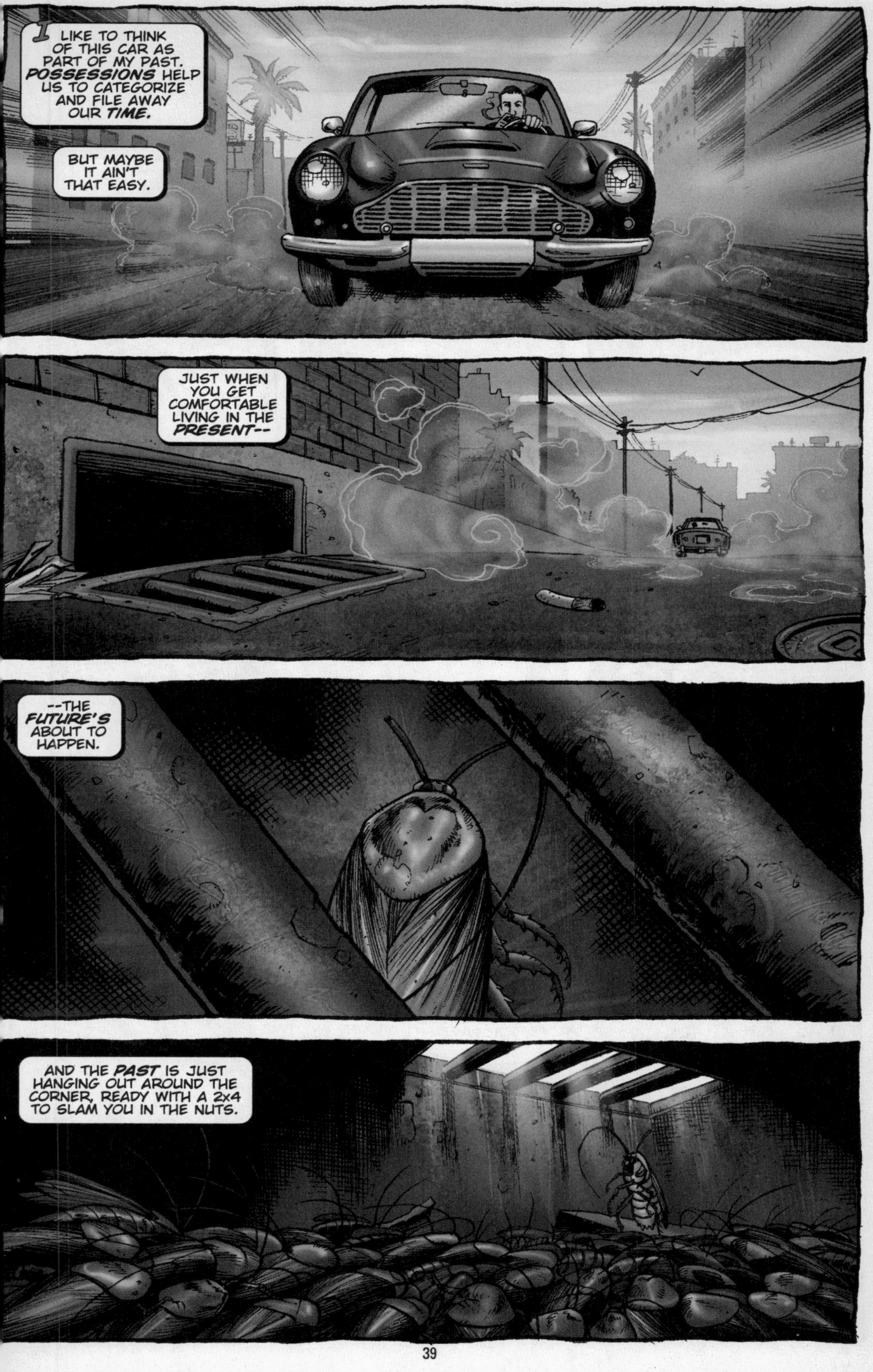
I LIKE TO THINK OF THIS CAR AS PART OF MY PAST. POSSESSIONS HELP US TO CATEGORIZE AND FILE AWAY OUR TIME.
BUT MAYBE IT AIN'T THAT EASY.
JUST WHEN YOU GET COMFORTABLE LIVING IN THE PRESENT--
--THE FUTURE'S ABOUT TO HAPPEN.
AND THE PAST IS JUST HANGING OUT AROUND THE CORNER, READY WITH A 2x4 TO SLAM YOU IN THE NUTS.

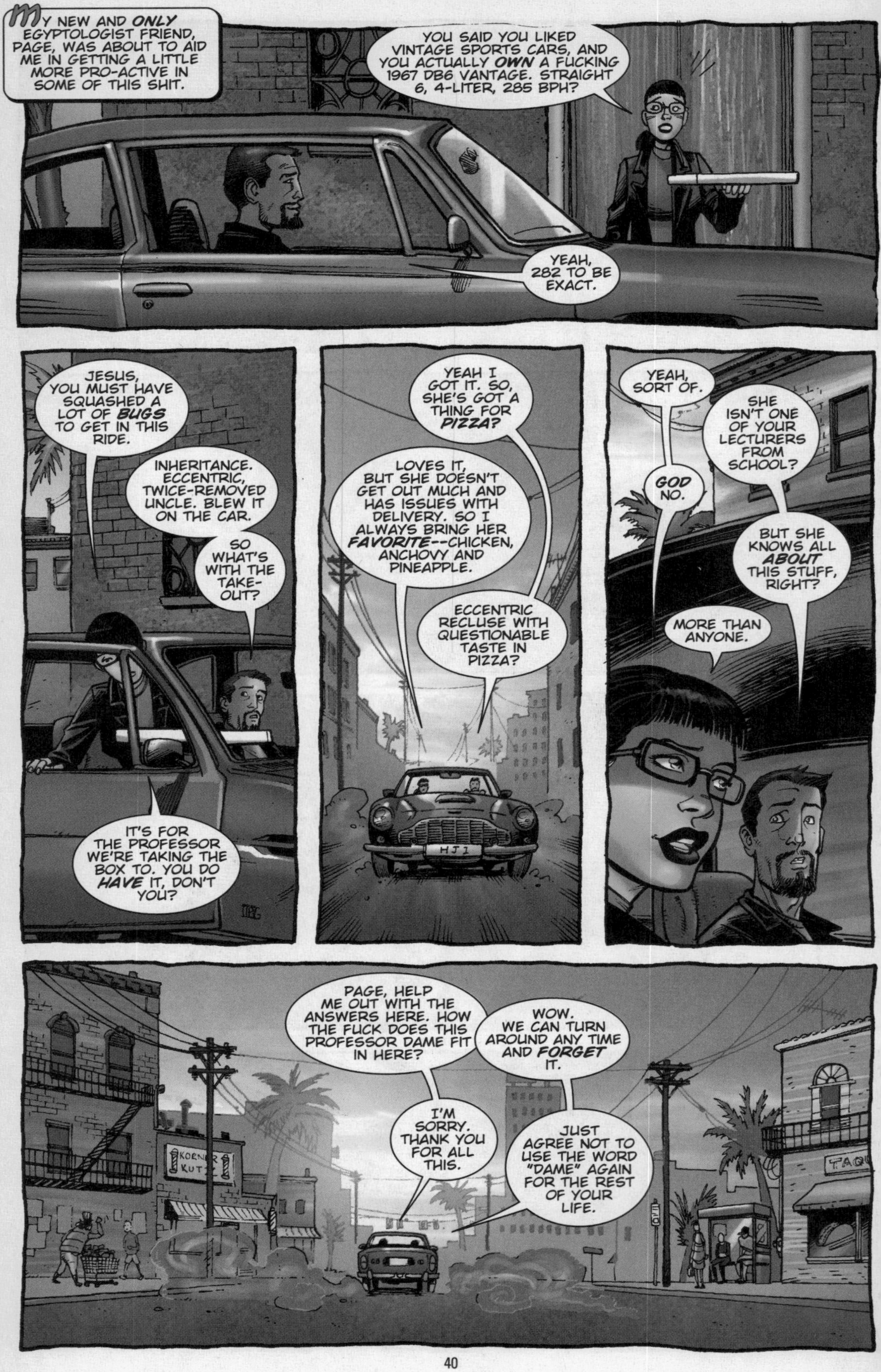
MY NEW AND ONLY EGYPTOLOGIST FRIEND, PAGE, WAS ABOUT TO AID ME IN GETTING A LITTLE MORE PRO-ACTIVE IN SOME OF THIS SHIT.
YOU SAID YOU LIKED VINTAGE SPORTS CARS, AND YOU ACTUALLY OWN A FUCKING 1967 DB6 VANTAGE. STRAIGHT 6, 4-LITER, 285 BPH?
YEAH, 282 TO BE EXACT.
JESUS, YOU MUST HAVE SQUASHED A LOT OF BUGS TO GET IN THIS RIDE.
INHERITANCE. ECCENTRIC, TWICE-REMOVED UNCLE. BLEW IT ON THE CAR.
SO WHAT'S WITH THE TAKE-OUT?
IT'S FOR THE PROFESSOR WE'RE TAKING THE BOX TO. YOU DO HAVE IT, DON'T YOU?
YEAH I GOT IT. SO, SHE'S GOT A THING FOR PIZZA?
LOVES IT, BUT SHE DOESN'T GET OUT MUCH AND HAS ISSUES WITH DELIVERY. SO I ALWAYS BRING HER FAVORITE--CHICKEN, ANCHOVY AND PINEAPPLE.
ECCENTRIC RECLUSE WITH QUESTIONABLE TASTE IN PIZZA?
HJ1
YEAH, SORT OF.
SHE ISN'T ONE OF YOUR LECTURERS FROM SCHOOL?
GOD NO.
BUT SHE KNOWS ALL ABOUT THIS STUFF, RIGHT?
MORE THAN ANYONE.
PAGE, HELP ME OUT WITH THE ANSWERS HERE. HOW THE FUCK DOES THIS PROFESSOR DAME FIT IN HERE?
WOW. WE CAN TURN AROUND ANY TIME AND FORGET IT.
I'M SORRY. THANK YOU FOR ALL THIS.
JUST AGREE NOT TO USE THE WORD "DAME" AGAIN FOR THE REST OF YOUR LIFE.
KORNER KUTS

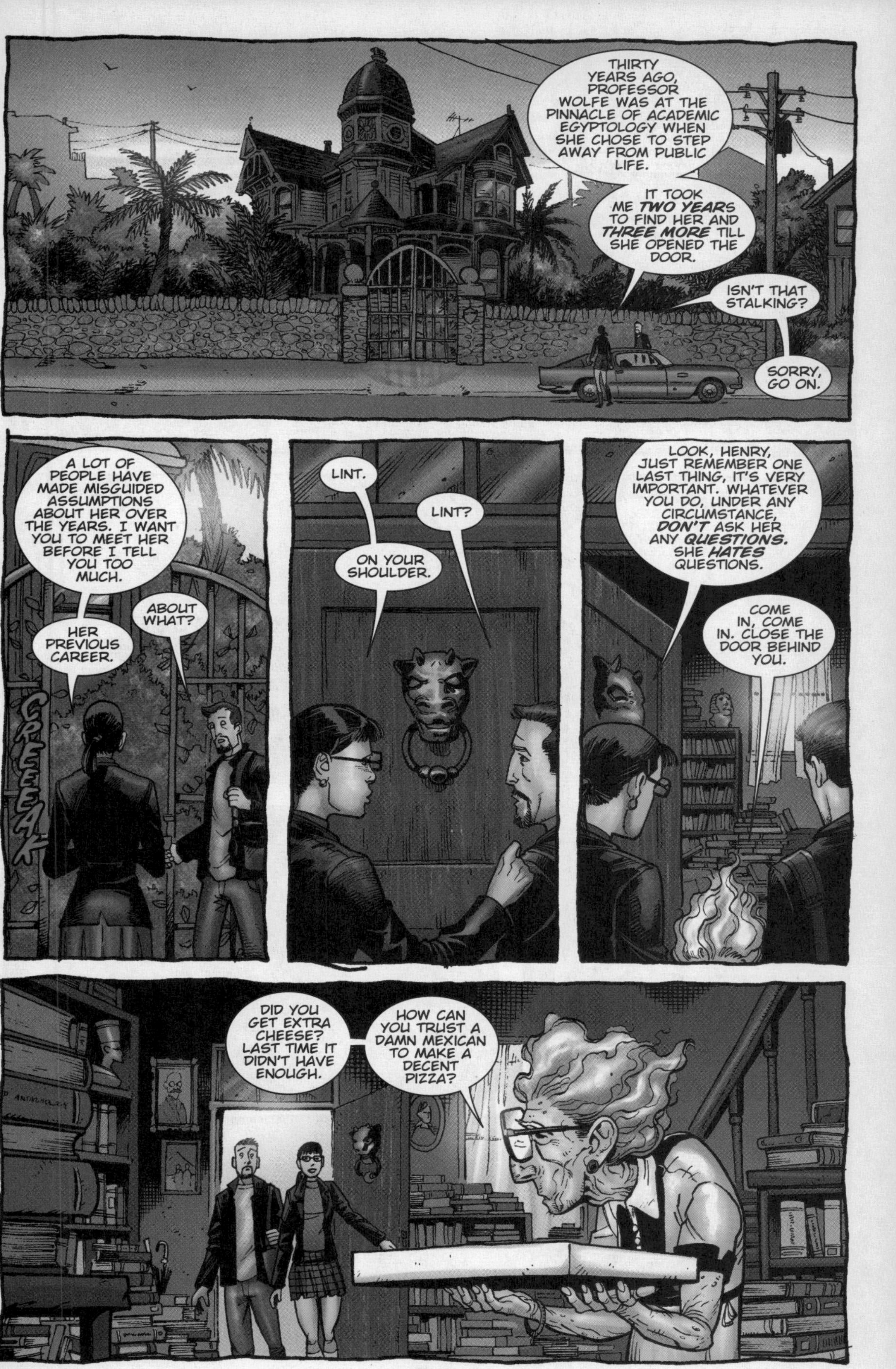
THIRTY YEARS AGO, PROFESSOR WOLFE WAS AT THE PINNACLE OF ACADEMIC EGYPTOLOGY WHEN SHE CHOSE TO STEP AWAY FROM PUBLIC LIFE.
IT TOOK ME TWO YEARS TO FIND HER AND THREE MORE TILL SHE OPENED THE DOOR.
ISN'T THAT STALKING?
SORRY, GO ON.
A LOT OF PEOPLE HAVE MADE MISGUIDED ASSUMPTIONS ABOUT HER OVER THE YEARS. I WANT YOU TO MEET HER BEFORE I TELL YOU TOO MUCH.
ABOUT WHAT?
HER PREVIOUS CAREER.
CREEEAK
LINT.
LINT?
ON YOUR SHOULDER.
LOOK, HENRY, JUST REMEMBER ONE LAST THING, IT'S VERY IMPORTANT. WHATEVER YOU DO, UNDER ANY CIRCUMSTANCE, DON'T ASK HER ANY QUESTIONS. SHE HATES QUESTIONS.
COME IN, COME IN. CLOSE THE DOOR BEHIND YOU.
DID YOU GET EXTRA CHEESE? LAST TIME IT DIDN'T HAVE ENOUGH.
HOW CAN YOU TRUST A DAMN MEXICAN TO MAKE A DECENT PIZZA?

THERE'S PROBABLY 80,000 SAD LITTLE APARTMENT BUILDINGS JUST LIKE THIS SCATTERED ALL OVER LOS ANGELES COUNTY. EACH ONE HOUSES AT LEAST A DOZEN LOST SOULS. I'LL LEAVE YOU TO DO THE MATH.

...WHY DO *BUGS* SUDDENLY APPEAR...

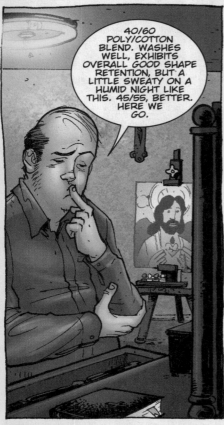

40/60 POLY/COTTON BLEND. WASHES WELL, EXHIBITS OVERALL GOOD SHAPE RETENTION, BUT A LITTLE SWEATY ON A HUMID NIGHT LIKE THIS. 45/55, BETTER. HERE WE GO.

70/30-- *PERFECT.*

GIMME-GIMME-GIMME A *BUG* AFTER MIDNIGHT...

COME ON THEN. LET'S SEE WHAT YOU'RE *UP* TO, FREAK BOY.

42

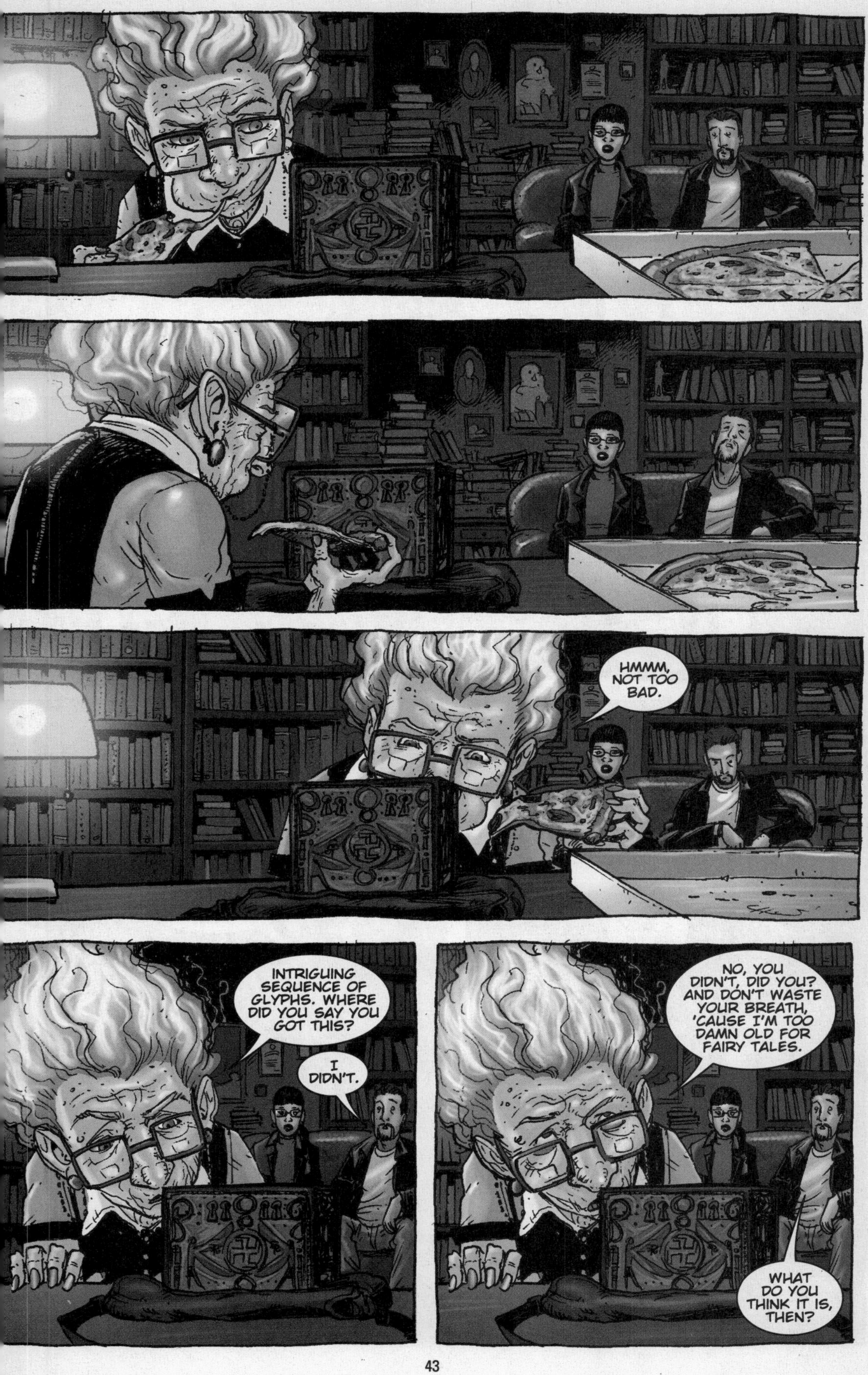
HMMM, NOT TOO BAD.
INTRIGUING SEQUENCE OF GLYPHS. WHERE DID YOU SAY YOU GOT THIS?
I DIDN'T.
NO, YOU DIDN'T, DID YOU? AND DON'T WASTE YOUR BREATH, 'CAUSE I'M TOO DAMN OLD FOR FAIRY TALES.
WHAT DO YOU THINK IT IS, THEN?

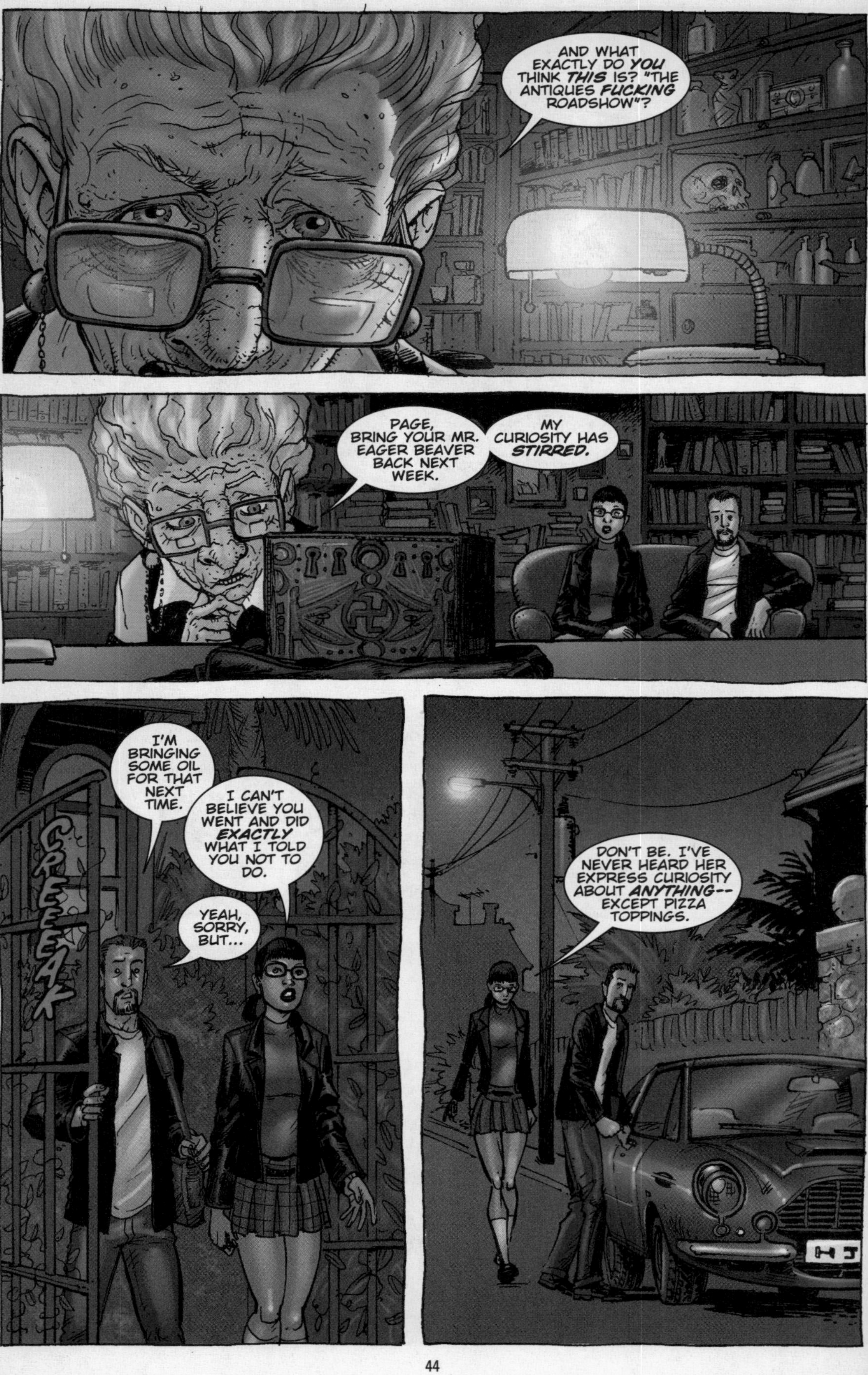
AND WHAT EXACTLY DO YOU THINK THIS IS? "THE ANTIQUES FUCKING ROADSHOW"?
PAGE, BRING YOUR MR. EAGER BEAVER BACK NEXT WEEK.
MY CURIOSITY HAS STIRRED.
I'M BRINGING SOME OIL FOR THAT NEXT TIME.
CREEEAK
I CAN'T BELIEVE YOU WENT AND DID EXACTLY WHAT I TOLD YOU NOT TO DO.
YEAH, SORRY, BUT...
DON'T BE. I'VE NEVER HEARD HER EXPRESS CURIOSITY ABOUT ANYTHING-- EXCEPT PIZZA TOPPINGS.

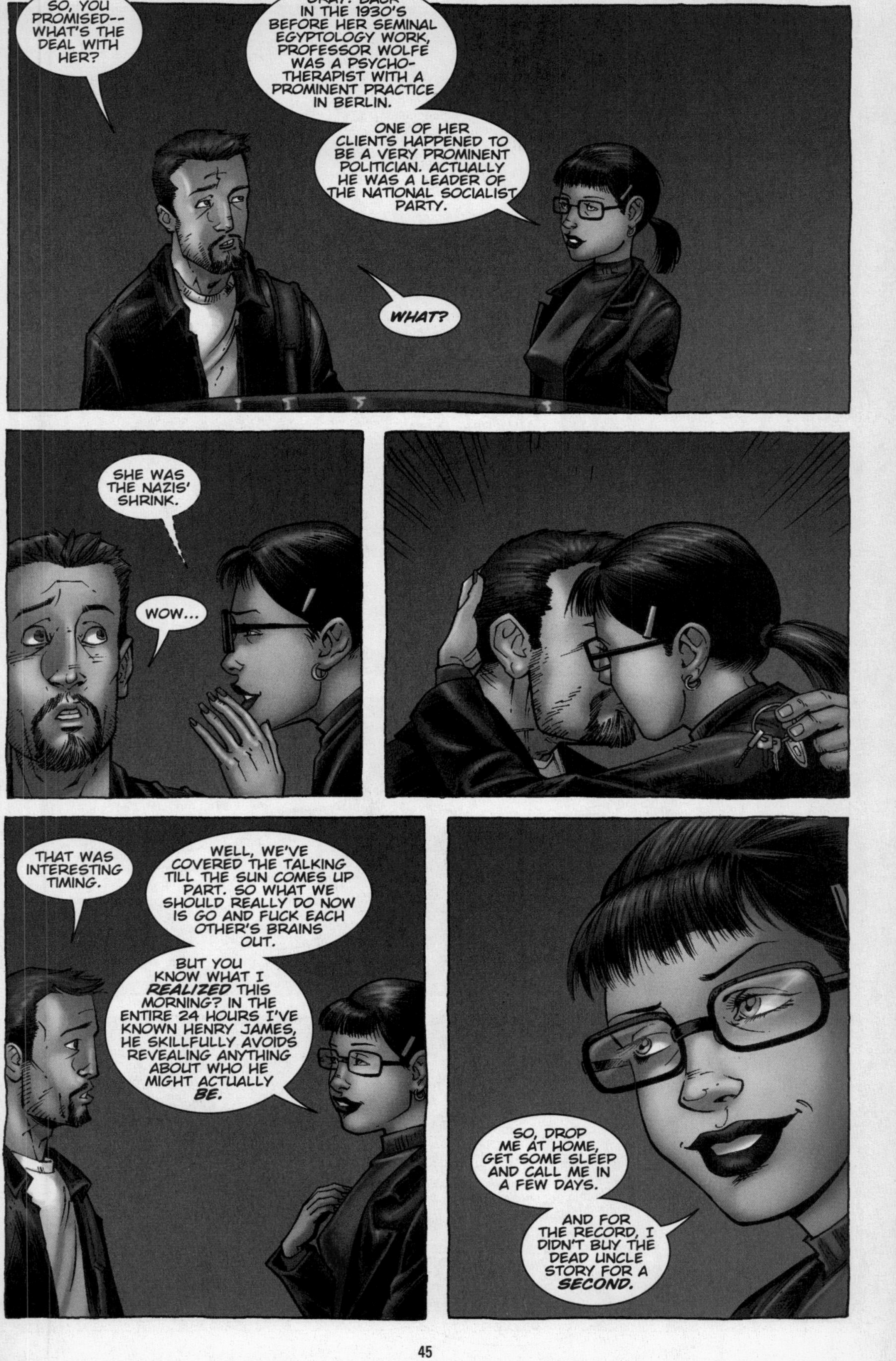
SO, YOU PROMISED-- WHAT'S THE DEAL WITH HER?
OKAY. BACK IN THE 1930'S BEFORE HER SEMINAL EGYPTOLOGY WORK, PROFESSOR WOLFE WAS A PSYCHO-THERAPIST WITH A PROMINENT PRACTICE IN BERLIN.
ONE OF HER CLIENTS HAPPENED TO BE A VERY PROMINENT POLITICIAN. ACTUALLY HE WAS A LEADER OF THE NATIONAL SOCIALIST PARTY.
WHAT?
SHE WAS THE NAZIS' SHRINK.
WOW...
THAT WAS INTERESTING TIMING.
WELL, WE'VE COVERED THE TALKING TILL THE SUN COMES UP PART. SO WHAT WE SHOULD REALLY DO NOW IS GO AND FUCK EACH OTHER'S BRAINS OUT.
BUT YOU KNOW WHAT I *REALIZED* THIS MORNING? IN THE ENTIRE 24 HOURS I'VE KNOWN HENRY JAMES, HE SKILLFULLY AVOIDS REVEALING ANYTHING ABOUT WHO HE MIGHT ACTUALLY *BE.*
SO, DROP ME AT HOME, GET SOME SLEEP AND CALL ME IN A FEW DAYS.
AND FOR THE RECORD, I DIDN'T BUY THE DEAD UNCLE STORY FOR A *SECOND.*

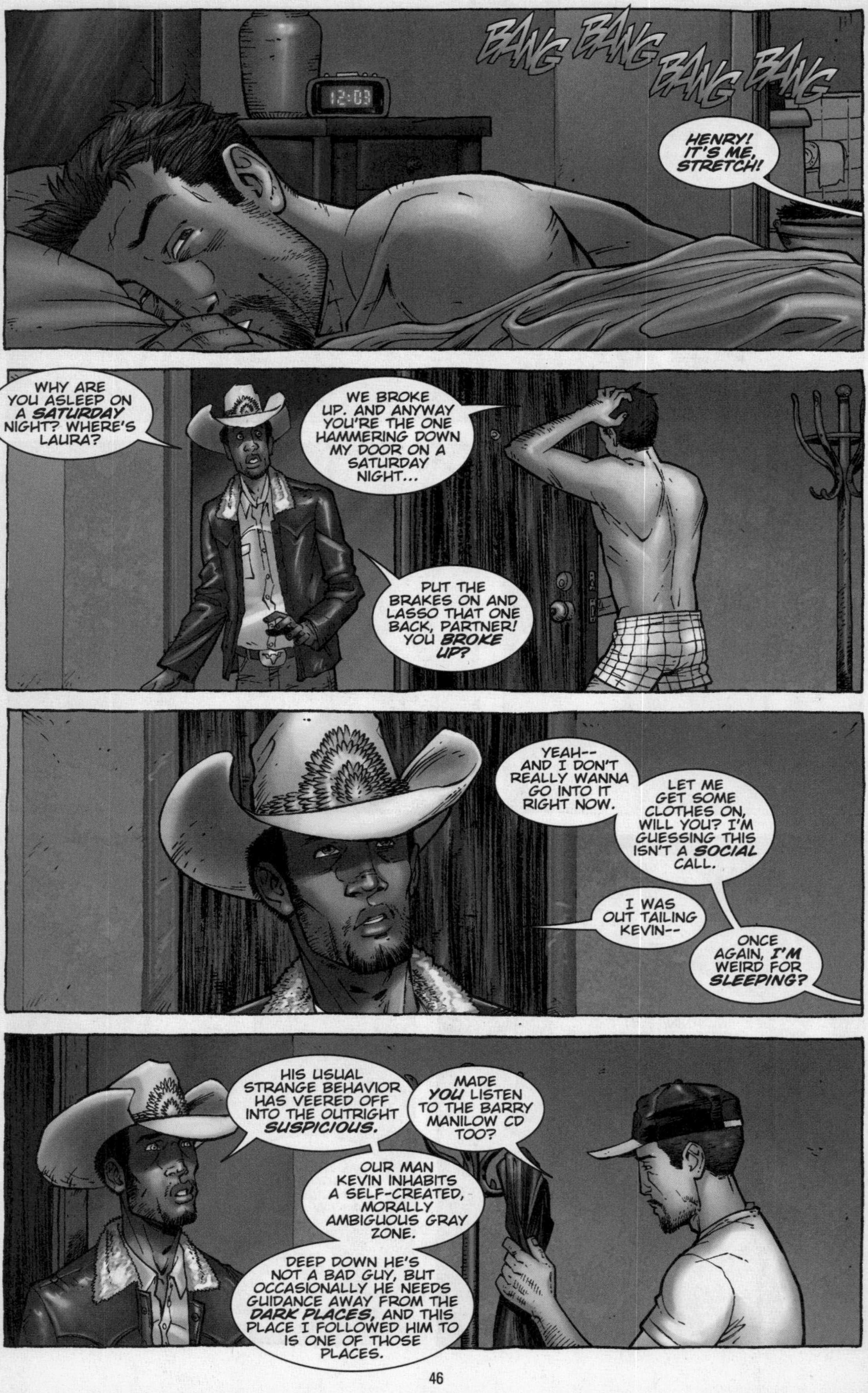
BANG BANG BANG BANG
HENRY! IT'S ME, STRETCH!
WHY ARE YOU ASLEEP ON A SATURDAY NIGHT? WHERE'S LAURA?
WE BROKE UP. AND ANYWAY YOU'RE THE ONE HAMMERING DOWN MY DOOR ON A SATURDAY NIGHT...
PUT THE BRAKES ON AND LASSO THAT ONE BACK, PARTNER! YOU BROKE UP?
YEAH-- AND I DON'T REALLY WANNA GO INTO IT RIGHT NOW.
LET ME GET SOME CLOTHES ON, WILL YOU? I'M GUESSING THIS ISN'T A SOCIAL CALL.
I WAS OUT TAILING KEVIN--
ONCE AGAIN, I'M WEIRD FOR SLEEPING?
HIS USUAL STRANGE BEHAVIOR HAS VEERED OFF INTO THE OUTRIGHT SUSPICIOUS.
MADE YOU LISTEN TO THE BARRY MANILOW CD TOO?
OUR MAN KEVIN INHABITS A SELF-CREATED, MORALLY AMBIGUOUS GRAY ZONE.
DEEP DOWN HE'S NOT A BAD GUY, BUT OCCASIONALLY HE NEEDS GUIDANCE AWAY FROM THE DARK PLACES, AND THIS PLACE I FOLLOWED HIM TO IS ONE OF THOSE PLACES.

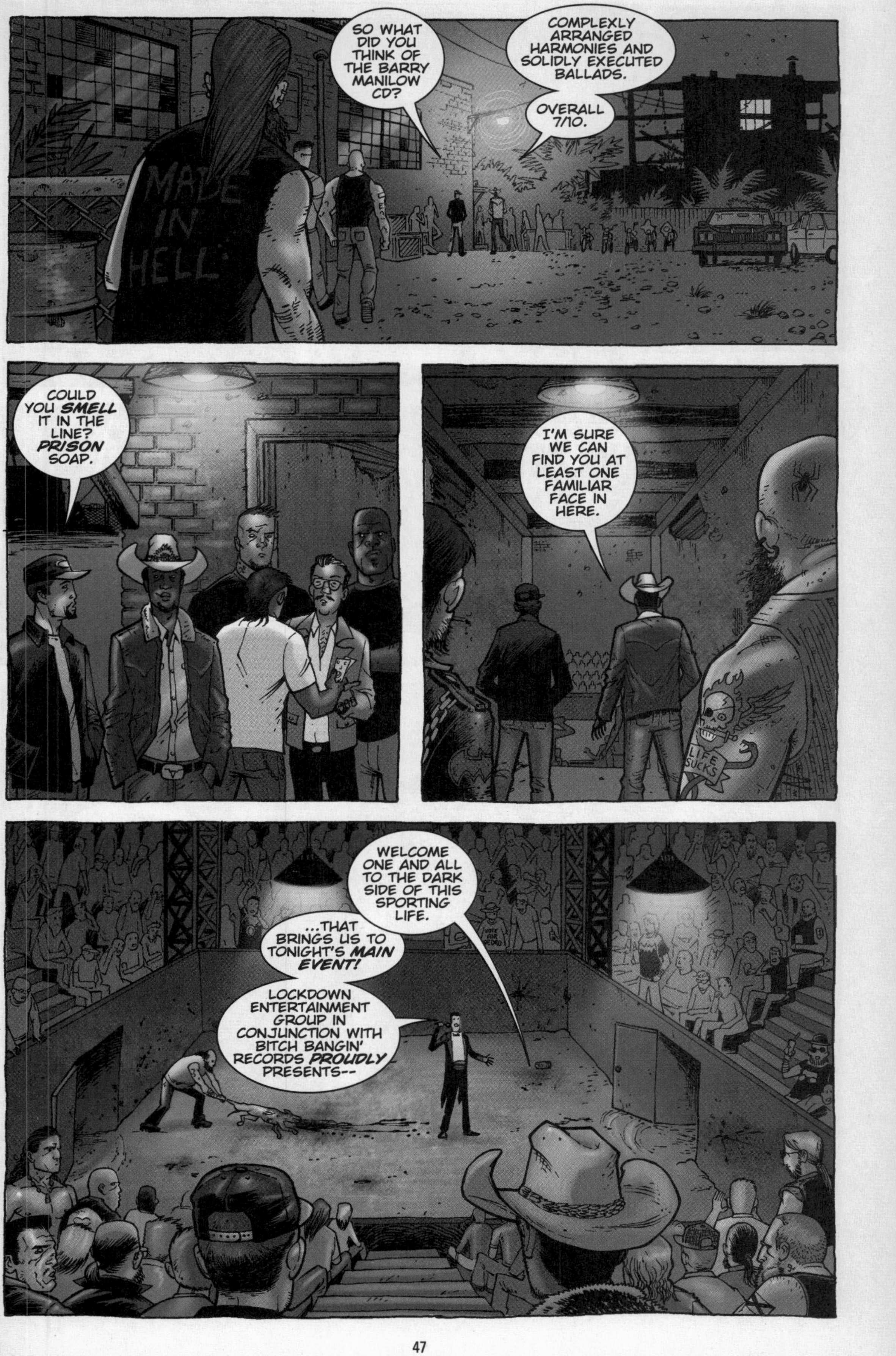
SO WHAT DID YOU THINK OF THE BARRY MANILOW CD?
COMPLEXLY ARRANGED HARMONIES AND SOLIDLY EXECUTED BALLADS.
OVERALL 7/10.
MADE IN HELL
COULD YOU SMELL IT IN THE LINE? PRISON SOAP.
I'M SURE WE CAN FIND YOU AT LEAST ONE FAMILIAR FACE IN HERE.
LIFE SUCKS
WELCOME ONE AND ALL TO THE DARK SIDE OF THIS SPORTING LIFE.
...THAT BRINGS US TO TONIGHT'S MAIN EVENT!
LOCKDOWN ENTERTAINMENT GROUP IN CONJUNCTION WITH BITCH BANGIN' RECORDS PROUDLY PRESENTS--

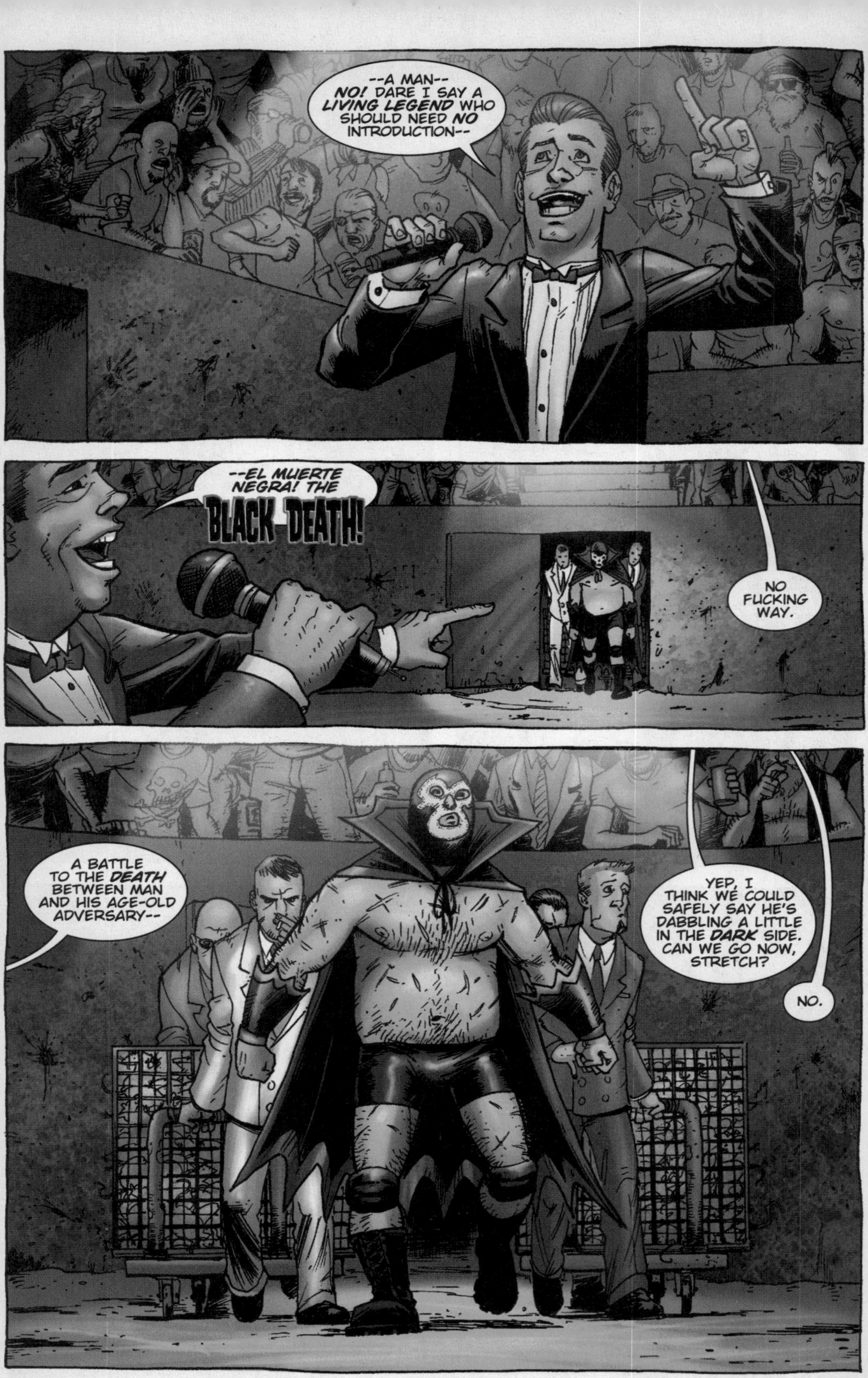
--A MAN--
NO! DARE I SAY A LIVING LEGEND WHO SHOULD NEED NO INTRODUCTION--
--EL MUERTE NEGRA! THE
BLACK DEATH!
NO FUCKING WAY.
A BATTLE TO THE DEATH BETWEEN MAN AND HIS AGE-OLD ADVERSARY--
YEP, I THINK WE COULD SAFELY SAY HE'S DABBLING A LITTLE IN THE DARK SIDE. CAN WE GO NOW, STRETCH?
NO.

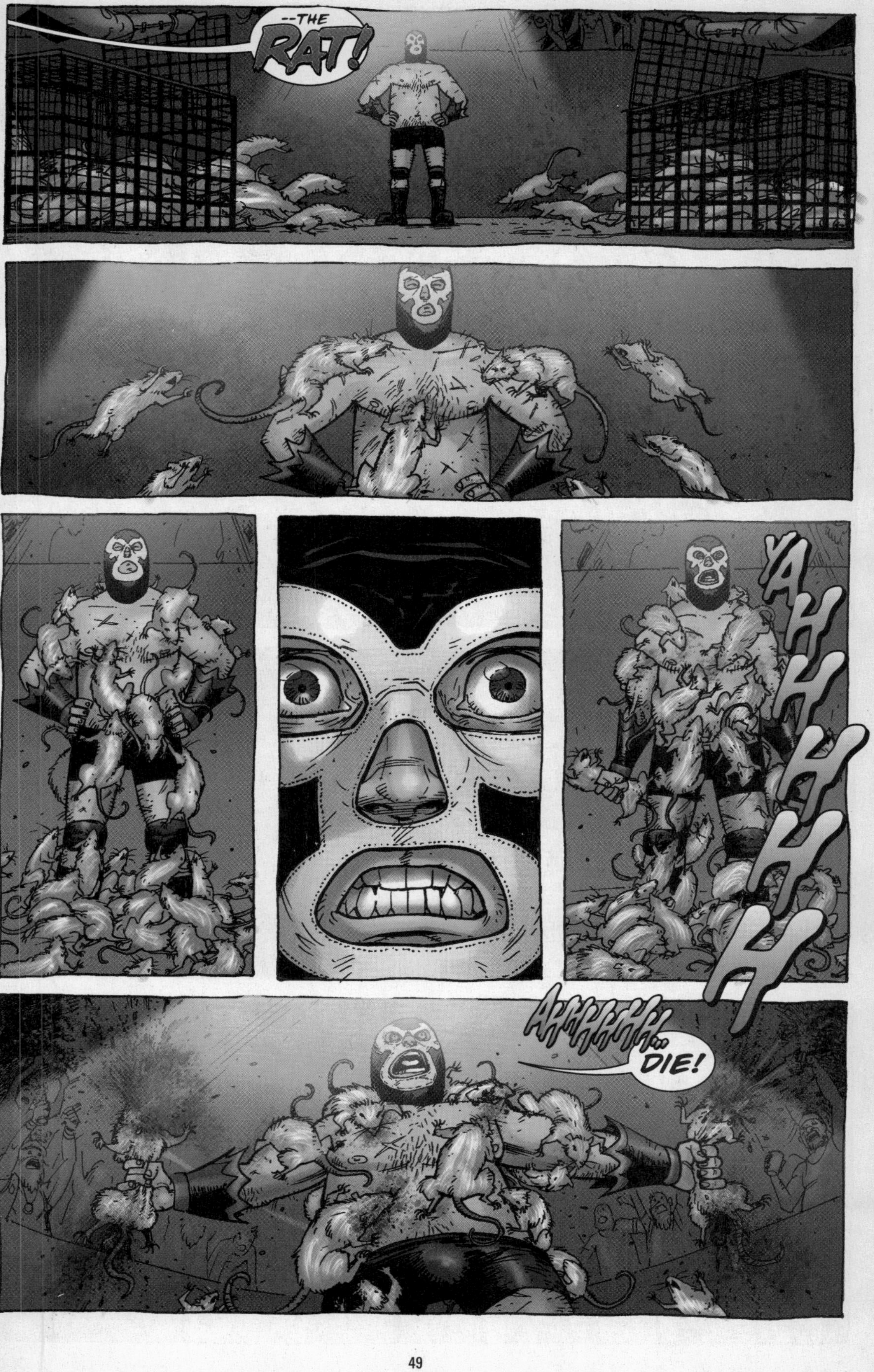
--THE RAT!
YAHHHHHH
AHHHHHHH... DIE!

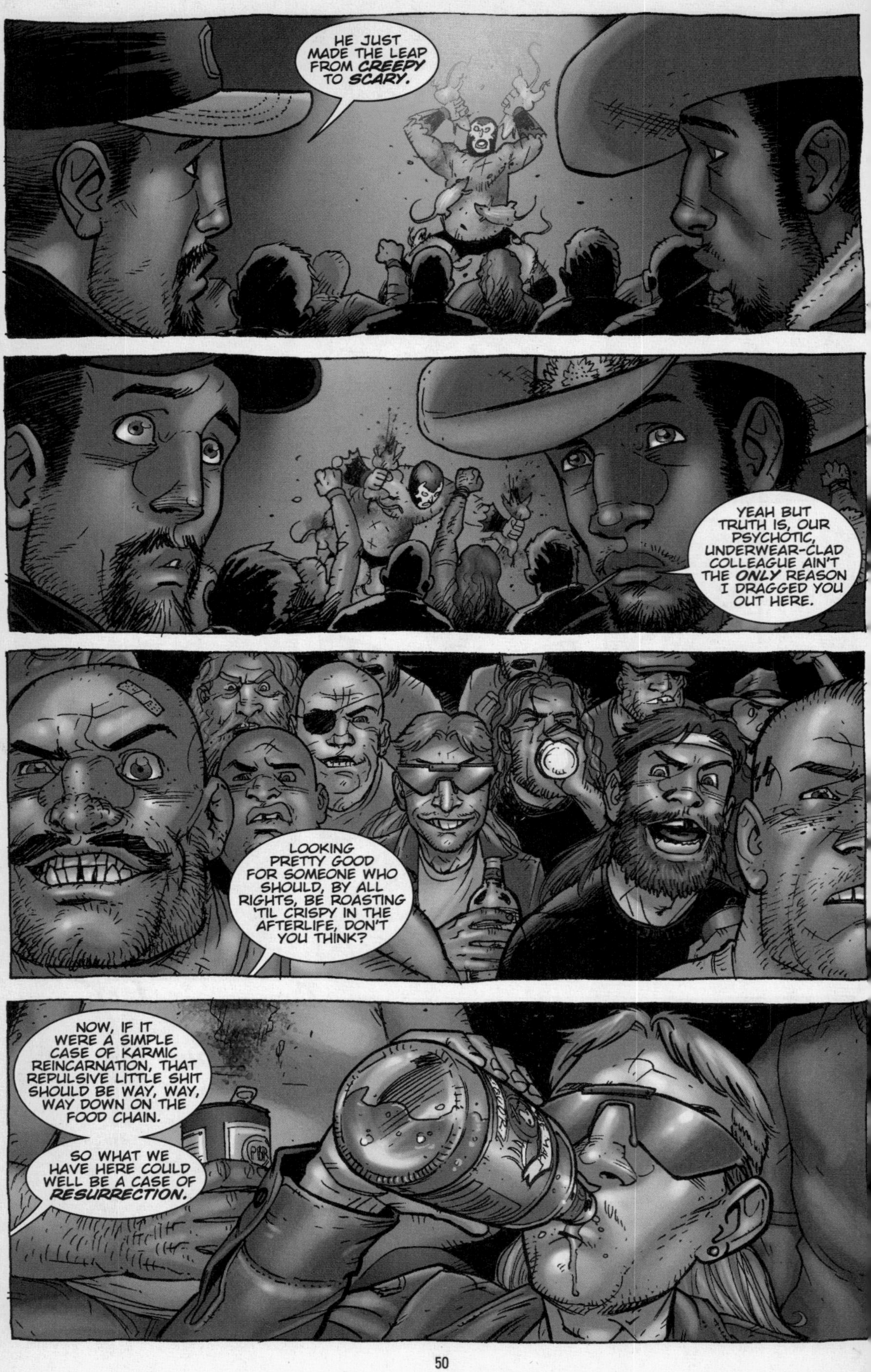
HE JUST MADE THE LEAP FROM CREEPY TO SCARY.
YEAH BUT TRUTH IS, OUR PSYCHOTIC, UNDERWEAR-CLAD COLLEAGUE AIN'T THE ONLY REASON I DRAGGED YOU OUT HERE.
LOOKING PRETTY GOOD FOR SOMEONE WHO SHOULD, BY ALL RIGHTS, BE ROASTING 'TIL CRISPY IN THE AFTERLIFE, DON'T YOU THINK?
NOW, IF IT WERE A SIMPLE CASE OF KARMIC REINCARNATION, THAT REPULSIVE LITTLE SHIT SHOULD BE WAY, WAY, WAY DOWN ON THE FOOD CHAIN.
SO WHAT WE HAVE HERE COULD WELL BE A CASE OF RESURRECTION.

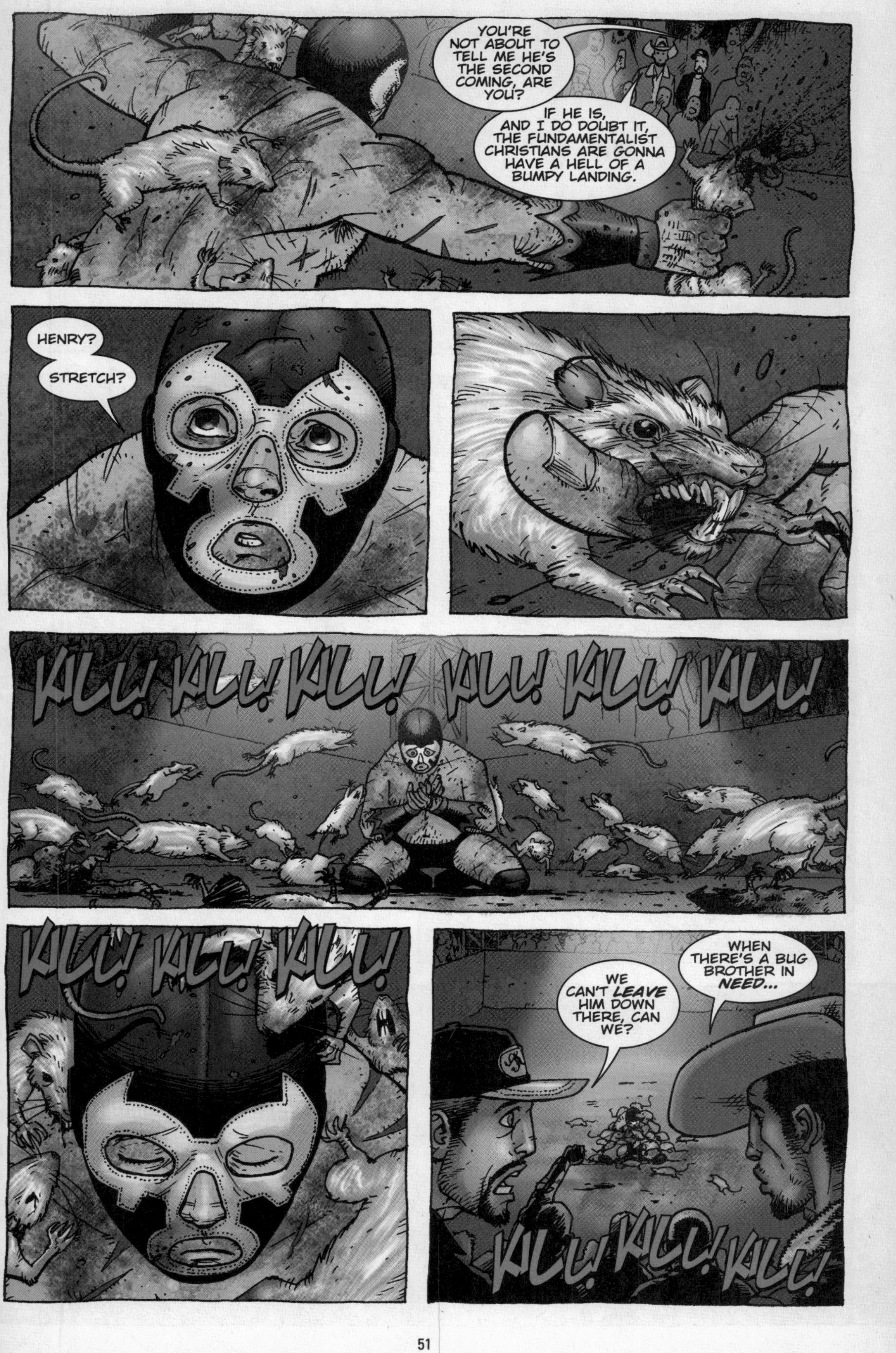
YOU'RE NOT ABOUT TO TELL ME HE'S THE SECOND COMING, ARE YOU?
IF HE IS, AND I DO DOUBT IT, THE FUNDAMENTALIST CHRISTIANS ARE GONNA HAVE A HELL OF A BUMPY LANDING.
HENRY?
STRETCH?
KLU! KLU! KLU! KLU! KLU! KLU!
KLU! KLU! KLU!
WE CAN'T *LEAVE* HIM DOWN THERE, CAN WE?
WHEN THERE'S A BUG BROTHER IN *NEED...*
KLU! KLU! KLU!

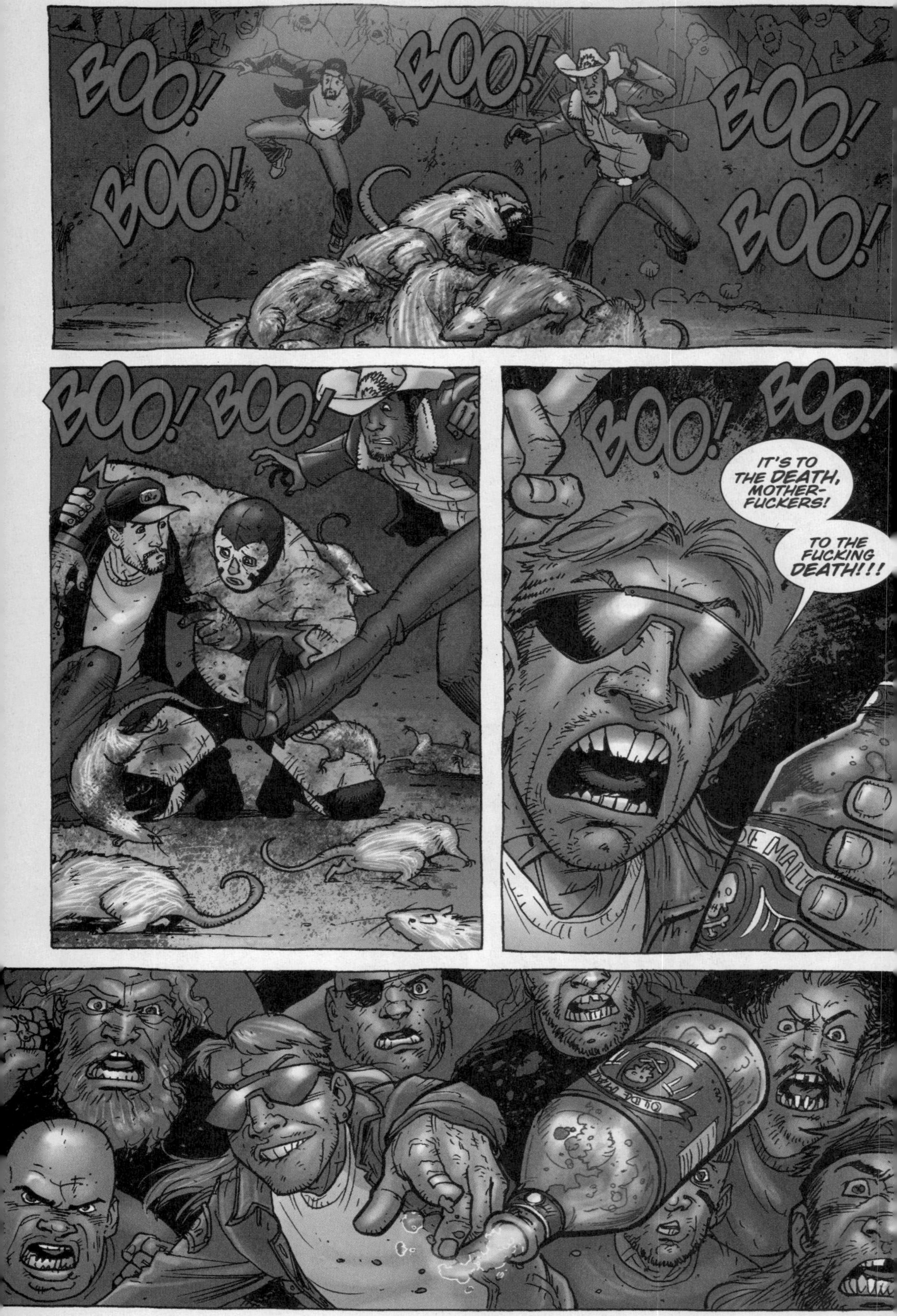
BOO!
BOO!
BOO!
BOO!
BOO!
BOO!
BOO!
BOO!
BOO!
IT'S TO THE DEATH, MOTHER-FUCKERS!
TO THE FUCKING DEATH!!!

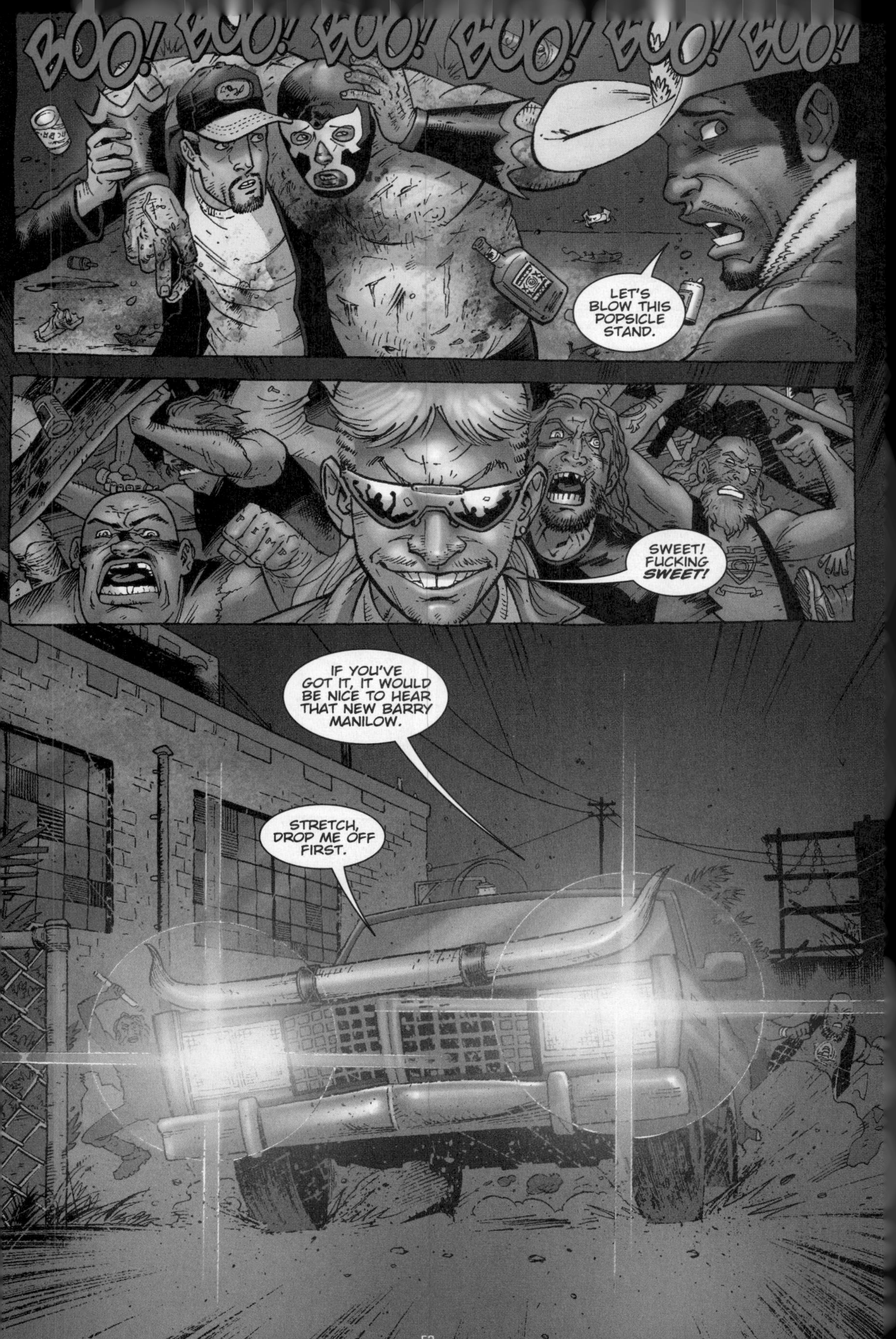
BOO! BOO! BOO! BOO! BOO! BOO!
LET'S BLOW THIS POPSICLE STAND.
SWEET! FUCKING SWEET!
IF YOU'VE GOT IT, IT WOULD BE NICE TO HEAR THAT NEW BARRY MANILOW.
STRETCH, DROP ME OFF FIRST.

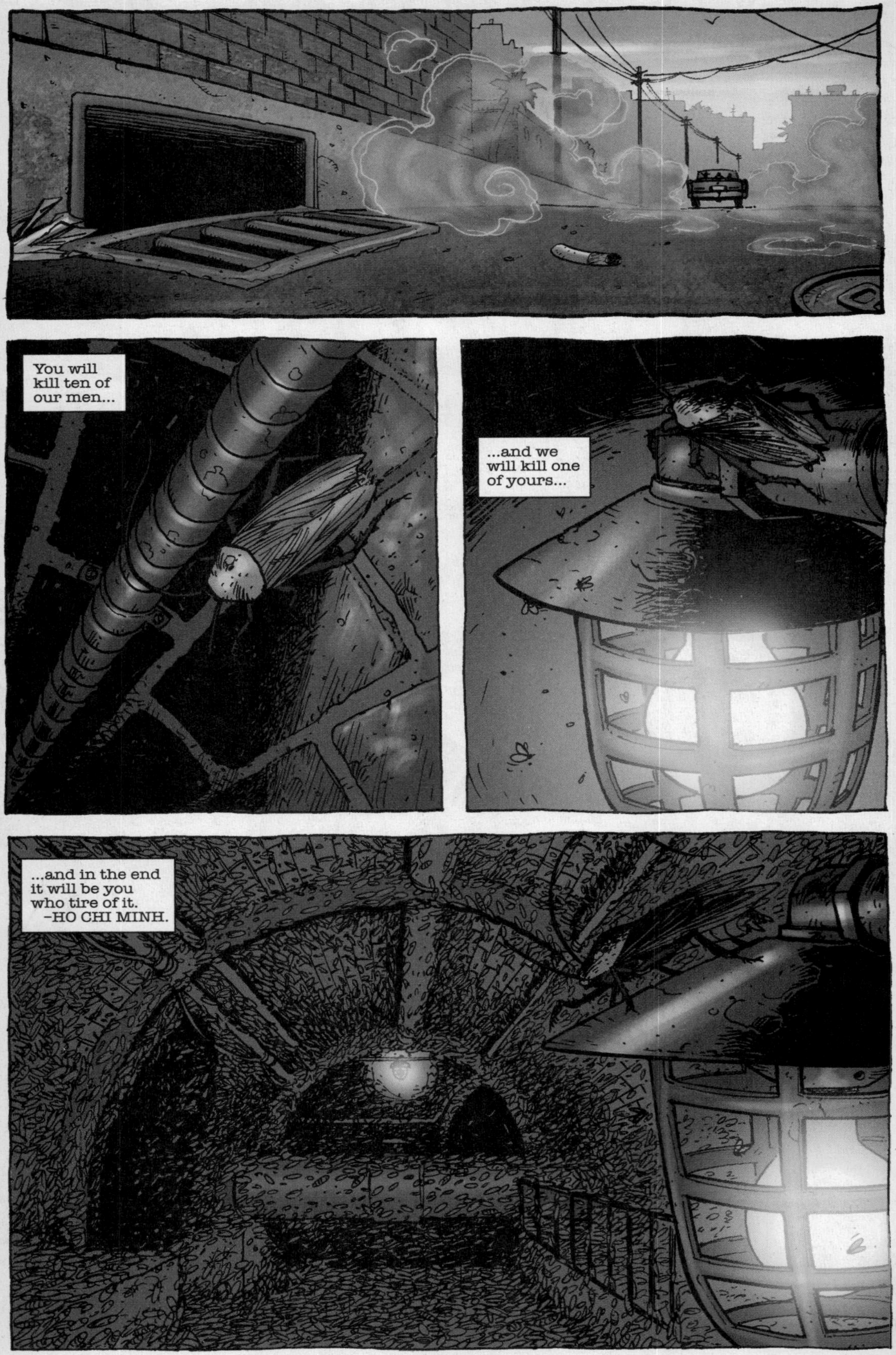
You will kill ten of our men...
...and we will kill one of yours...
...and in the end it will be you who tire of it.
–HO CHI MINH.

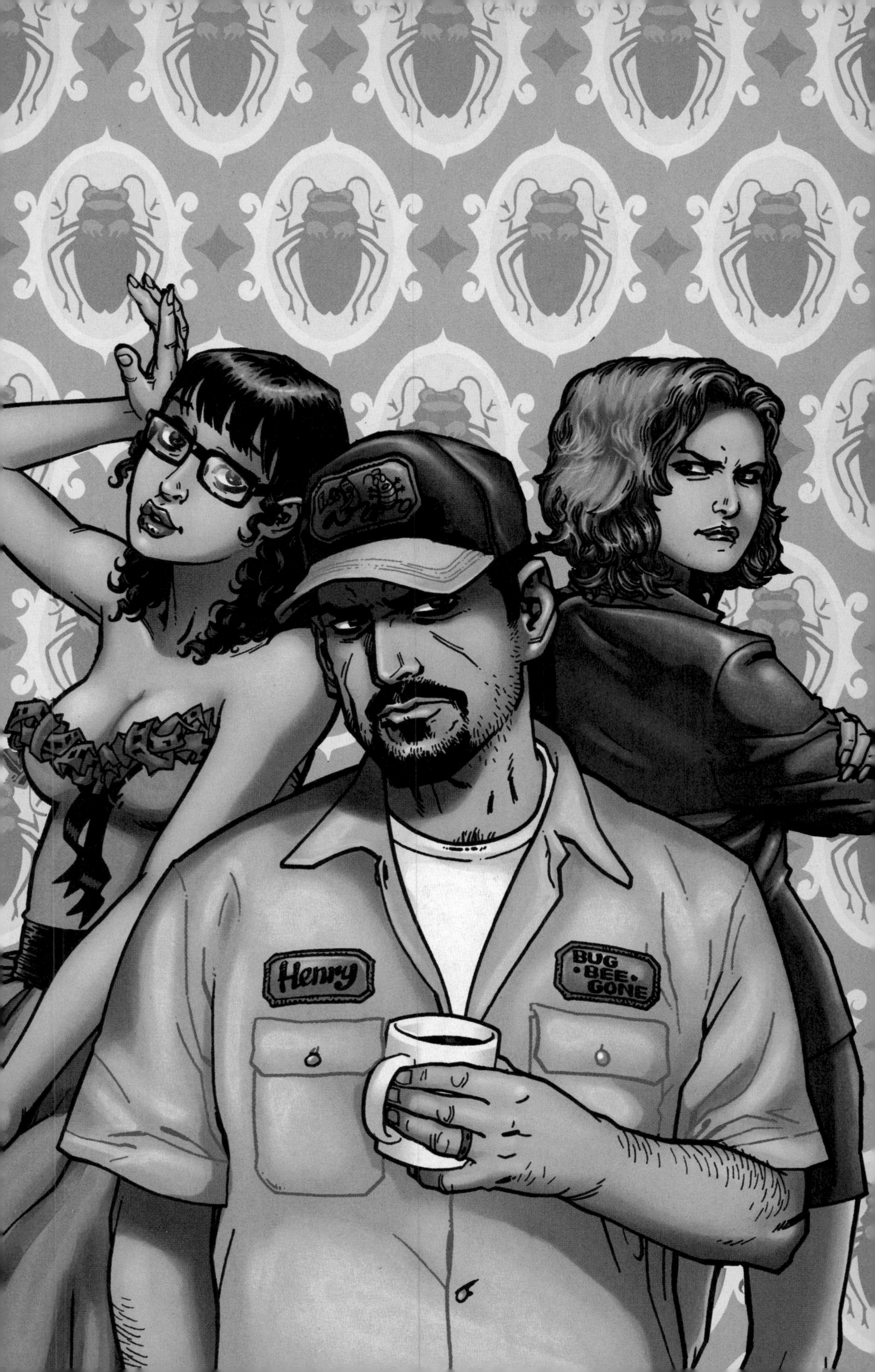
Henry
BUG
BEE
GONE

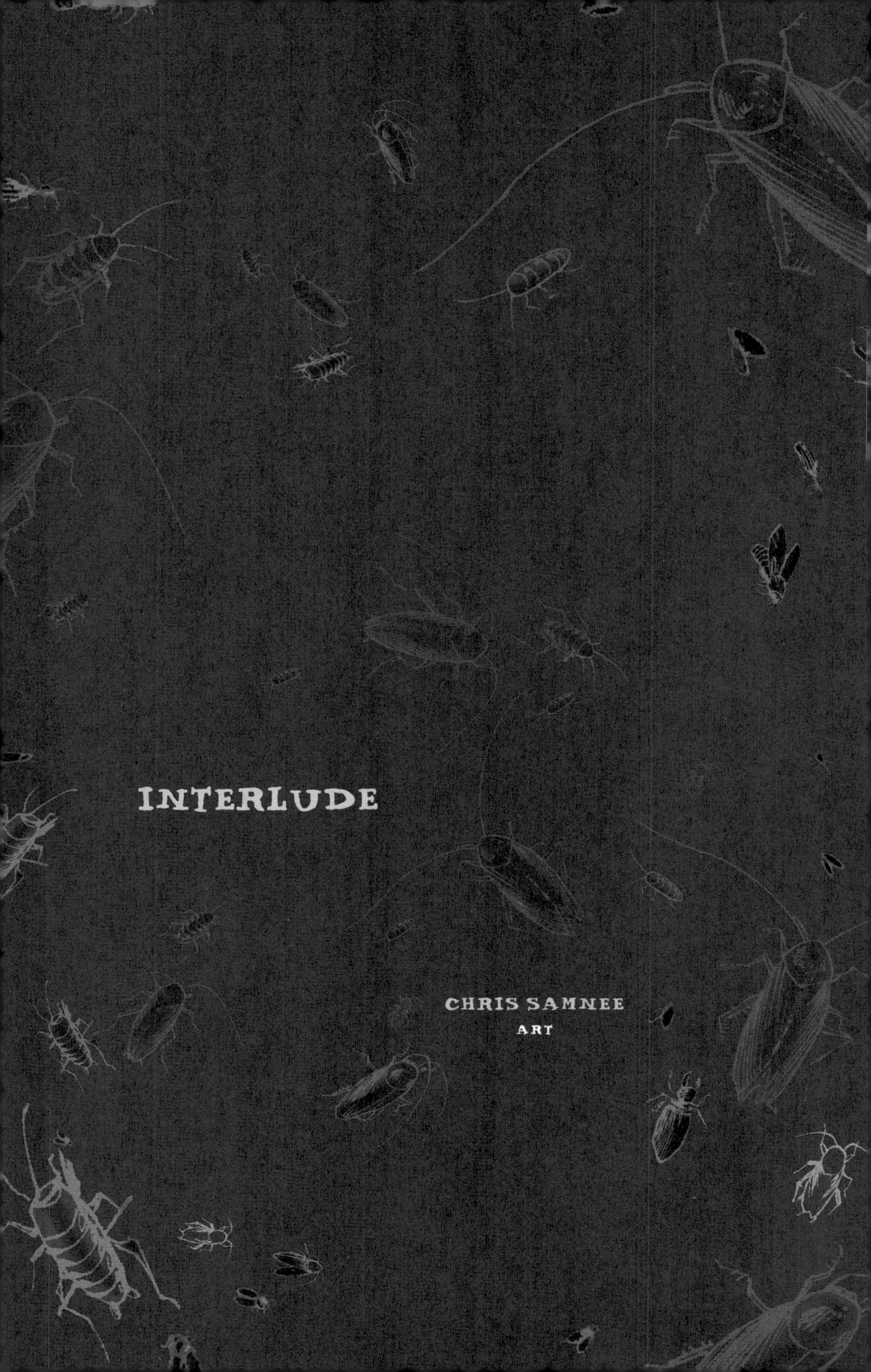

INTERLUDE

CHRIS SAMNEE
ART

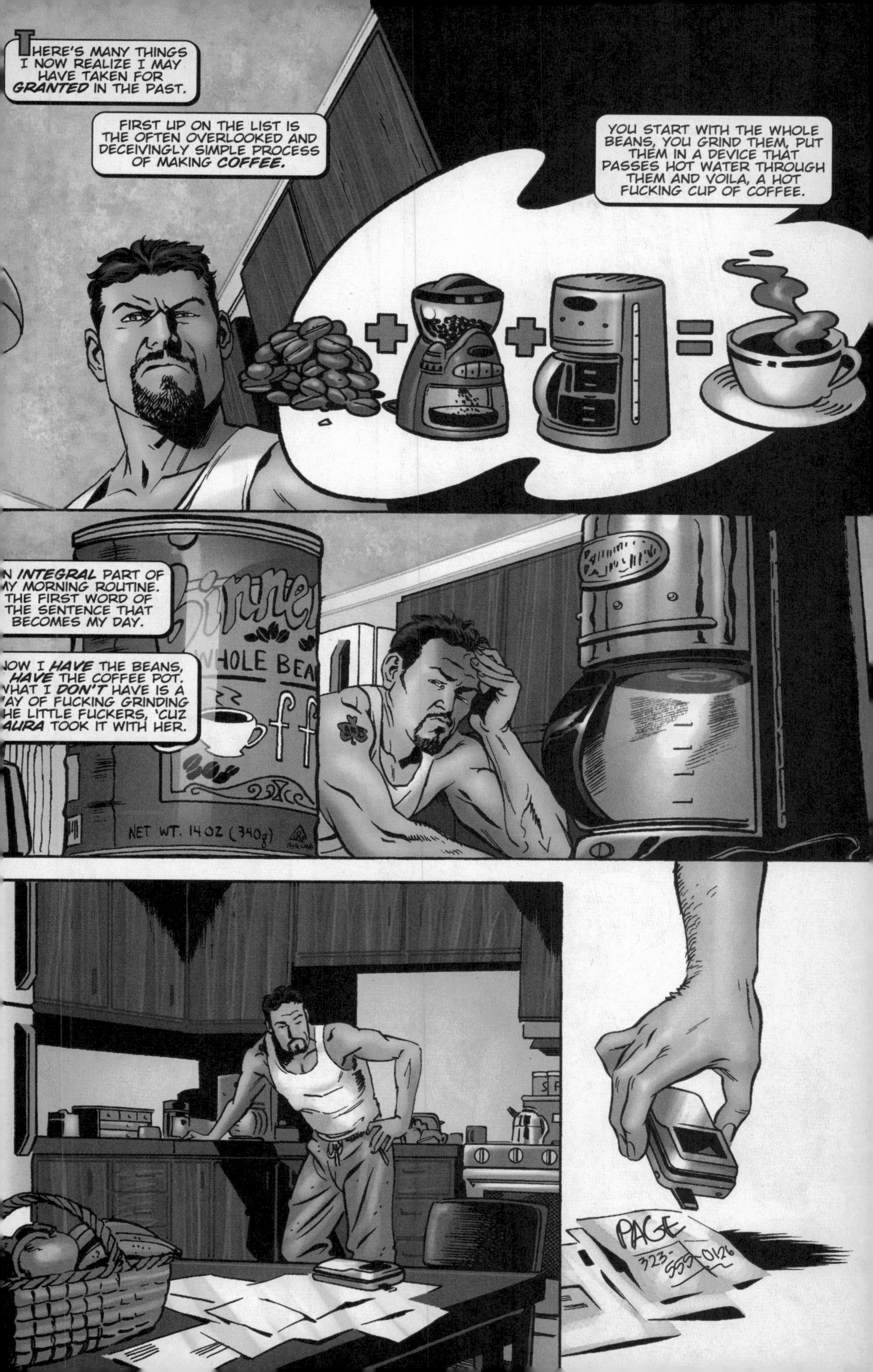
THERE'S MANY THINGS I NOW REALIZE I MAY HAVE TAKEN FOR GRANTED IN THE PAST.
FIRST UP ON THE LIST IS THE OFTEN OVERLOOKED AND DECEIVINGLY SIMPLE PROCESS OF MAKING COFFEE.
YOU START WITH THE WHOLE BEANS, YOU GRIND THEM, PUT THEM IN A DEVICE THAT PASSES HOT WATER THROUGH THEM AND VOILA, A HOT FUCKING CUP OF COFFEE.
N INTEGRAL PART OF MY MORNING ROUTINE. THE FIRST WORD OF THE SENTENCE THAT BECOMES MY DAY.
NOW I HAVE THE BEANS, HAVE THE COFFEE POT. WHAT I DON'T HAVE IS A AY OF FUCKING GRINDING HE LITTLE FUCKERS, 'CUZ AURA TOOK IT WITH HER.
WHOLE BEA
NET WT. 14 OZ (340g)
PAGE
323-555-0126

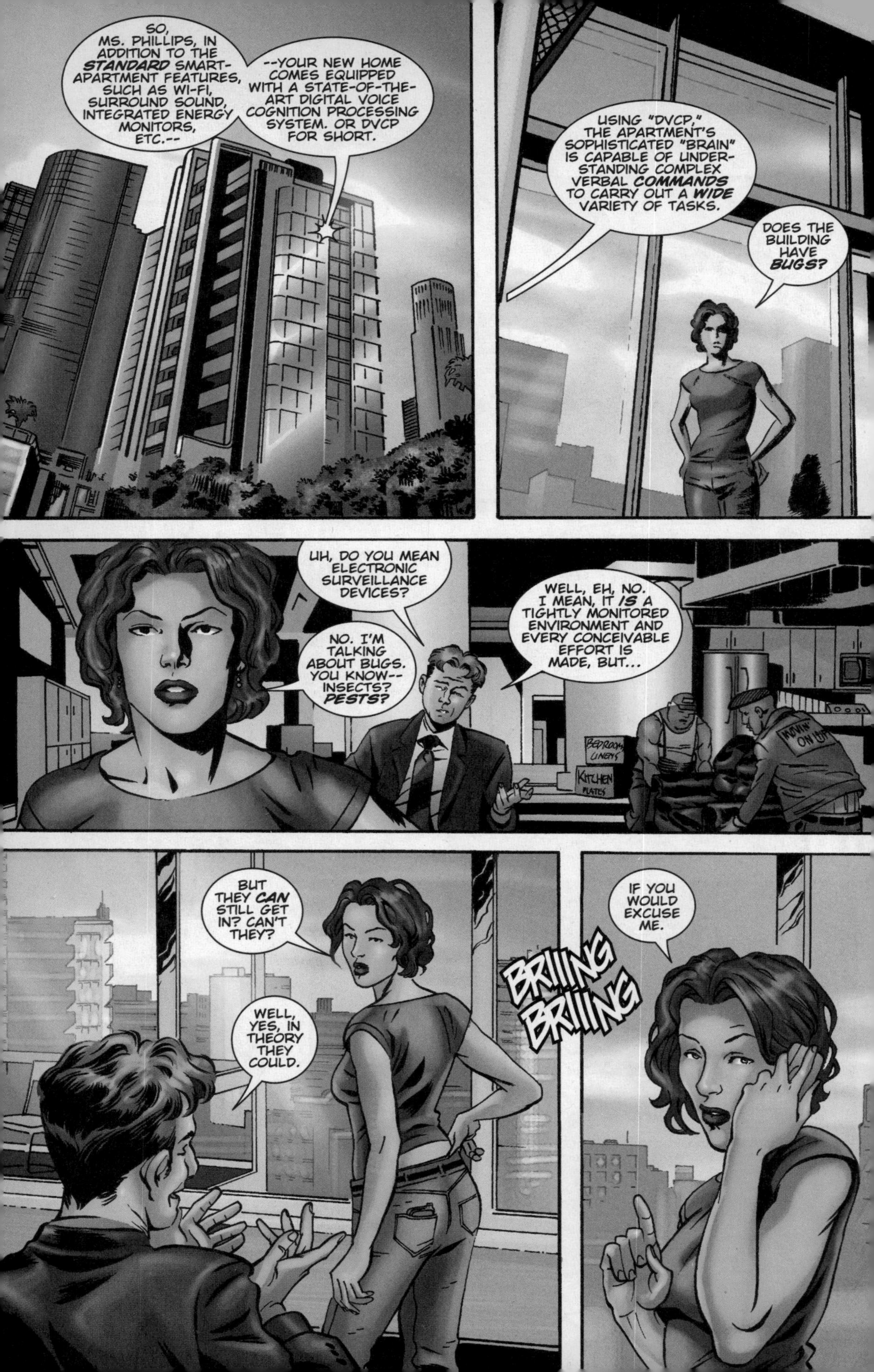
SO, MS. PHILLIPS, IN ADDITION TO THE STANDARD SMART-APARTMENT FEATURES, SUCH AS WI-FI, SURROUND SOUND, INTEGRATED ENERGY MONITORS, ETC.--
--YOUR NEW HOME COMES EQUIPPED WITH A STATE-OF-THE-ART DIGITAL VOICE COGNITION PROCESSING SYSTEM. OR DVCP FOR SHORT.
USING "DVCP," THE APARTMENT'S SOPHISTICATED "BRAIN" IS CAPABLE OF UNDER-STANDING COMPLEX VERBAL COMMANDS TO CARRY OUT A WIDE VARIETY OF TASKS.
DOES THE BUILDING HAVE BUGS?
UH, DO YOU MEAN ELECTRONIC SURVEILLANCE DEVICES?
NO. I'M TALKING ABOUT BUGS. YOU KNOW--INSECTS? PESTS?
WELL, EH, NO. I MEAN, IT IS A TIGHTLY MONITORED ENVIRONMENT AND EVERY CONCEIVABLE EFFORT IS MADE, BUT...
BEDROOM LINENS
KITCHEN PLATES
MOVIN' ON UP
BUT THEY CAN STILL GET IN? CAN'T THEY?
WELL, YES, IN THEORY THEY COULD.
BRIIING BRIIING
IF YOU WOULD EXCUSE ME.

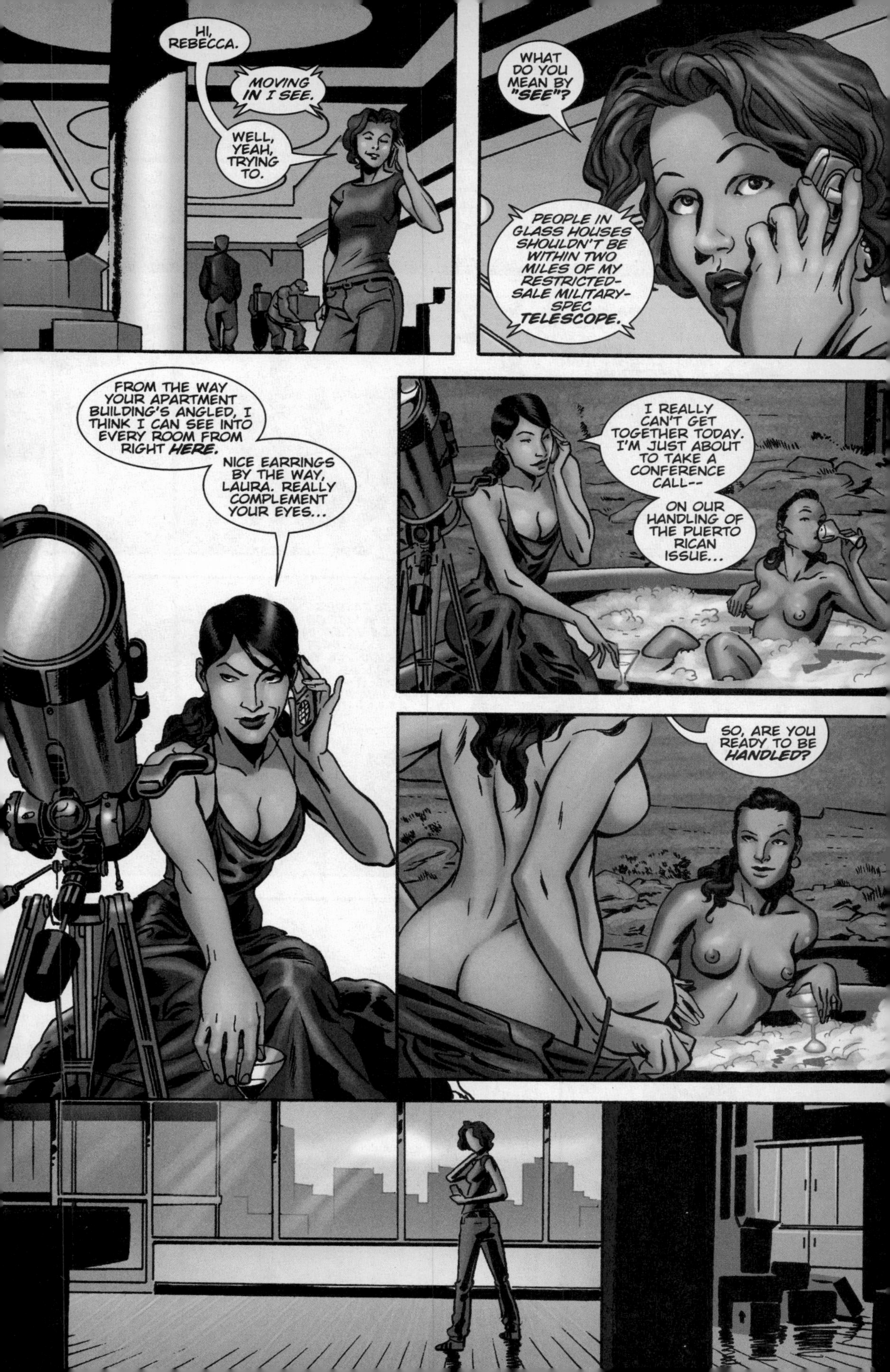
HI, REBECCA.
MOVING IN I SEE.
WELL, YEAH, TRYING TO.
WHAT DO YOU MEAN BY "SEE"?
PEOPLE IN GLASS HOUSES SHOULDN'T BE WITHIN TWO MILES OF MY RESTRICTED-SALE MILITARY-SPEC TELESCOPE.
FROM THE WAY YOUR APARTMENT BUILDING'S ANGLED, I THINK I CAN SEE INTO EVERY ROOM FROM RIGHT HERE.
NICE EARRINGS BY THE WAY, LAURA. REALLY COMPLEMENT YOUR EYES...
I REALLY CAN'T GET TOGETHER TODAY. I'M JUST ABOUT TO TAKE A CONFERENCE CALL--
ON OUR HANDLING OF THE PUERTO RICAN ISSUE...
SO, ARE YOU READY TO BE HANDLED?

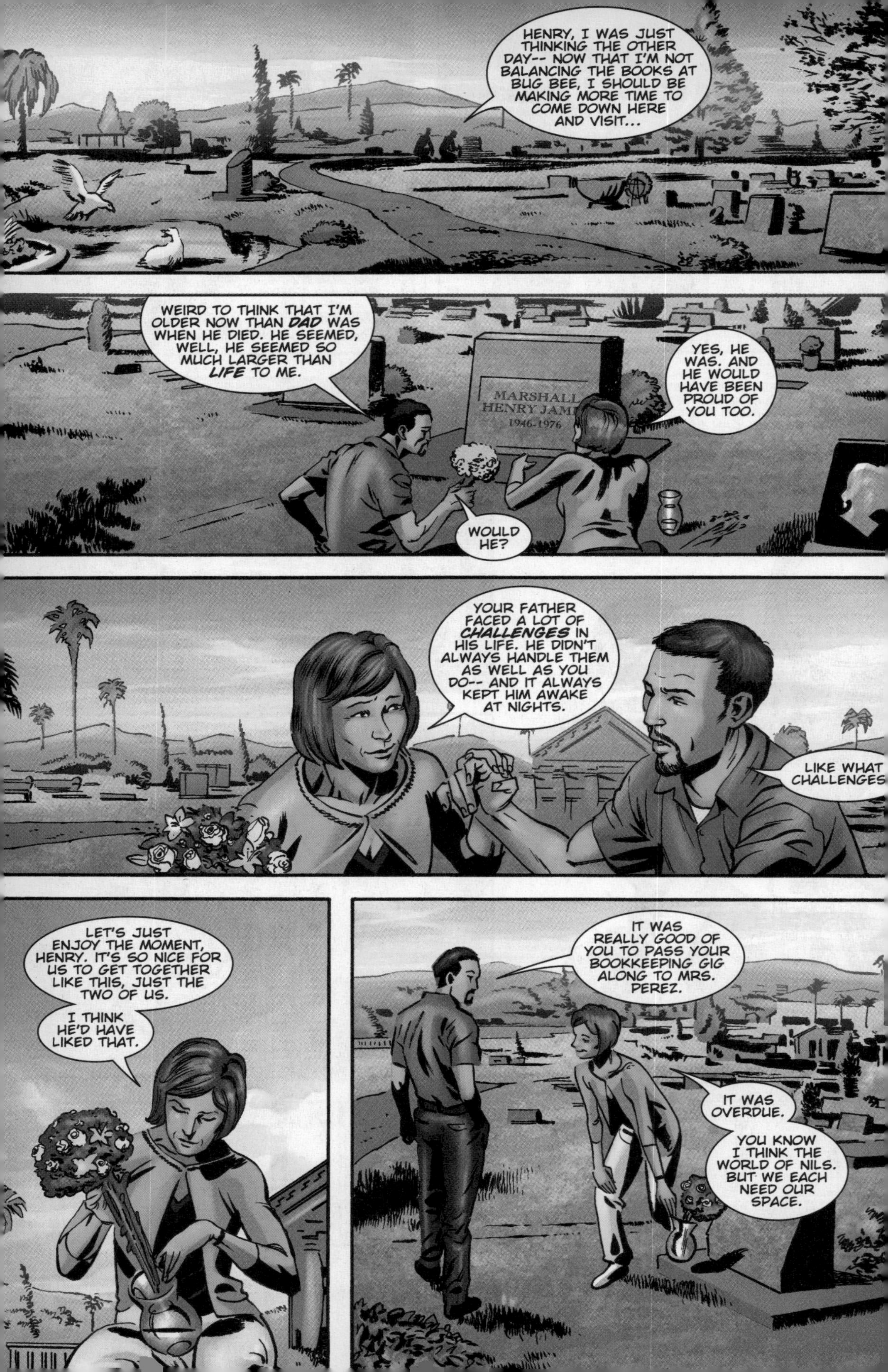
HENRY, I WAS JUST THINKING THE OTHER DAY-- NOW THAT I'M NOT BALANCING THE BOOKS AT BUG BEE, I SHOULD BE MAKING MORE TIME TO COME DOWN HERE AND VISIT...
WEIRD TO THINK THAT I'M OLDER NOW THAN DAD WAS WHEN HE DIED. HE SEEMED, WELL, HE SEEMED SO MUCH LARGER THAN LIFE TO ME.
MARSHALL
HENRY JAM
1946-1976
YES, HE WAS. AND HE WOULD HAVE BEEN PROUD OF YOU TOO.
WOULD HE?
YOUR FATHER FACED A LOT OF CHALLENGES IN HIS LIFE. HE DIDN'T ALWAYS HANDLE THEM AS WELL AS YOU DO-- AND IT ALWAYS KEPT HIM AWAKE AT NIGHTS.
LIKE WHAT CHALLENGES
LET'S JUST ENJOY THE MOMENT, HENRY. IT'S SO NICE FOR US TO GET TOGETHER LIKE THIS, JUST THE TWO OF US.
I THINK HE'D HAVE LIKED THAT.
IT WAS REALLY GOOD OF YOU TO PASS YOUR BOOKKEEPING GIG ALONG TO MRS. PEREZ.
IT WAS OVERDUE.
YOU KNOW I THINK THE WORLD OF NILS. BUT WE EACH NEED OUR SPACE.

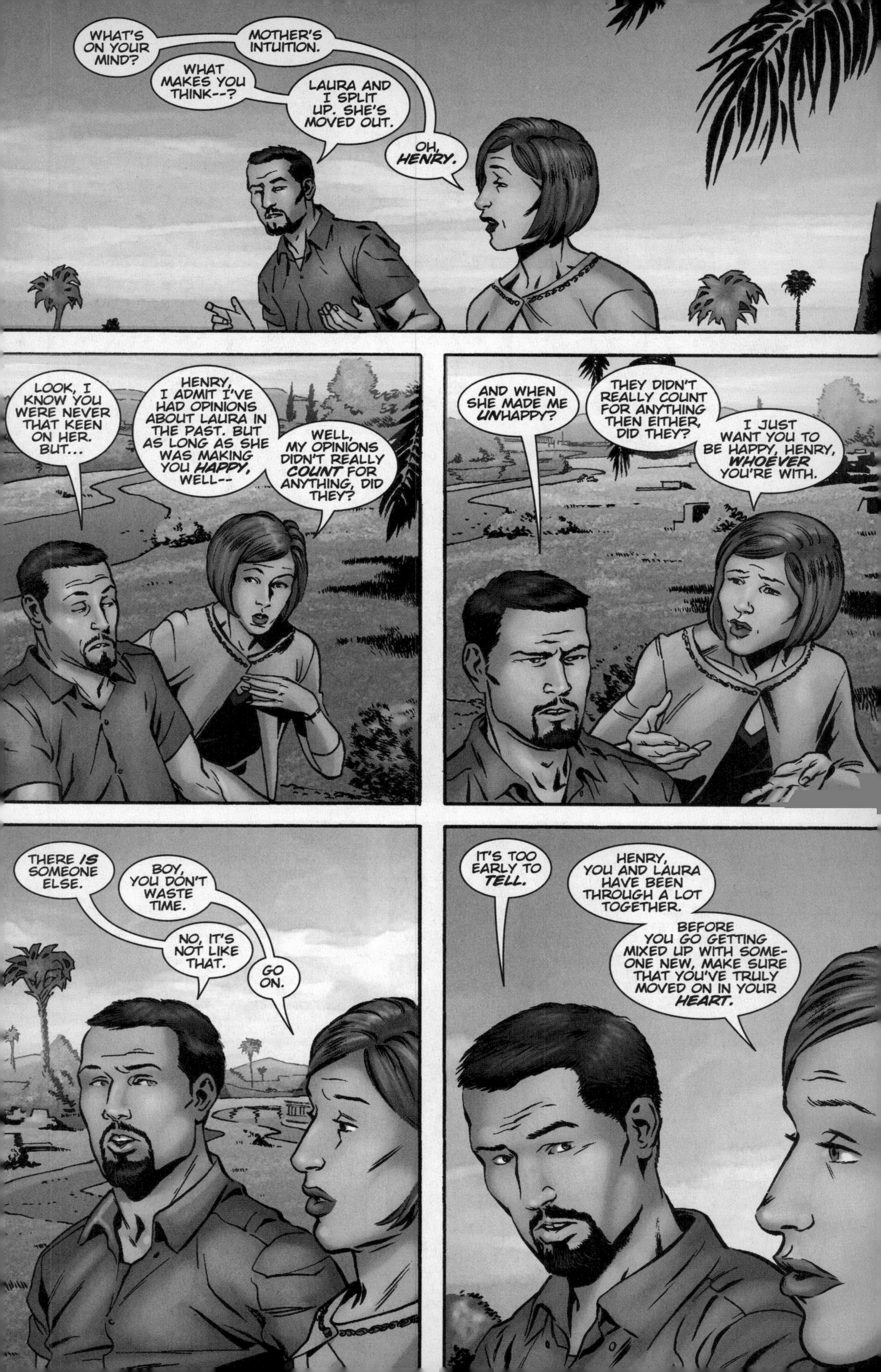
WHAT'S ON YOUR MIND?
MOTHER'S INTUITION.
WHAT MAKES YOU THINK--?
LAURA AND I SPLIT UP. SHE'S MOVED OUT.
OH, HENRY.
LOOK, I KNOW YOU WERE NEVER THAT KEEN ON HER. BUT...
HENRY, I ADMIT I'VE HAD OPINIONS ABOUT LAURA IN THE PAST. BUT AS LONG AS SHE WAS MAKING YOU HAPPY, WELL--
WELL, MY OPINIONS DIDN'T REALLY COUNT FOR ANYTHING, DID THEY?
AND WHEN SHE MADE ME UNHAPPY?
THEY DIDN'T REALLY COUNT FOR ANYTHING THEN EITHER, DID THEY?
I JUST WANT YOU TO BE HAPPY, HENRY, WHOEVER YOU'RE WITH.
THERE IS SOMEONE ELSE.
BOY, YOU DON'T WASTE TIME.
NO, IT'S NOT LIKE THAT.
GO ON.
IT'S TOO EARLY TO TELL.
HENRY, YOU AND LAURA HAVE BEEN THROUGH A LOT TOGETHER.
BEFORE YOU GO GETTING MIXED UP WITH SOME-ONE NEW, MAKE SURE THAT YOU'VE TRULY MOVED ON IN YOUR HEART.

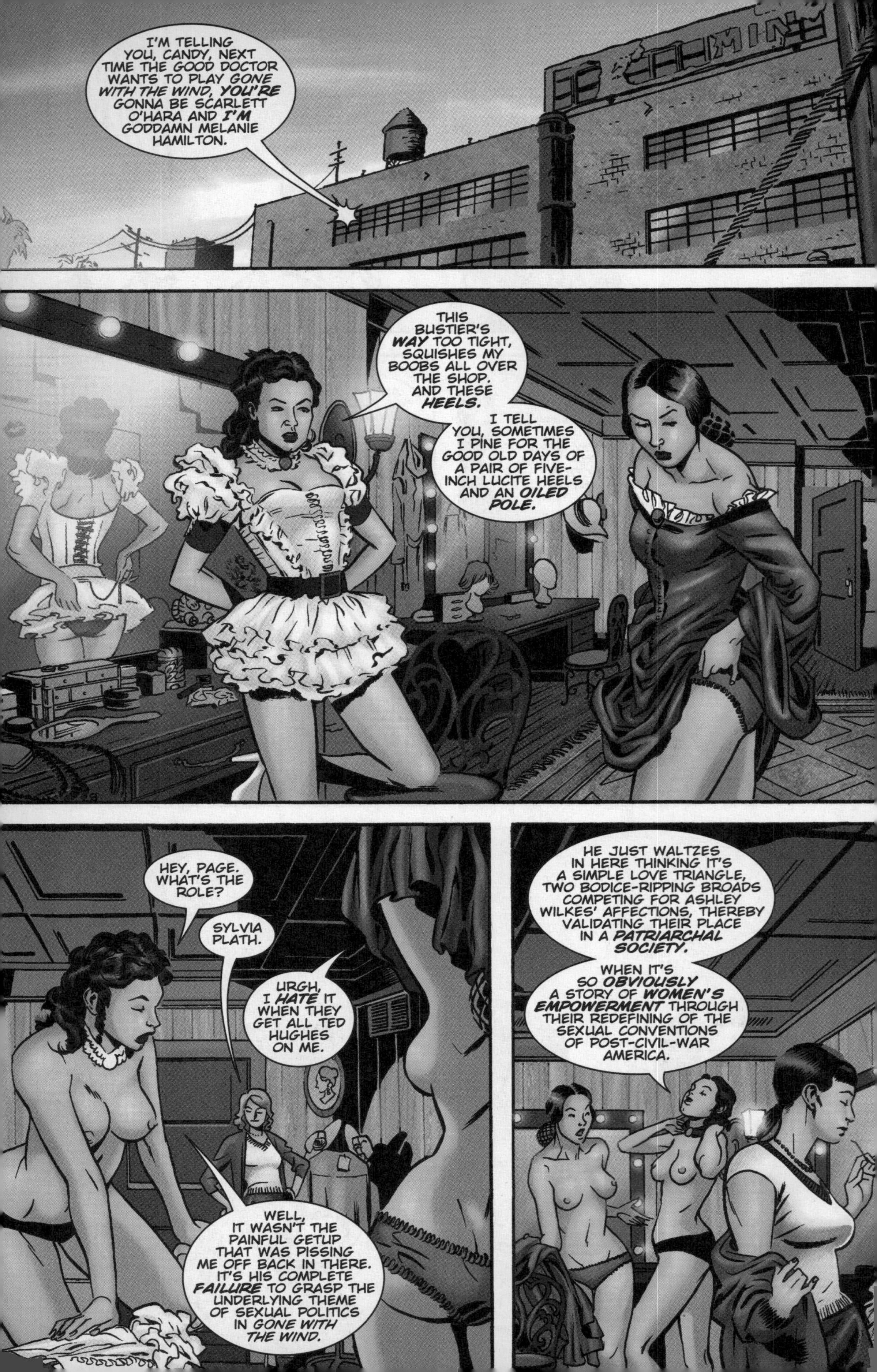
I'M TELLING YOU, CANDY, NEXT TIME THE GOOD DOCTOR WANTS TO PLAY *GONE WITH THE WIND*, ***YOU'RE*** GONNA BE SCARLETT O'HARA AND ***I'M*** GODDAMN MELANIE HAMILTON.
THIS BUSTIER'S ***WAY*** TOO TIGHT, SQUISHES MY BOOBS ALL OVER THE SHOP. AND THESE ***HEELS.***
I TELL YOU, SOMETIMES I PINE FOR THE GOOD OLD DAYS OF A PAIR OF FIVE-INCH LUCITE HEELS AND AN ***OILED POLE.***
HEY, PAGE. WHAT'S THE ROLE?
SYLVIA PLATH.
URGH, I ***HATE*** IT WHEN THEY GET ALL TED HUGHES ON ME.
WELL, IT WASN'T THE PAINFUL GETUP THAT WAS PISSING ME OFF BACK IN THERE. IT'S HIS COMPLETE ***FAILURE*** TO GRASP THE UNDERLYING THEME OF SEXUAL POLITICS IN *GONE WITH THE WIND.*
HE JUST WALTZES IN HERE THINKING IT'S A SIMPLE LOVE TRIANGLE, TWO BODICE-RIPPING BROADS COMPETING FOR ASHLEY WILKES' AFFECTIONS, THEREBY VALIDATING THEIR PLACE IN A ***PATRIARCHAL SOCIETY.***
WHEN IT'S SO ***OBVIOUSLY*** A STORY OF ***WOMEN'S EMPOWERMENT*** THROUGH THEIR REDEFINING OF THE SEXUAL CONVENTIONS OF POST-CIVIL-WAR AMERICA.

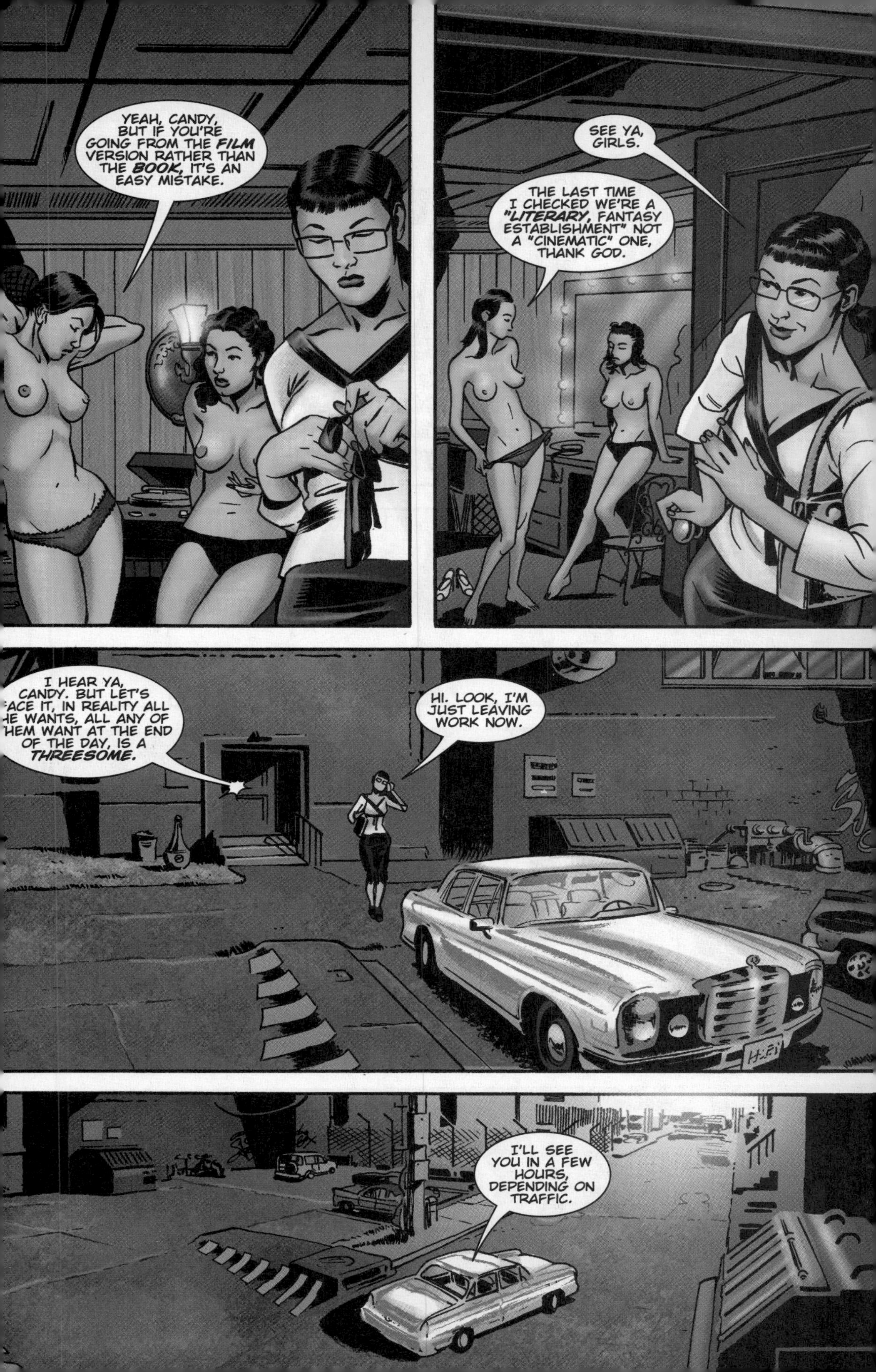
YEAH, CANDY, BUT IF YOU'RE GOING FROM THE FILM VERSION RATHER THAN THE BOOK, IT'S AN EASY MISTAKE.
SEE YA, GIRLS.
THE LAST TIME I CHECKED WE'RE A "LITERARY, FANTASY ESTABLISHMENT" NOT A "CINEMATIC" ONE, THANK GOD.
I HEAR YA, CANDY. BUT LET'S FACE IT, IN REALITY ALL HE WANTS, ALL ANY OF THEM WANT AT THE END OF THE DAY, IS A THREESOME.
HI. LOOK, I'M JUST LEAVING WORK NOW.
I'LL SEE YOU IN A FEW HOURS, DEPENDING ON TRAFFIC.

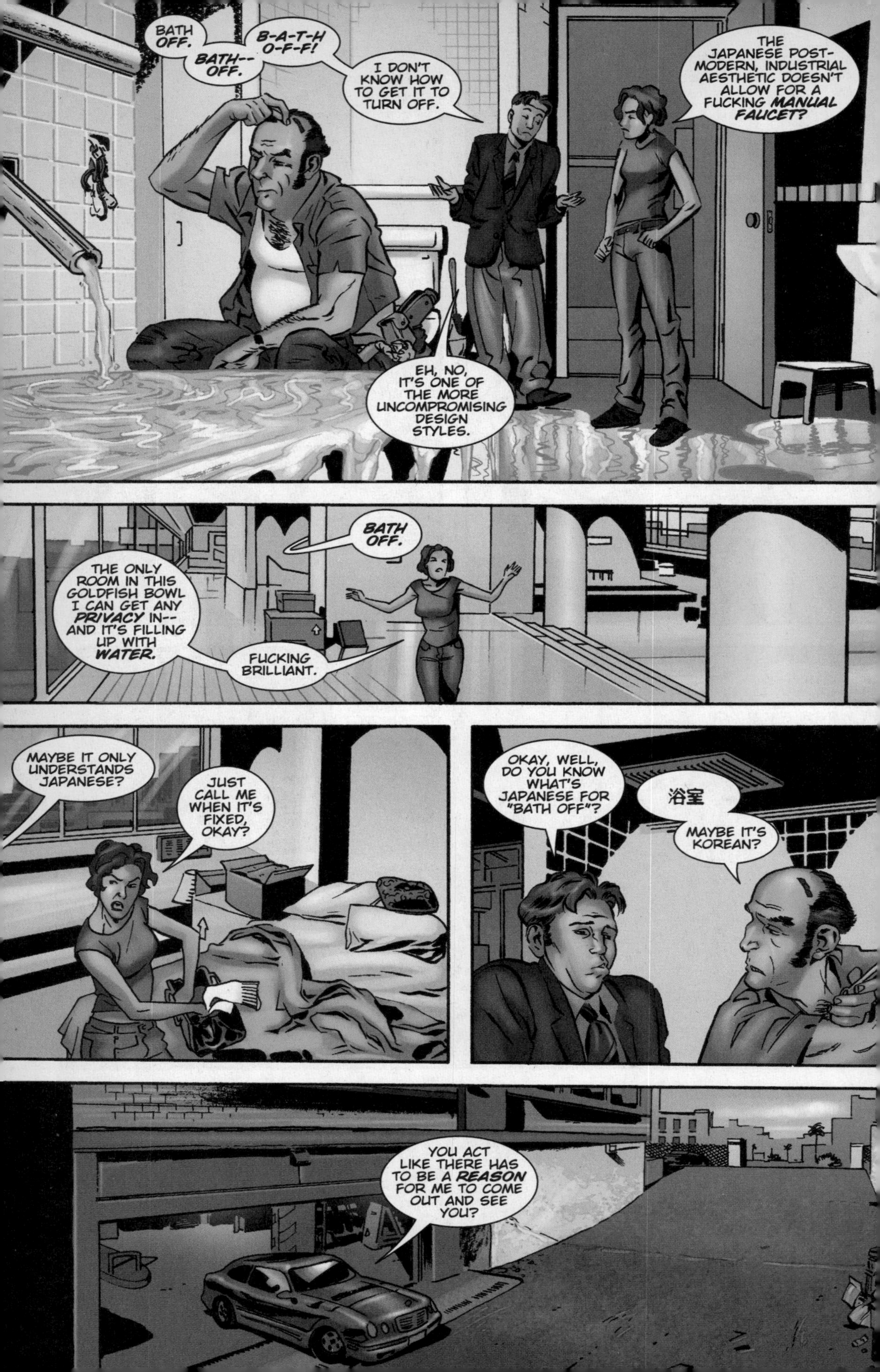

BATH OFF.
BATH-- OFF.
B-A-T-H O-F-F!
I DON'T KNOW HOW TO GET IT TO TURN OFF.
THE JAPANESE POST-MODERN, INDUSTRIAL AESTHETIC DOESN'T ALLOW FOR A FUCKING MANUAL FAUCET?
EH, NO, IT'S ONE OF THE MORE UNCOMPROMISING DESIGN STYLES.
BATH OFF.
THE ONLY ROOM IN THIS GOLDFISH BOWL I CAN GET ANY PRIVACY IN-- AND IT'S FILLING UP WITH WATER.
FUCKING BRILLIANT.
MAYBE IT ONLY UNDERSTANDS JAPANESE?
JUST CALL ME WHEN IT'S FIXED, OKAY?
OKAY, WELL, DO YOU KNOW WHAT'S JAPANESE FOR "BATH OFF"?
浴室
MAYBE IT'S KOREAN?
YOU ACT LIKE THERE HAS TO BE A REASON FOR ME TO COME OUT AND SEE YOU?

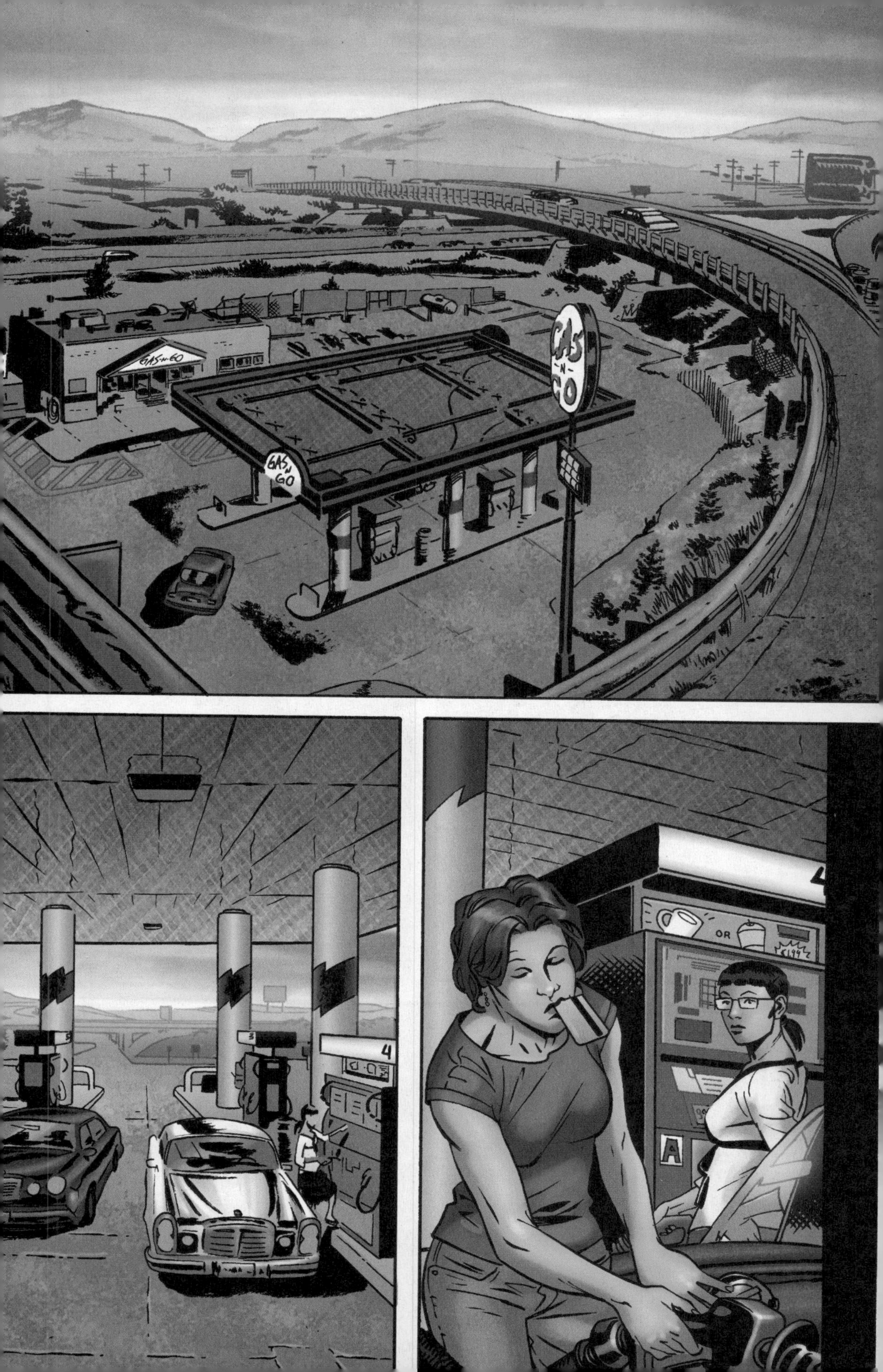
GAS-N-GO
GAS -N- GO
GAS N GO
4
OR
A

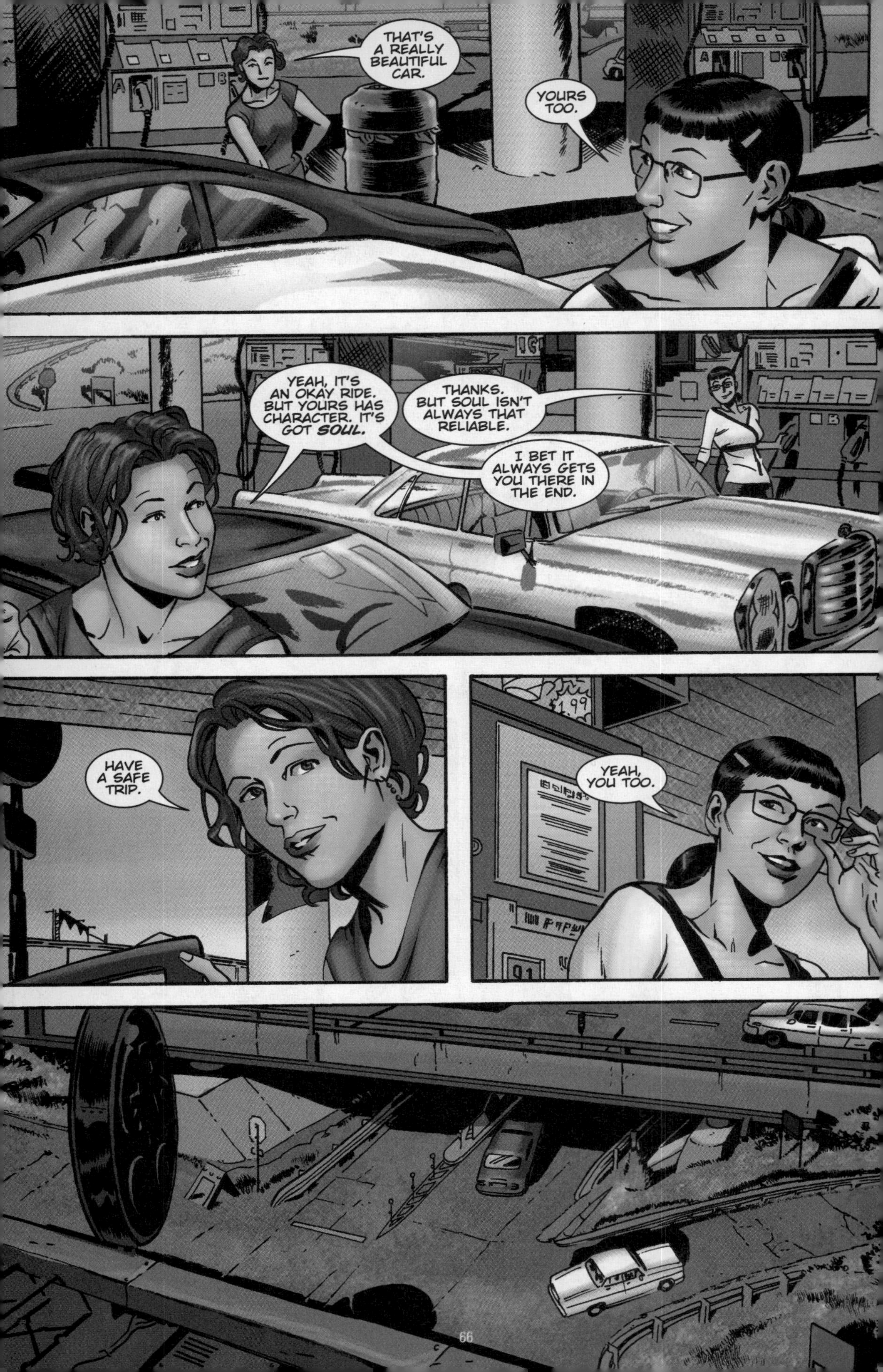
THAT'S A REALLY BEAUTIFUL CAR.
YOURS TOO.
YEAH, IT'S AN OKAY RIDE. BUT YOURS HAS CHARACTER. IT'S GOT SOUL.
THANKS. BUT SOUL ISN'T ALWAYS THAT RELIABLE.
I BET IT ALWAYS GETS YOU THERE IN THE END.
HAVE A SAFE TRIP.
YEAH, YOU TOO.

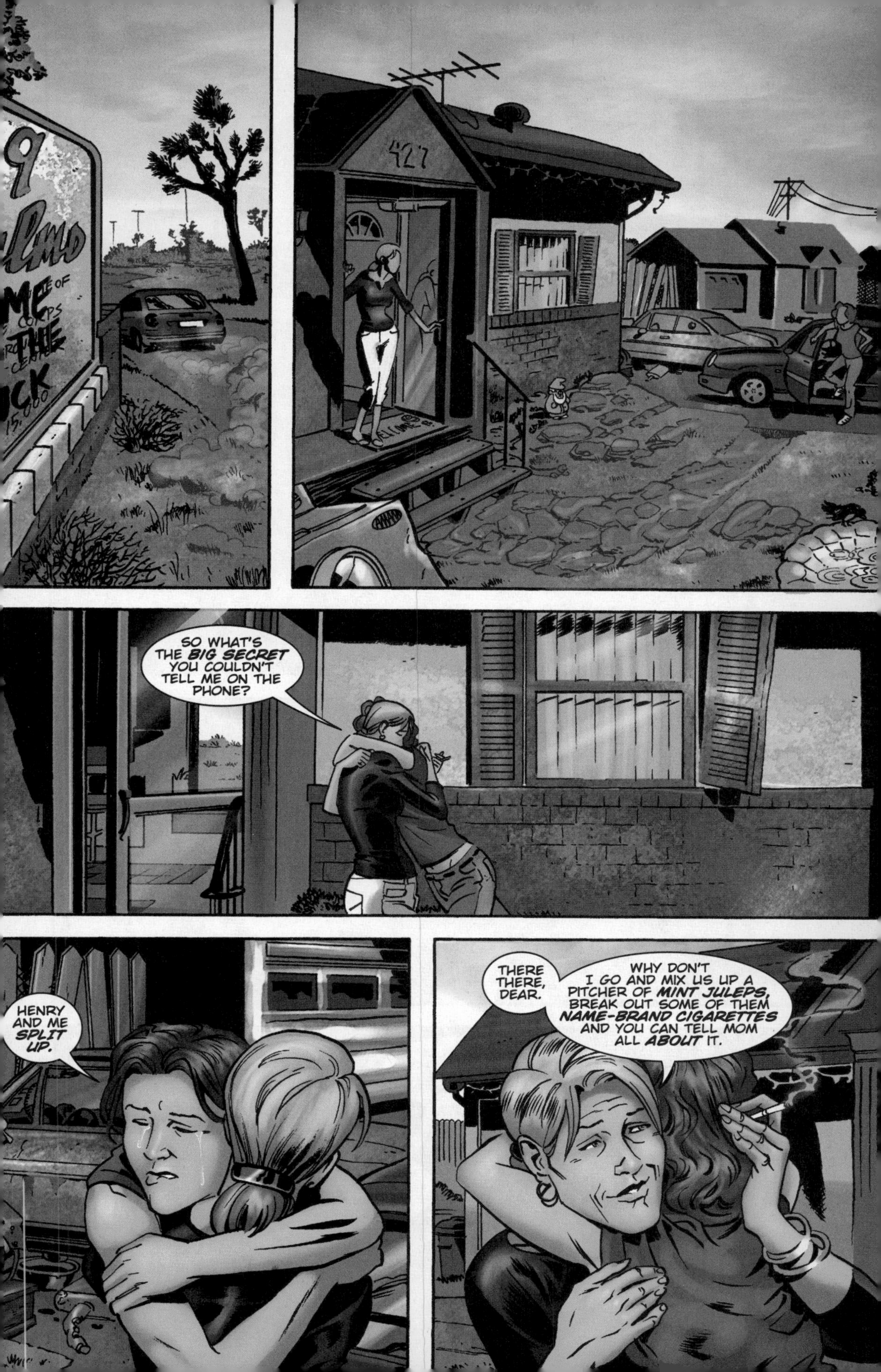
427
SO WHAT'S THE BIG SECRET YOU COULDN'T TELL ME ON THE PHONE?
HENRY AND ME SPLIT UP.
THERE THERE, DEAR.
WHY DON'T I GO AND MIX US UP A PITCHER OF MINT JULEPS, BREAK OUT SOME OF THEM NAME-BRAND CIGARETTES AND YOU CAN TELL MOM ALL ABOUT IT.

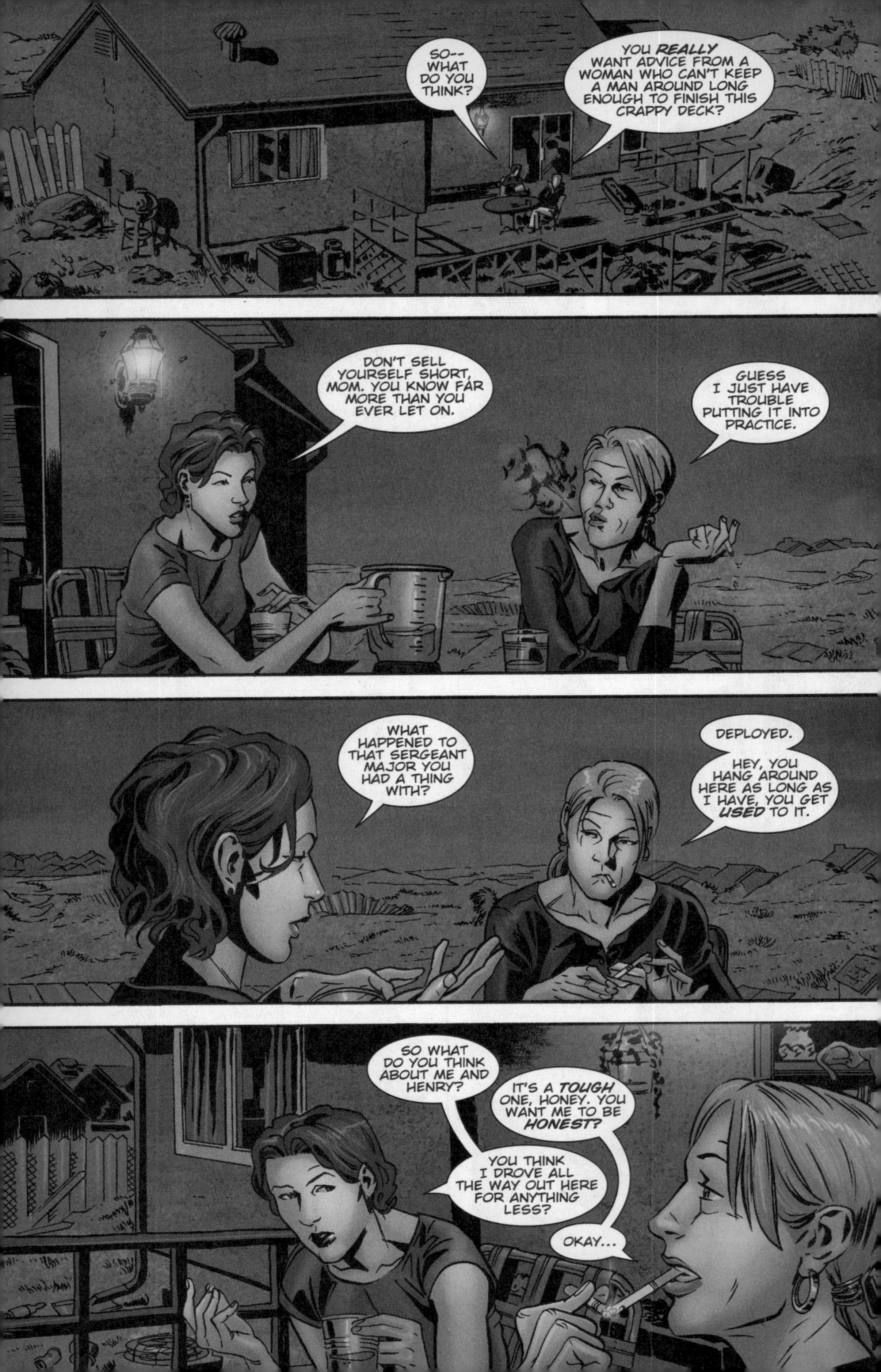
SO-- WHAT DO YOU THINK?
YOU REALLY WANT ADVICE FROM A WOMAN WHO CAN'T KEEP A MAN AROUND LONG ENOUGH TO FINISH THIS CRAPPY DECK?
DON'T SELL YOURSELF SHORT, MOM. YOU KNOW FAR MORE THAN YOU EVER LET ON.
GUESS I JUST HAVE TROUBLE PUTTING IT INTO PRACTICE.
WHAT HAPPENED TO THAT SERGEANT MAJOR YOU HAD A THING WITH?
DEPLOYED.
HEY, YOU HANG AROUND HERE AS LONG AS I HAVE, YOU GET USED TO IT.
SO WHAT DO YOU THINK ABOUT ME AND HENRY?
IT'S A TOUGH ONE, HONEY. YOU WANT ME TO BE HONEST?
YOU THINK I DROVE ALL THE WAY OUT HERE FOR ANYTHING LESS?
OKAY...

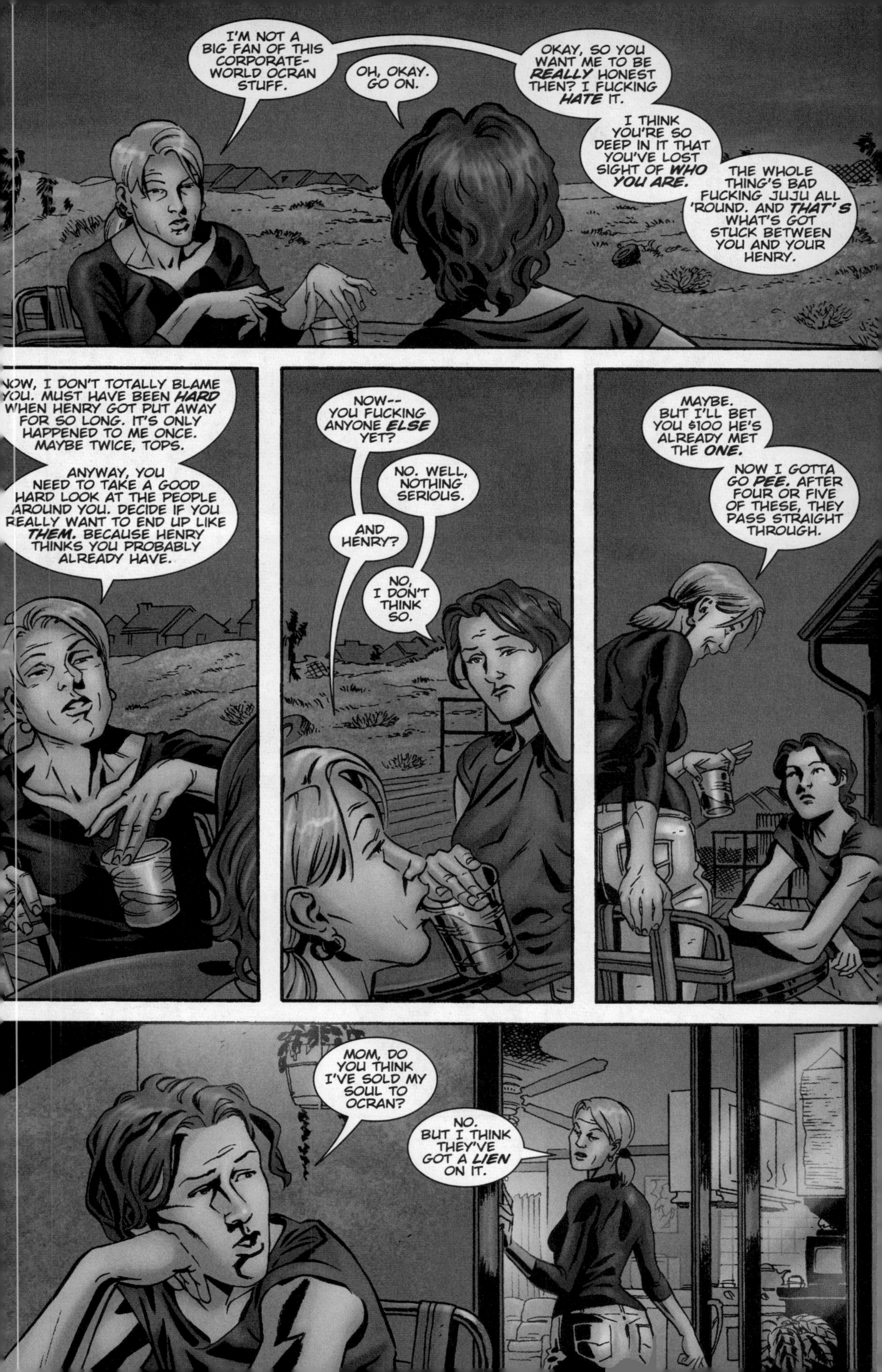
I'M NOT A BIG FAN OF THIS CORPORATE-WORLD OCRAN STUFF.
OH, OKAY. GO ON.
OKAY, SO YOU WANT ME TO BE REALLY HONEST THEN? I FUCKING HATE IT.
I THINK YOU'RE SO DEEP IN IT THAT YOU'VE LOST SIGHT OF WHO YOU ARE.
THE WHOLE THING'S BAD FUCKING JUJU ALL 'ROUND. AND THAT'S WHAT'S GOT STUCK BETWEEN YOU AND YOUR HENRY.
NOW, I DON'T TOTALLY BLAME YOU. MUST HAVE BEEN HARD WHEN HENRY GOT PUT AWAY FOR SO LONG. IT'S ONLY HAPPENED TO ME ONCE. MAYBE TWICE, TOPS.
ANYWAY, YOU NEED TO TAKE A GOOD HARD LOOK AT THE PEOPLE AROUND YOU. DECIDE IF YOU REALLY WANT TO END UP LIKE THEM. BECAUSE HENRY THINKS YOU PROBABLY ALREADY HAVE.
NOW-- YOU FUCKING ANYONE ELSE YET?
NO. WELL, NOTHING SERIOUS.
AND HENRY?
NO, I DON'T THINK SO.
MAYBE. BUT I'LL BET YOU $100 HE'S ALREADY MET THE ONE.
NOW I GOTTA GO PEE. AFTER FOUR OR FIVE OF THESE, THEY PASS STRAIGHT THROUGH.
MOM, DO YOU THINK I'VE SOLD MY SOUL TO OCRAN?
NO. BUT I THINK THEY'VE GOT A LIEN ON IT.

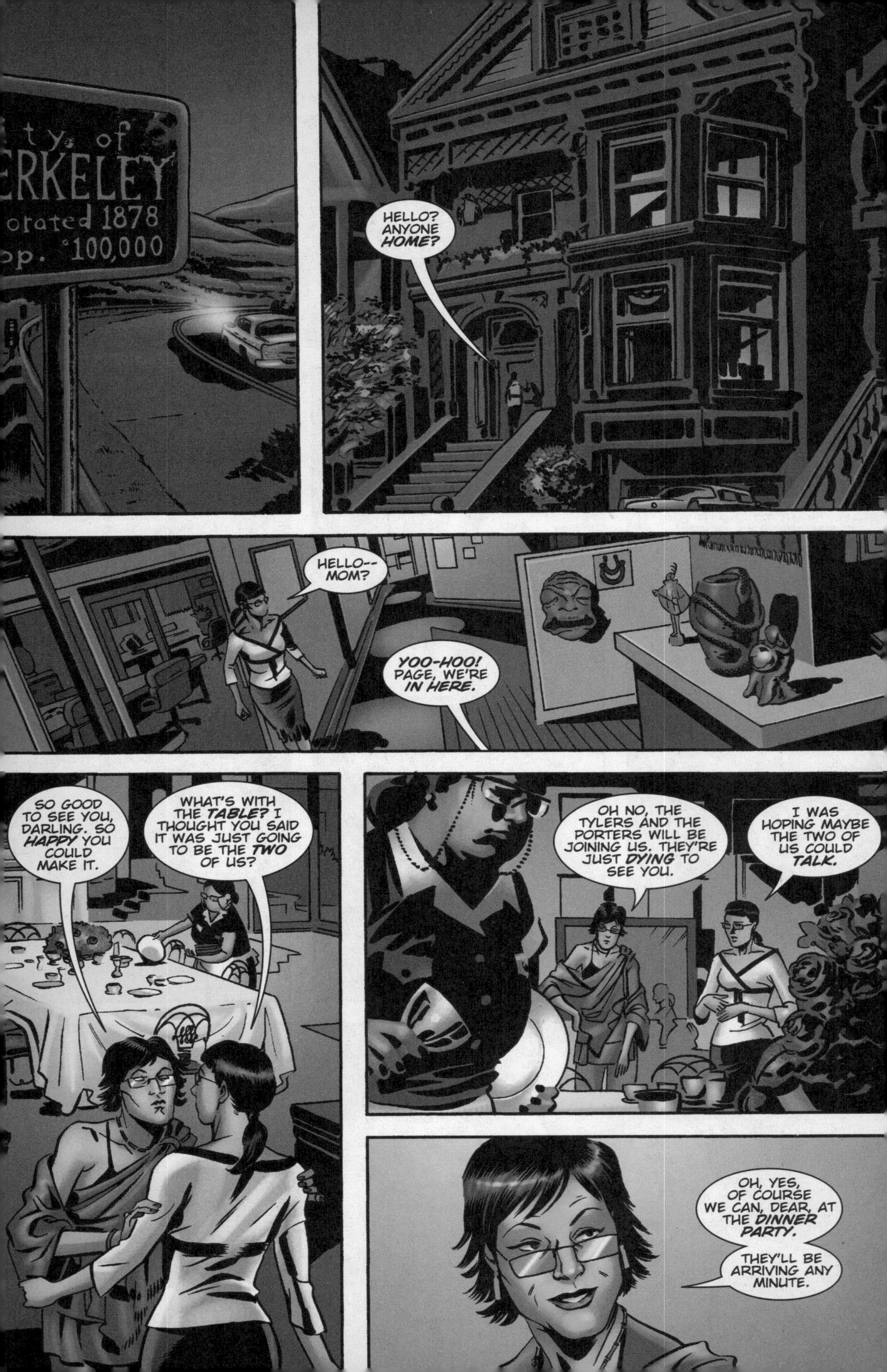

...TY OF
...ERKELEY
...ORATED 1878
...OP. 100,000
HELLO? ANYONE *HOME?*
HELLO-- MOM?
YOO-HOO! PAGE, WE'RE *IN HERE.*
SO GOOD TO SEE YOU, DARLING. SO *HAPPY* YOU COULD MAKE IT.
WHAT'S WITH THE *TABLE?* I THOUGHT YOU SAID IT WAS JUST GOING TO BE THE *TWO* OF US?
OH NO, THE TYLERS AND THE PORTERS WILL BE JOINING US. THEY'RE JUST *DYING* TO SEE YOU.
I WAS HOPING MAYBE THE TWO OF US COULD *TALK.*
OH, YES, OF COURSE WE CAN, DEAR, AT THE *DINNER PARTY.*
THEY'LL BE ARRIVING ANY MINUTE.

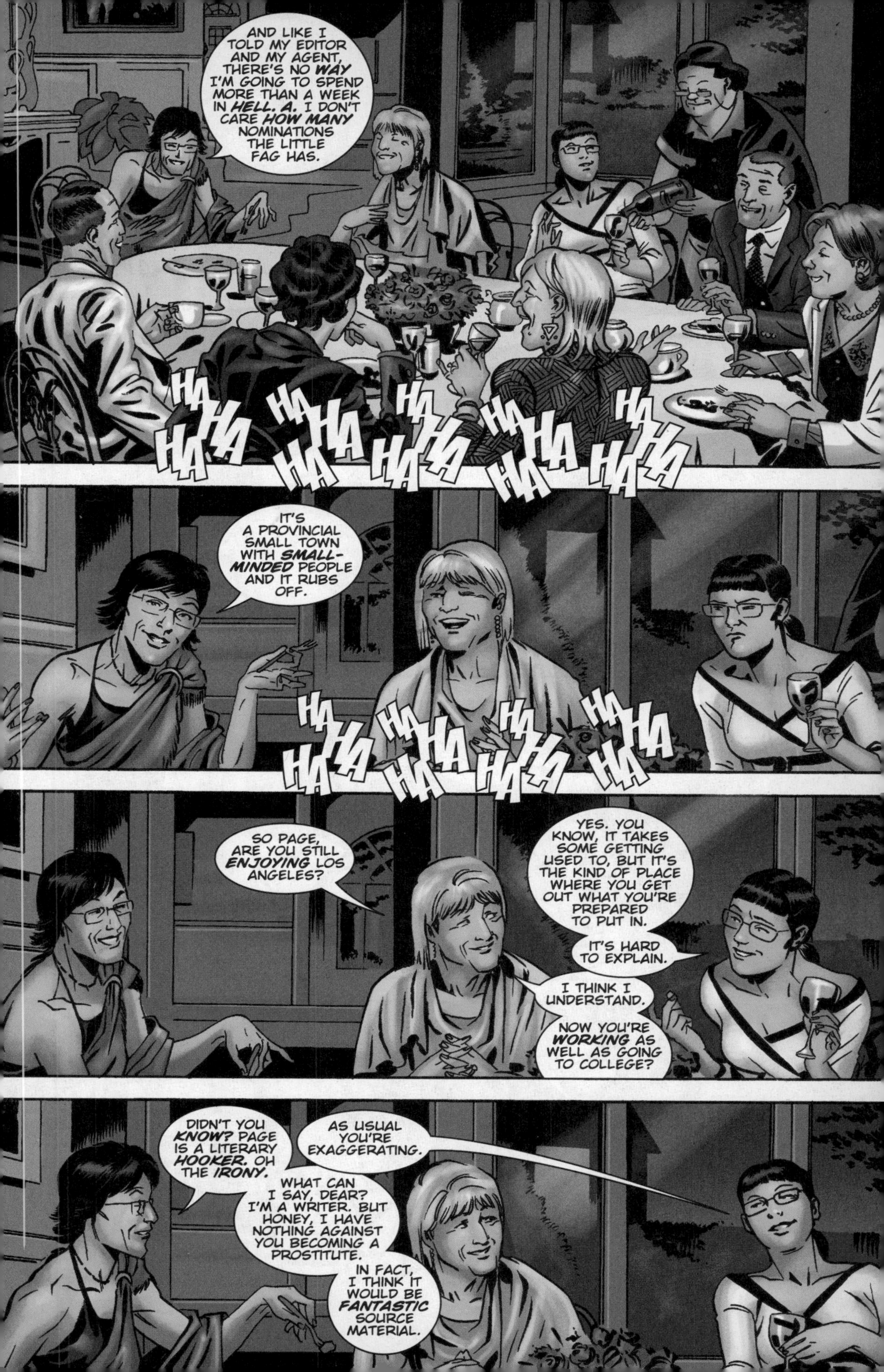
AND LIKE I TOLD MY EDITOR AND MY AGENT, THERE'S NO WAY I'M GOING TO SPEND MORE THAN A WEEK IN HELL. A. I DON'T CARE HOW MANY NOMINATIONS THE LITTLE FAG HAS.
HA HA HA HA HA HA HA HA HA HA HA HA HA HA HA
IT'S A PROVINCIAL SMALL TOWN WITH SMALL-MINDED PEOPLE AND IT RUBS OFF.
HA HA HA HA HA HA HA HA HA HA HA HA
SO PAGE, ARE YOU STILL ENJOYING LOS ANGELES?
YES. YOU KNOW, IT TAKES SOME GETTING USED TO, BUT IT'S THE KIND OF PLACE WHERE YOU GET OUT WHAT YOU'RE PREPARED TO PUT IN.
IT'S HARD TO EXPLAIN.
I THINK I UNDERSTAND.
NOW YOU'RE WORKING AS WELL AS GOING TO COLLEGE?
DIDN'T YOU KNOW? PAGE IS A LITERARY HOOKER. OH THE IRONY.
AS USUAL YOU'RE EXAGGERATING.
WHAT CAN I SAY, DEAR? I'M A WRITER. BUT HONEY, I HAVE NOTHING AGAINST YOU BECOMING A PROSTITUTE.
IN FACT, I THINK IT WOULD BE FANTASTIC SOURCE MATERIAL.

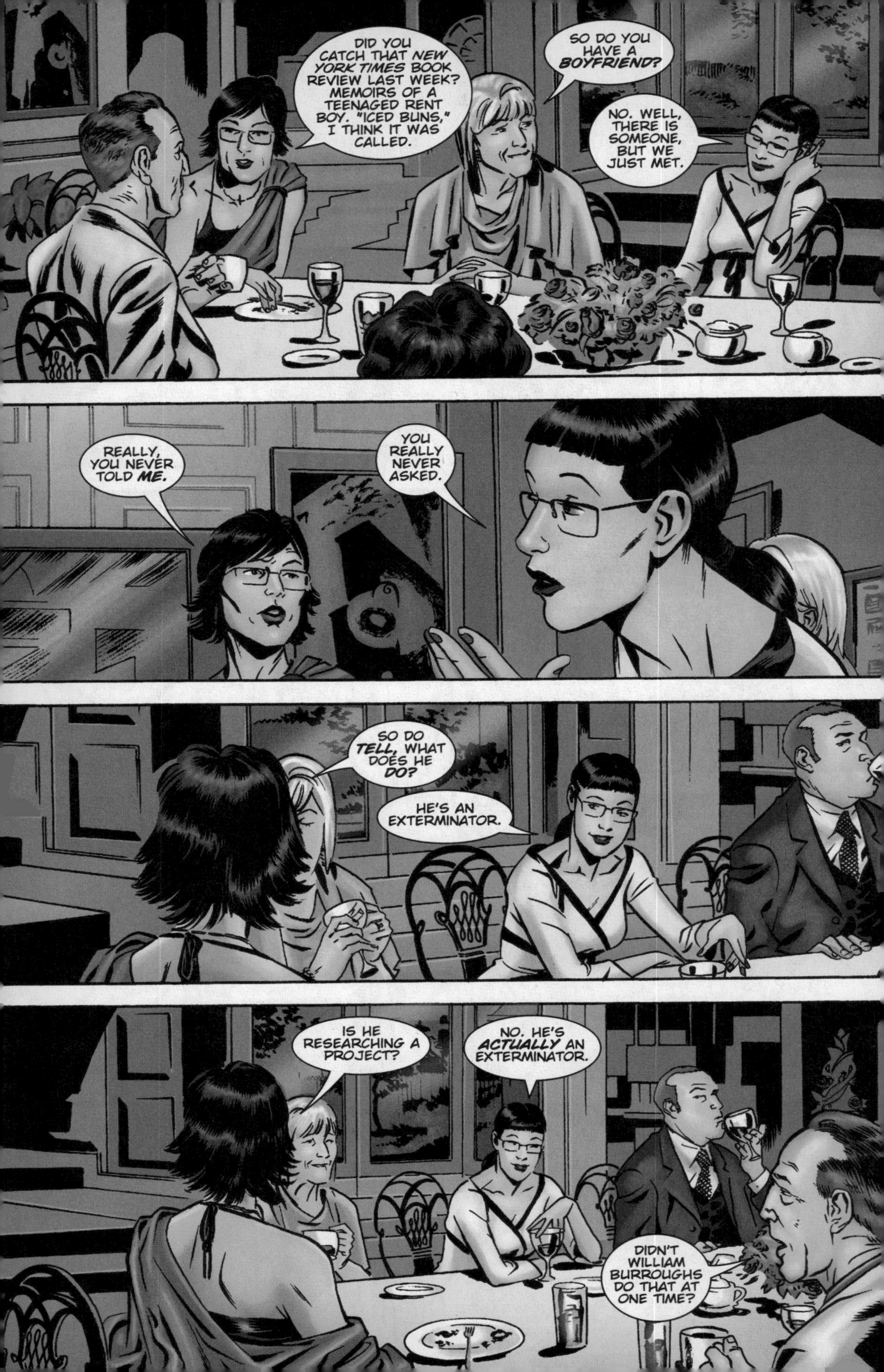
DID YOU CATCH THAT *NEW YORK TIMES* BOOK REVIEW LAST WEEK? MEMOIRS OF A TEENAGED RENT BOY. "ICED BUNS," I THINK IT WAS CALLED.
SO DO YOU HAVE A ***BOYFRIEND?***
NO. WELL, THERE IS SOMEONE, BUT WE JUST MET.
REALLY, YOU NEVER TOLD ***ME.***
YOU REALLY NEVER ASKED.
SO DO ***TELL,*** WHAT DOES HE ***DO?***
HE'S AN EXTERMINATOR.
IS HE RESEARCHING A PROJECT?
NO. HE'S ***ACTUALLY*** AN EXTERMINATOR.
DIDN'T WILLIAM BURROUGHS DO THAT AT ONE TIME?

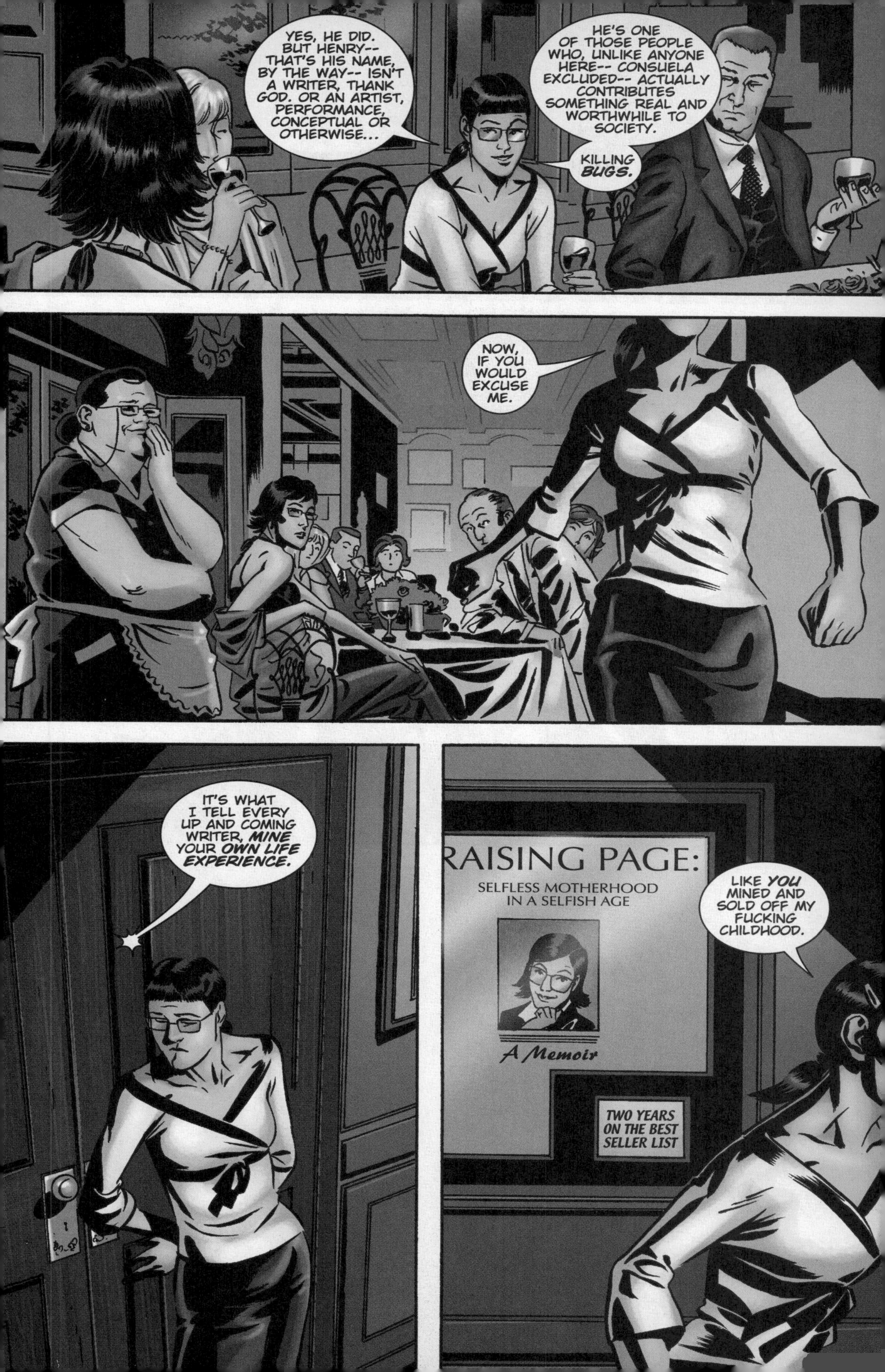
YES, HE DID. BUT HENRY-- THAT'S HIS NAME, BY THE WAY-- ISN'T A WRITER, THANK GOD. OR AN ARTIST, PERFORMANCE, CONCEPTUAL OR OTHERWISE...
HE'S ONE OF THOSE PEOPLE WHO, UNLIKE ANYONE HERE-- CONSUELA EXCLUDED-- ACTUALLY CONTRIBUTES SOMETHING REAL AND WORTHWHILE TO SOCIETY.
KILLING BUGS.
NOW, IF YOU WOULD EXCUSE ME.
IT'S WHAT I TELL EVERY UP AND COMING WRITER, MINE YOUR OWN LIFE EXPERIENCE.
RAISING PAGE:
SELFLESS MOTHERHOOD IN A SELFISH AGE
A Memoir
TWO YEARS ON THE BEST SELLER LIST
LIKE YOU MINED AND SOLD OFF MY FUCKING CHILDHOOD.

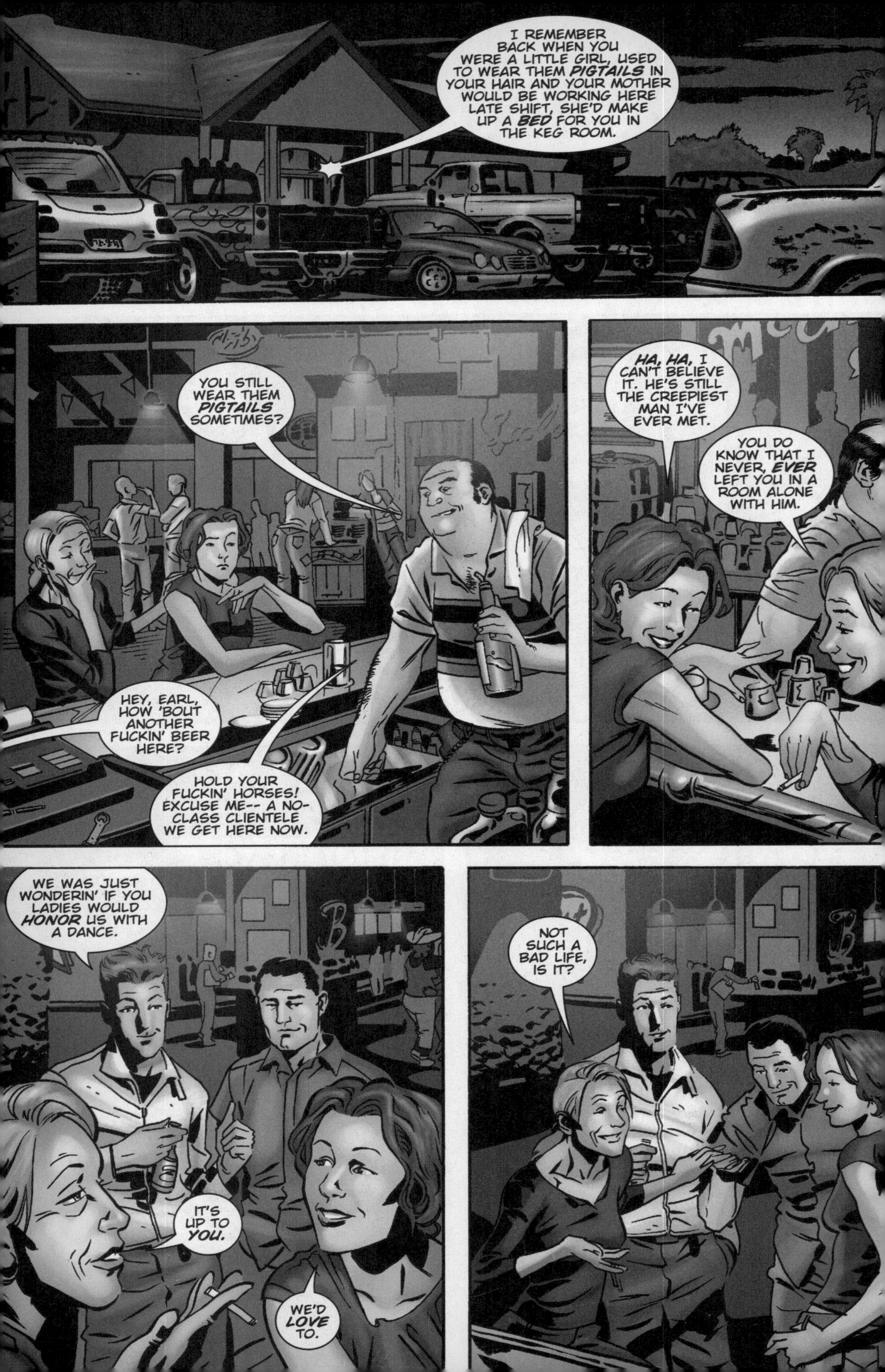
I REMEMBER BACK WHEN YOU WERE A LITTLE GIRL, USED TO WEAR THEM PIGTAILS IN YOUR HAIR AND YOUR MOTHER WOULD BE WORKING HERE LATE SHIFT, SHE'D MAKE UP A BED FOR YOU IN THE KEG ROOM.
YOU STILL WEAR THEM PIGTAILS SOMETIMES?
HEY, EARL, HOW 'BOUT ANOTHER FUCKIN' BEER HERE?
HOLD YOUR FUCKIN' HORSES! EXCUSE ME-- A NO-CLASS CLIENTELE WE GET HERE NOW.
HA, HA, I CAN'T BELIEVE IT. HE'S STILL THE CREEPIEST MAN I'VE EVER MET.
YOU DO KNOW THAT I NEVER, EVER LEFT YOU IN A ROOM ALONE WITH HIM.
WE WAS JUST WONDERIN' IF YOU LADIES WOULD HONOR US WITH A DANCE.
IT'S UP TO YOU.
WE'D LOVE TO.
NOT SUCH A BAD LIFE, IS IT?

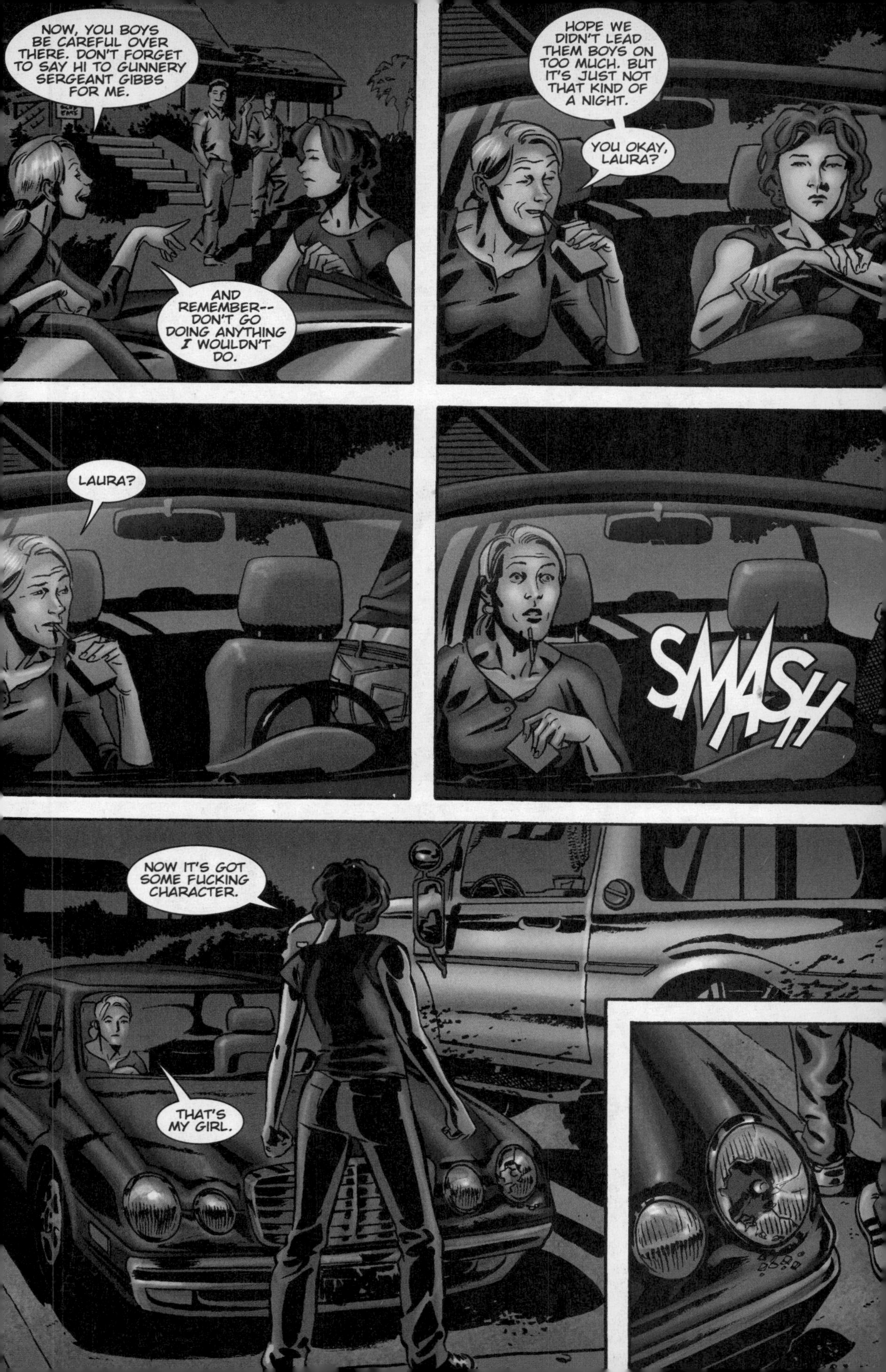
NOW, YOU BOYS BE CAREFUL OVER THERE. DON'T FORGET TO SAY HI TO GUNNERY SERGEANT GIBBS FOR ME.
AND REMEMBER-- DON'T GO DOING ANYTHING I WOULDN'T DO.
HOPE WE DIDN'T LEAD THEM BOYS ON TOO MUCH. BUT IT'S JUST NOT THAT KIND OF A NIGHT.
YOU OKAY, LAURA?
LAURA?
SMASH
NOW IT'S GOT SOME FUCKING CHARACTER.
THAT'S MY GIRL.

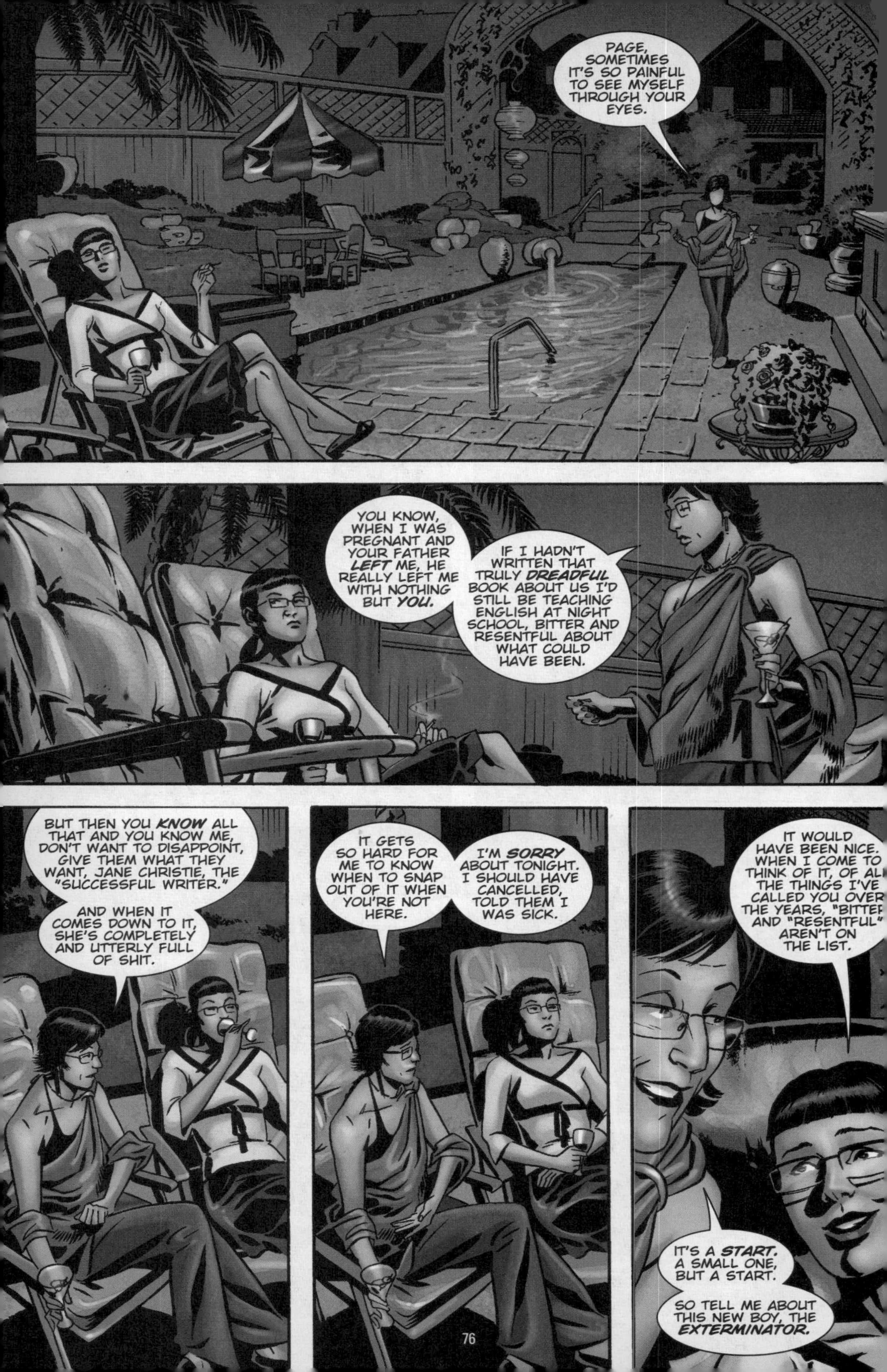

PAGE, SOMETIMES IT'S SO PAINFUL TO SEE MYSELF THROUGH YOUR EYES.
YOU KNOW, WHEN I WAS PREGNANT AND YOUR FATHER LEFT ME, HE REALLY LEFT ME WITH NOTHING BUT YOU.
IF I HADN'T WRITTEN THAT TRULY DREADFUL BOOK ABOUT US I'D STILL BE TEACHING ENGLISH AT NIGHT SCHOOL, BITTER AND RESENTFUL ABOUT WHAT COULD HAVE BEEN.
BUT THEN YOU KNOW ALL THAT AND YOU KNOW ME, DON'T WANT TO DISAPPOINT, GIVE THEM WHAT THEY WANT, JANE CHRISTIE, THE "SUCCESSFUL WRITER."
AND WHEN IT COMES DOWN TO IT, SHE'S COMPLETELY AND UTTERLY FULL OF SHIT.
IT GETS SO HARD FOR ME TO KNOW WHEN TO SNAP OUT OF IT WHEN YOU'RE NOT HERE.
I'M SORRY ABOUT TONIGHT. I SHOULD HAVE CANCELLED, TOLD THEM I WAS SICK.
IT WOULD HAVE BEEN NICE. WHEN I COME TO THINK OF IT, OF AL THE THINGS I'VE CALLED YOU OVER THE YEARS, "BITTEF AND "RESENTFUL" AREN'T ON THE LIST.
IT'S A START. A SMALL ONE, BUT A START.
SO TELL ME ABOUT THIS NEW BOY, THE EXTERMINATOR.

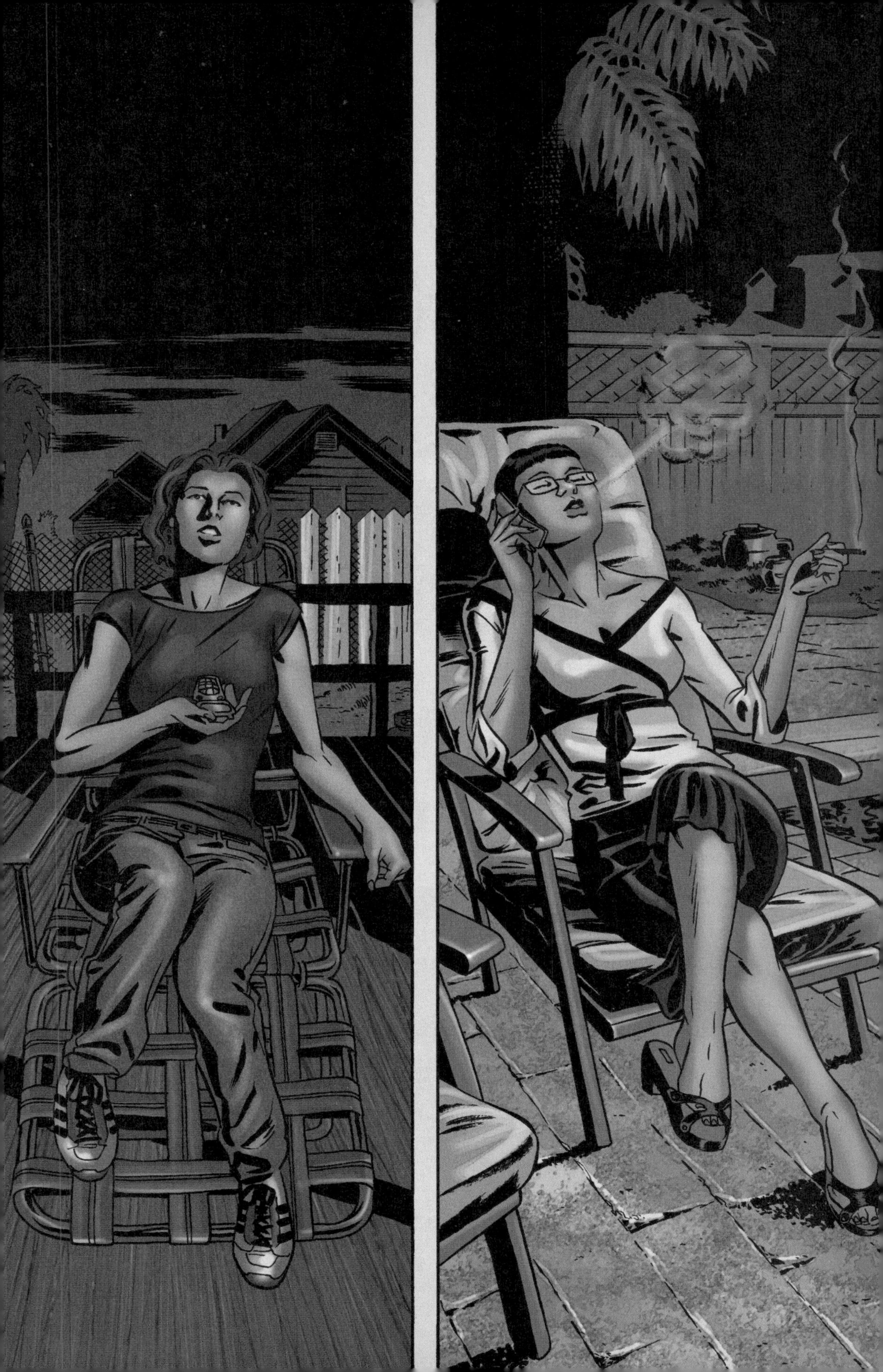

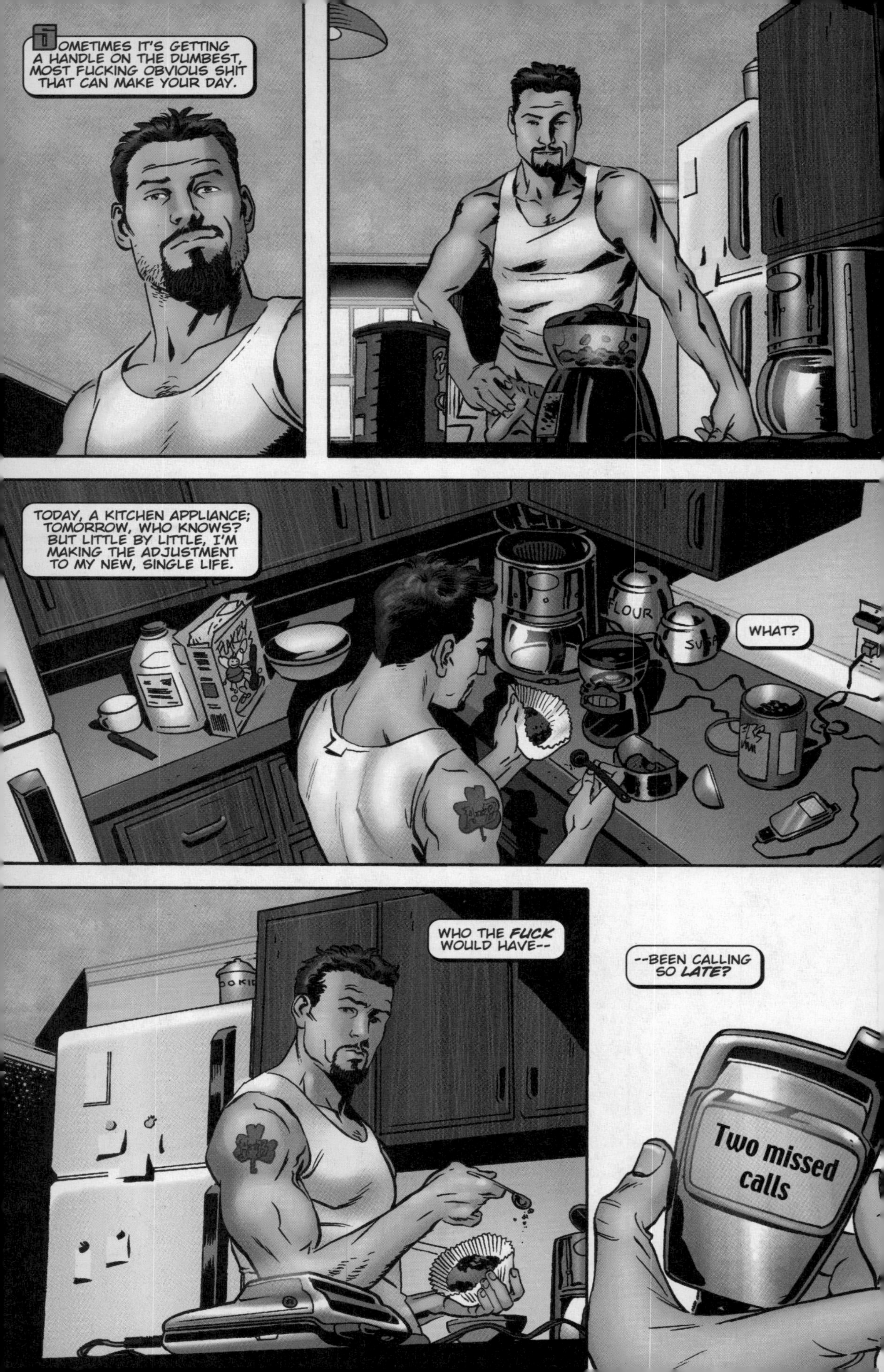
SOMETIMES IT'S GETTING A HANDLE ON THE DUMBEST, MOST FUCKING OBVIOUS SHIT THAT CAN MAKE YOUR DAY.
TODAY, A KITCHEN APPLIANCE; TOMORROW, WHO KNOWS? BUT LITTLE BY LITTLE, I'M MAKING THE ADJUSTMENT TO MY NEW, SINGLE LIFE.
FLOUR
WHAT?
WHO THE *FUCK* WOULD HAVE--
--BEEN CALLING SO *LATE?*
Two missed calls

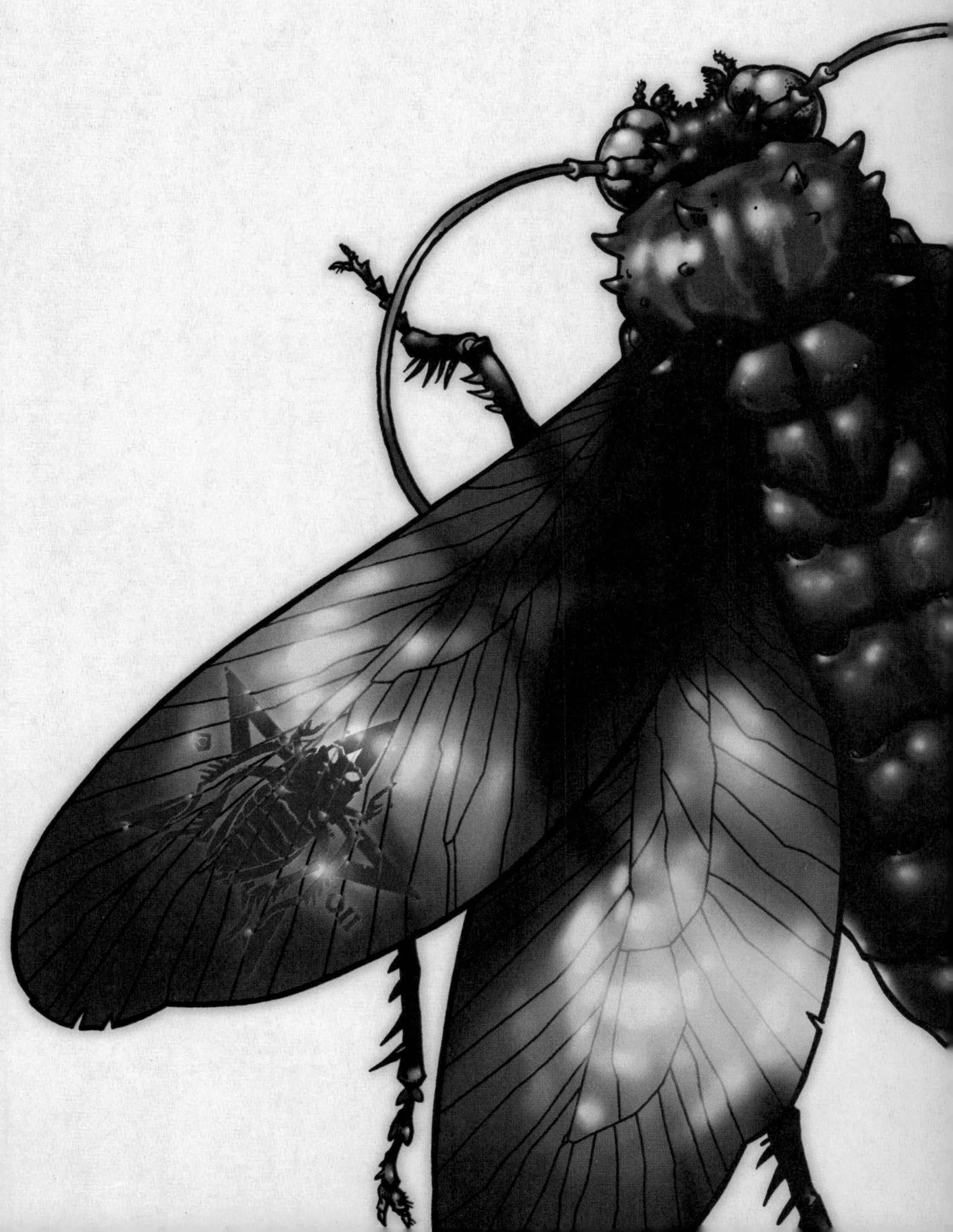

CHAPTER THREE

TONY MOORE
PENCILLER

ANDE PARKS
(pgs. 83-90, 94-95, 97-102)

TONY MOORE
(pgs. 82, 92-93)

SEAN PARSONS
(pgs. 81, 91, 96)

INKERS

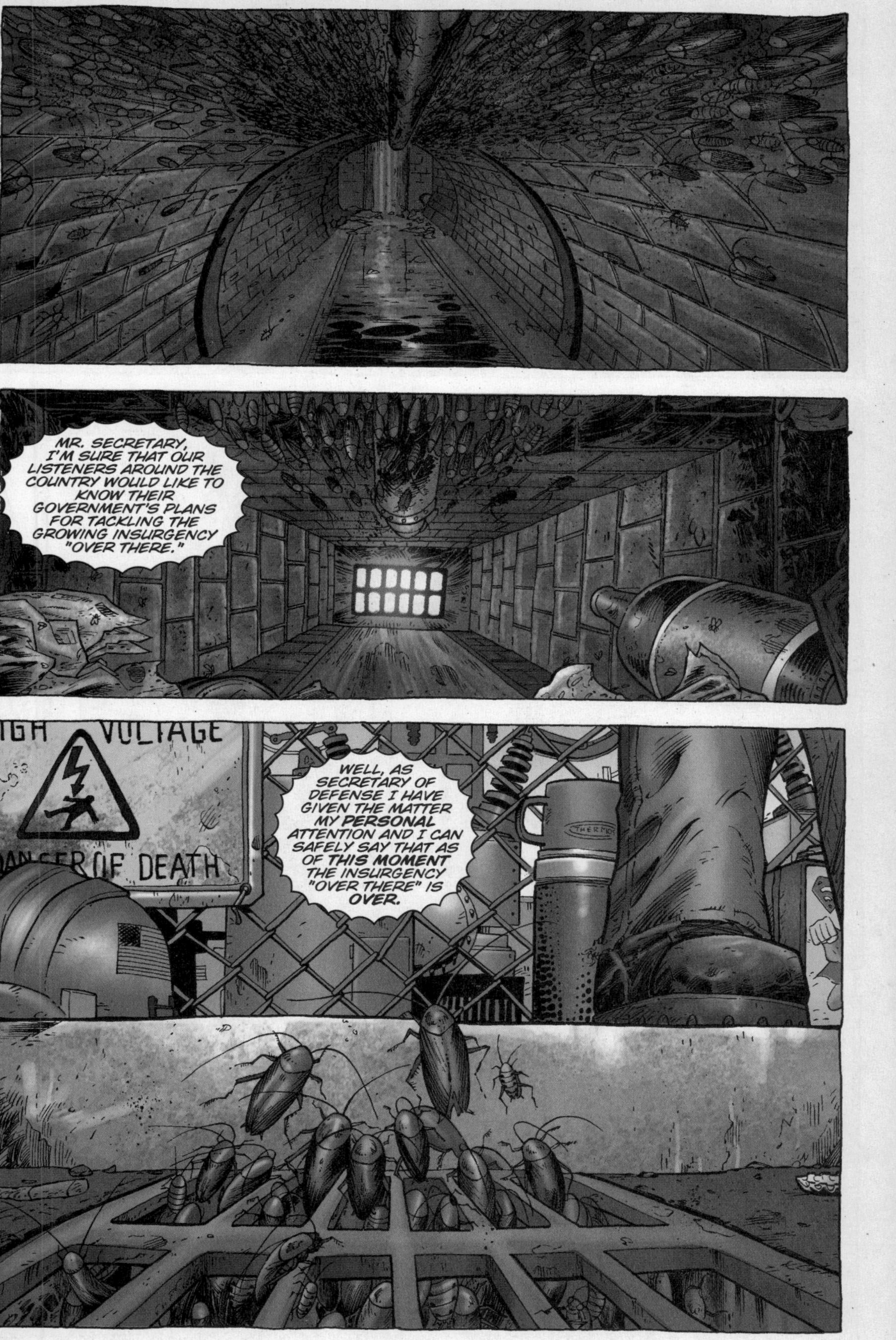
MR. SECRETARY, I'M SURE THAT OUR LISTENERS AROUND THE COUNTRY WOULD LIKE TO KNOW THEIR GOVERNMENT'S PLANS FOR TACKLING THE GROWING INSURGENCY "OVER THERE."
IGH VOLTAGE
DANGER OF DEATH
WELL, AS SECRETARY OF DEFENSE I HAVE GIVEN THE MATTER MY PERSONAL ATTENTION AND I CAN SAFELY SAY THAT AS OF THIS MOMENT THE INSURGENCY "OVER THERE" IS OVER.
THERMOS

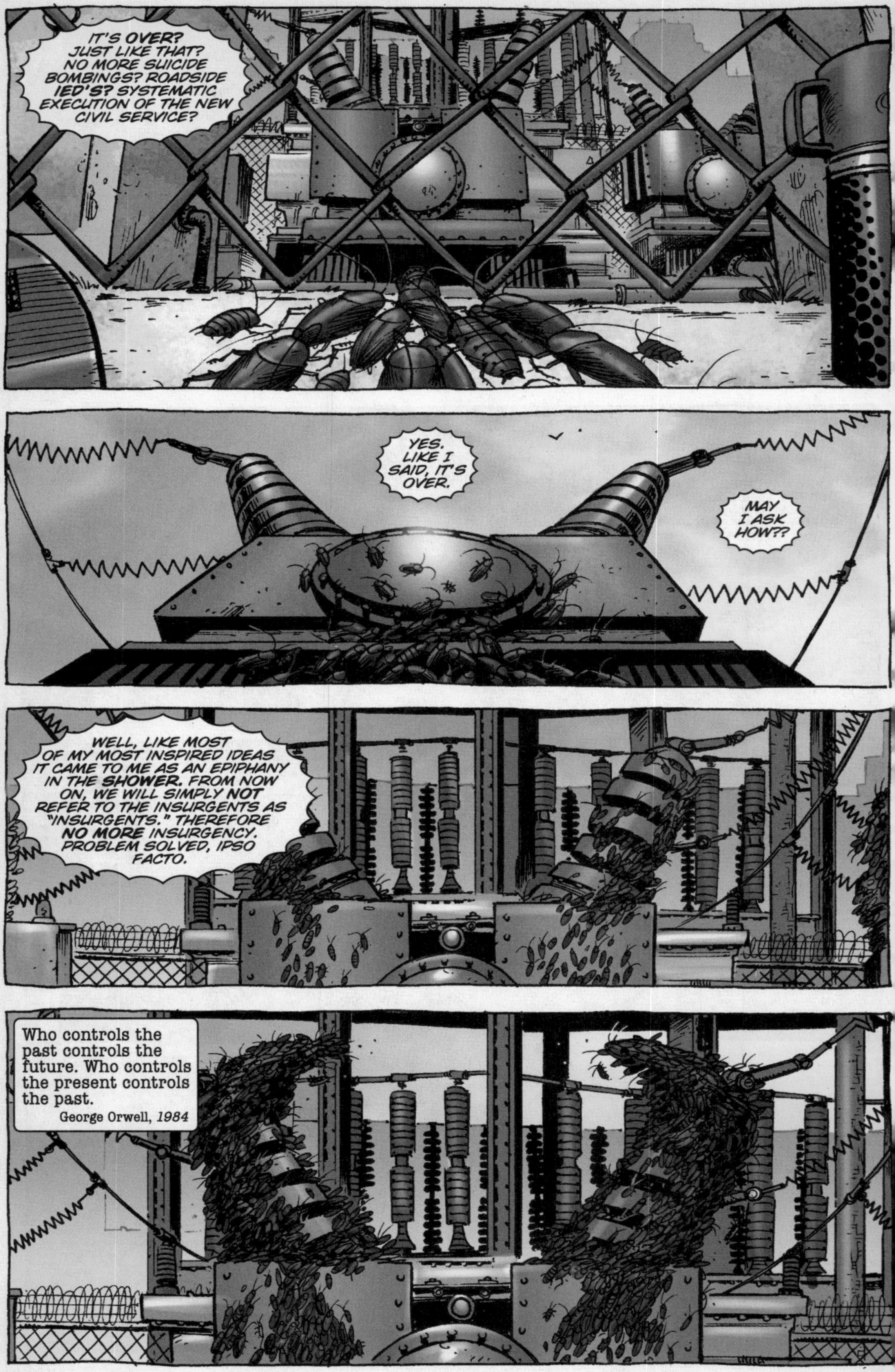
IT'S OVER? JUST LIKE THAT? NO MORE SUICIDE BOMBINGS? ROADSIDE IED'S? SYSTEMATIC EXECUTION OF THE NEW CIVIL SERVICE?
YES. LIKE I SAID, IT'S OVER.
MAY I ASK HOW??
WELL, LIKE MOST OF MY MOST INSPIRED IDEAS IT CAME TO ME AS AN EPIPHANY IN THE SHOWER. FROM NOW ON, WE WILL SIMPLY NOT REFER TO THE INSURGENTS AS "INSURGENTS." THEREFORE NO MORE INSURGENCY. PROBLEM SOLVED, IPSO FACTO.
Who controls the past controls the future. Who controls the present controls the past.
George Orwell, 1984

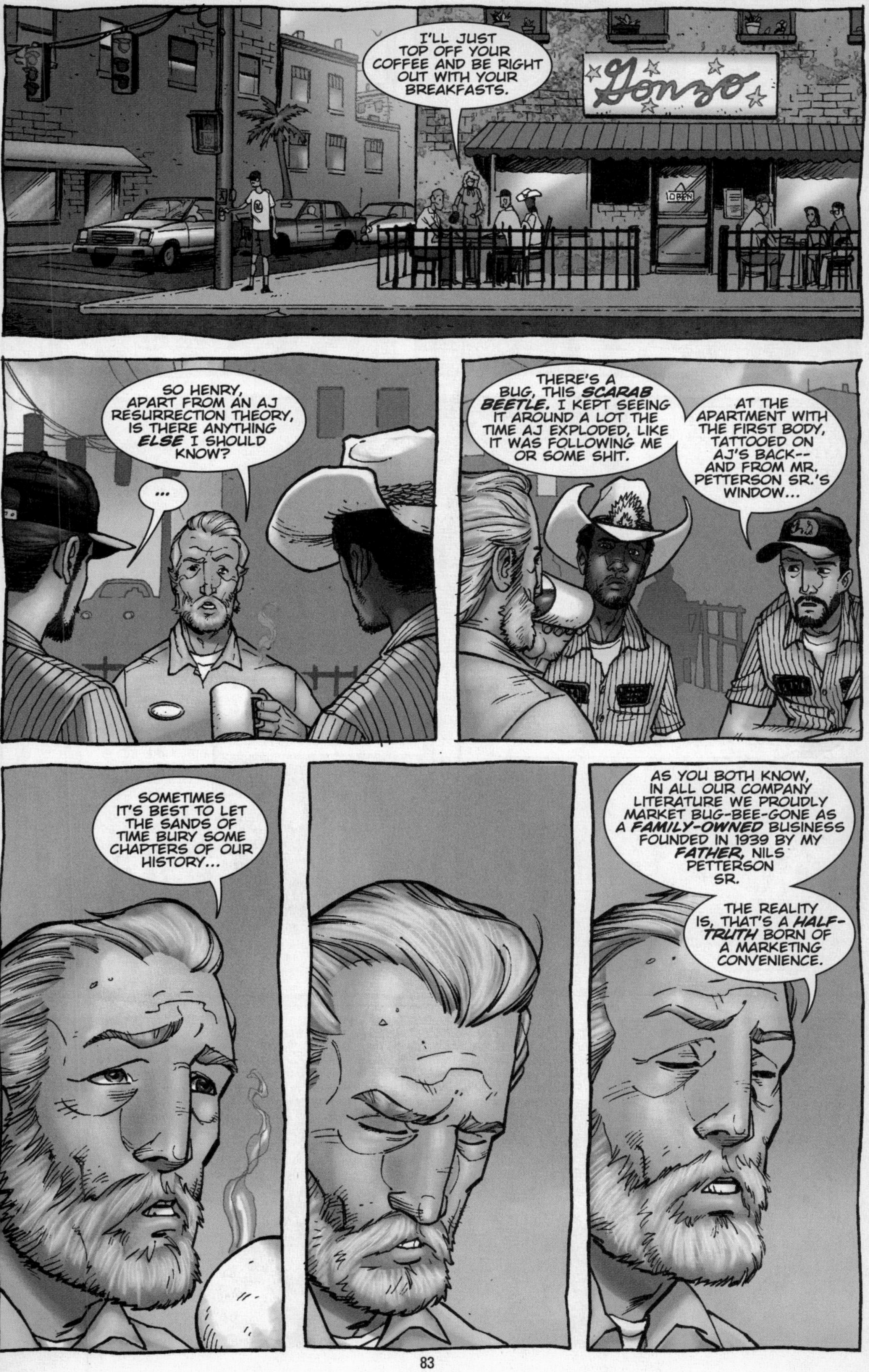
I'LL JUST TOP OFF YOUR COFFEE AND BE RIGHT OUT WITH YOUR BREAKFASTS.
Gonzo
OPEN
SO HENRY, APART FROM AN AJ RESURRECTION THEORY, IS THERE ANYTHING *ELSE* I SHOULD KNOW?
...
THERE'S A BUG, THIS *SCARAB BEETLE.* I KEPT SEEING IT AROUND A LOT THE TIME AJ EXPLODED, LIKE IT WAS FOLLOWING ME OR SOME SHIT.
AT THE APARTMENT WITH THE FIRST BODY, TATTOOED ON AJ'S BACK-- AND FROM MR. PETTERSON SR.'S WINDOW...
SOMETIMES IT'S BEST TO LET THE SANDS OF TIME BURY SOME CHAPTERS OF OUR HISTORY...
AS YOU BOTH KNOW, IN ALL OUR COMPANY LITERATURE WE PROUDLY MARKET BUG-BEE-GONE AS A *FAMILY-OWNED* BUSINESS FOUNDED IN 1939 BY MY *FATHER,* NILS PETTERSON SR.
THE REALITY IS, THAT'S A *HALF-TRUTH* BORN OF A MARKETING CONVENIENCE.

IN 1936, MY FATHER ARRIVED IN THE U.S.A. FROM GRIMSTAD, NORWAY EAGER TO START A *NEW LIFE*.

FOR TWO YEARS HE WORKED AS A STEEL MONKEY, SAW A GOOD NUMBER OF HIS FRIENDS PEELED OFF THE SIDEWALKS.

AHHHHHH...

HE WANTED OUT. AND WITH THE MEALYBUG PLAGUE OF 1937 AND BALDFACED HORNETS OF THE FOLLOWING YEAR IT WAS OBVIOUS TO HIM THAT THE *SMART* MONEY WAS IN EXTERMINATING.

AND IT WOULD HAVE REMAINED ANOTHER AMERICAN DREAM DASHED ON THE COLD ROCKS OF REALITY UNLESS A PARTNER WITH CAPITAL HAD STEPPED IN--*MR. CRAWLEY*.

SAL

THEY COULDN'T HAVE BEEN MORE *MISMATCHED*: NILS THE *HARD-WORKING*, SALT-OF-THE-EARTH, MAKE-A-GO-OF-IT *IMMIGRANT* AND CRAWLEY, THE PAMPERED, *BISEXUAL* SON OF AN EAST COAST INDUSTRIAL *ROBBER BARON*.

HE HAD INHERITED A FAMILY FORTUNE BUILT ON THE BLOOD, SWEAT AND TEARS OF OTHERS.

BUT WHAT HAD TAKEN HIS LATE FATHER A LIFETIME TO STEAL AND CHEAT FROM HIS EXPLOITED WORKERS--

--CRAWLEY JR. *PISSED AWAY* IN TEN YEARS ON BOOZE, DRUGS, HOOKERS, ELABORATE SADOMASOCHISTIC ORGIES THAT LASTED FOR DAYS, AND THE MOST PRODIGIOUS COLLECTION OF *PORNOGRAPHY* AMASSED OUTSIDE OF THE BRITISH ROYAL FAMILY.

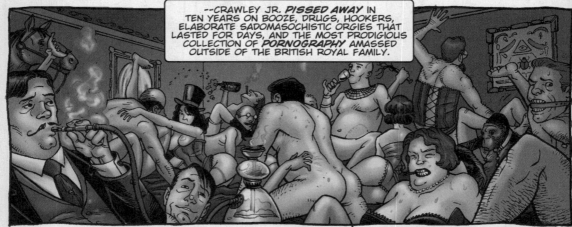

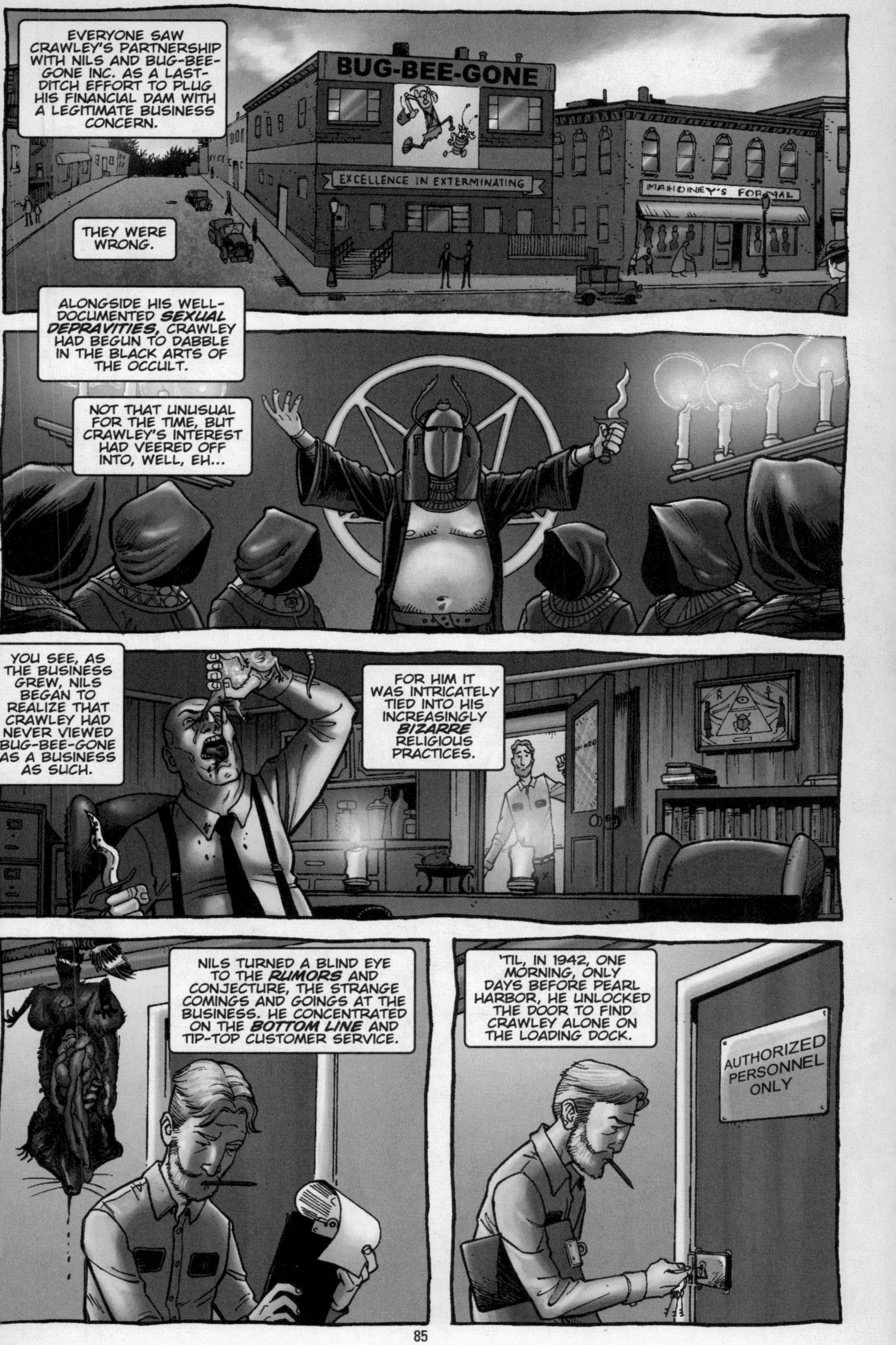
EVERYONE SAW CRAWLEY'S PARTNERSHIP WITH NILS AND BUG-BEE-GONE INC. AS A LAST-DITCH EFFORT TO PLUG HIS FINANCIAL DAM WITH A LEGITIMATE BUSINESS CONCERN.
BUG-BEE-GONE
EXCELLENCE IN EXTERMINATING
THEY WERE WRONG.
ALONGSIDE HIS WELL-DOCUMENTED SEXUAL DEPRAVITIES, CRAWLEY HAD BEGUN TO DABBLE IN THE BLACK ARTS OF THE OCCULT.
NOT THAT UNUSUAL FOR THE TIME, BUT CRAWLEY'S INTEREST HAD VEERED OFF INTO, WELL, EH...
YOU SEE, AS THE BUSINESS GREW, NILS BEGAN TO REALIZE THAT CRAWLEY HAD NEVER VIEWED BUG-BEE-GONE AS A BUSINESS AS SUCH.
FOR HIM IT WAS INTRICATELY TIED INTO HIS INCREASINGLY BIZARRE RELIGIOUS PRACTICES.
NILS TURNED A BLIND EYE TO THE RUMORS AND CONJECTURE, THE STRANGE COMINGS AND GOINGS AT THE BUSINESS. HE CONCENTRATED ON THE BOTTOM LINE AND TIP-TOP CUSTOMER SERVICE.
'TIL, IN 1942, ONE MORNING, ONLY DAYS BEFORE PEARL HARBOR, HE UNLOCKED THE DOOR TO FIND CRAWLEY ALONE ON THE LOADING DOCK.
AUTHORIZED PERSONNEL ONLY

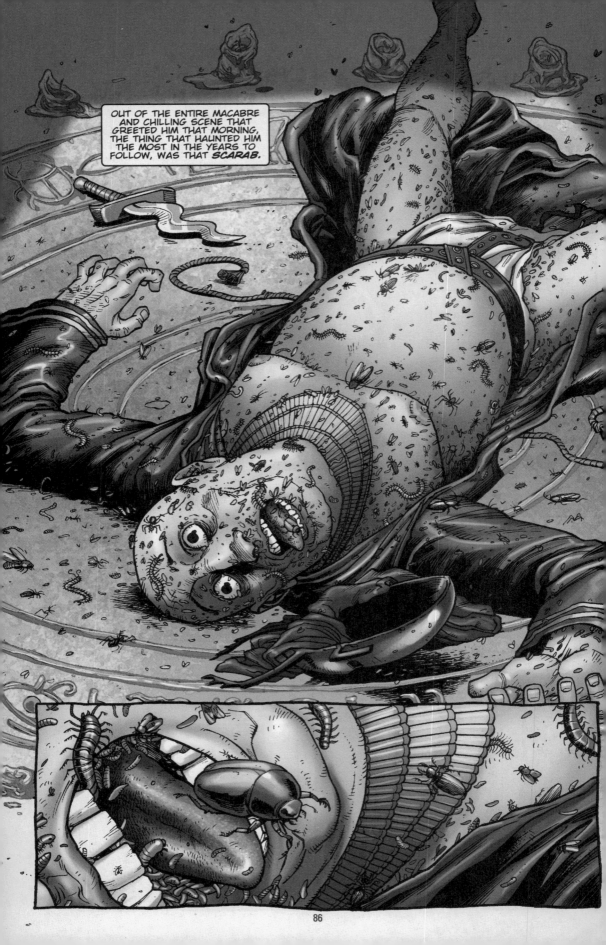

OUT OF THE ENTIRE MACABRE AND CHILLING SCENE THAT GREETED HIM THAT MORNING, THE THING THAT HAUNTED HIM THE MOST IN THE YEARS TO FOLLOW, WAS THAT *SCARAB.*

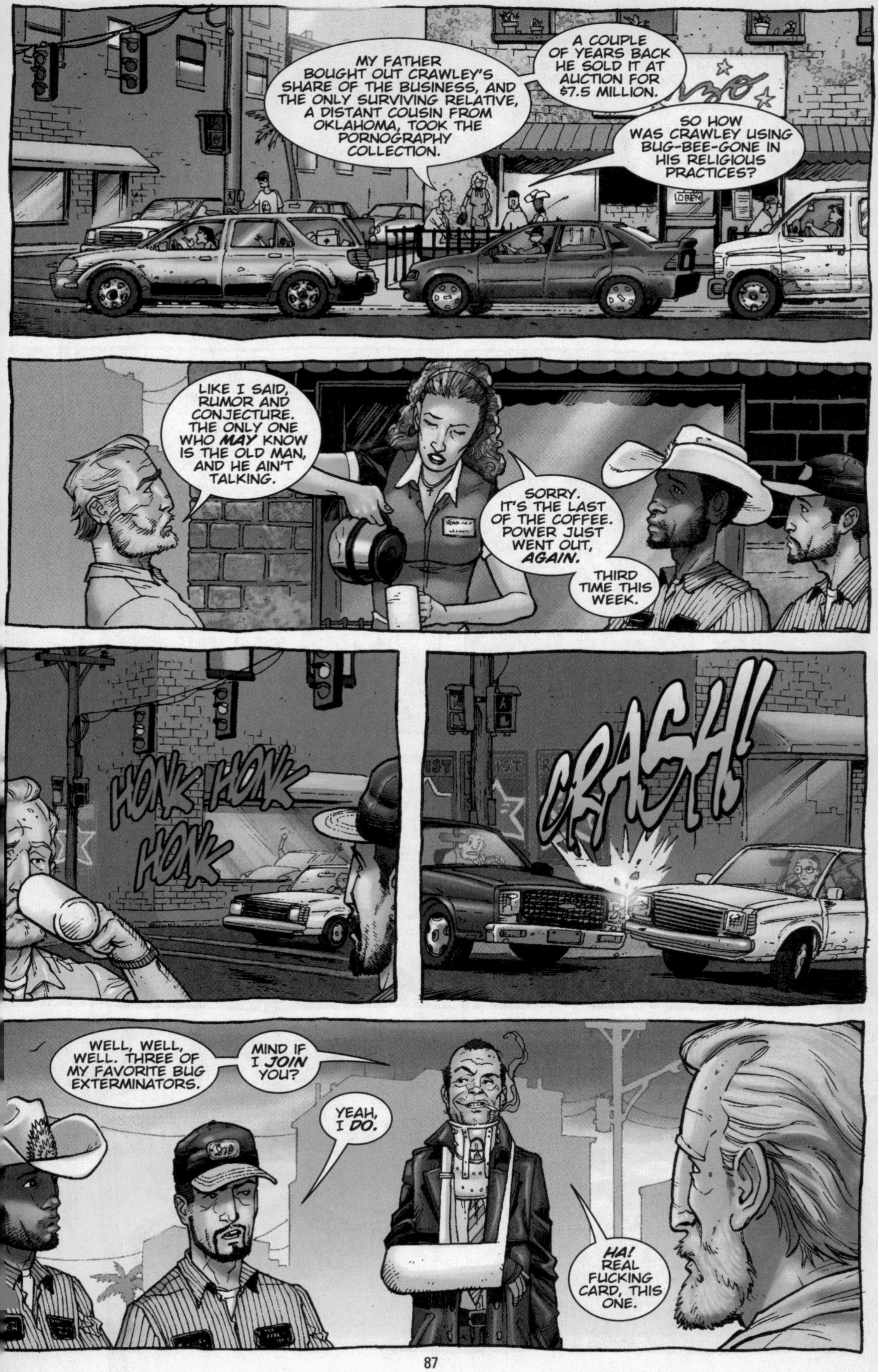
MY FATHER BOUGHT OUT CRAWLEY'S SHARE OF THE BUSINESS, AND THE ONLY SURVIVING RELATIVE, A DISTANT COUSIN FROM OKLAHOMA, TOOK THE PORNOGRAPHY COLLECTION.
A COUPLE OF YEARS BACK HE SOLD IT AT AUCTION FOR $7.5 MILLION.
SO HOW WAS CRAWLEY USING BUG-BEE-GONE IN HIS RELIGIOUS PRACTICES?
OPEN
LIKE I SAID, RUMOR AND CONJECTURE. THE ONLY ONE WHO MAY KNOW IS THE OLD MAN, AND HE AIN'T TALKING.
SORRY. IT'S THE LAST OF THE COFFEE. POWER JUST WENT OUT, AGAIN.
THIRD TIME THIS WEEK.
HONK HONK
HONK
CRASH!
WELL, WELL, WELL. THREE OF MY FAVORITE BUG EXTERMINATORS.
MIND IF I JOIN YOU?
YEAH, I DO.
HA! REAL FUCKING CARD, THIS ONE.

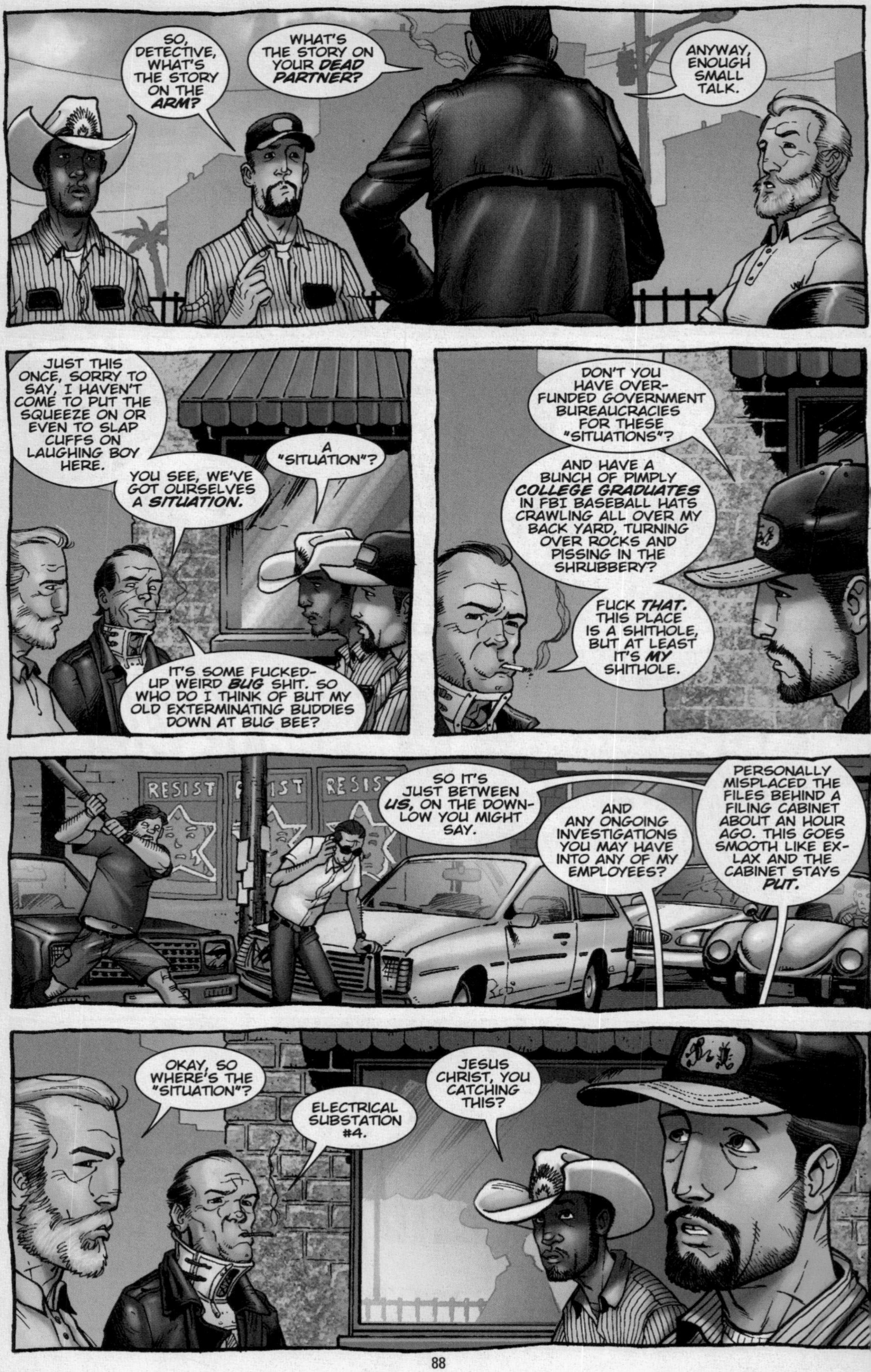
SO, DETECTIVE, WHAT'S THE STORY ON THE ARM?
WHAT'S THE STORY ON YOUR DEAD PARTNER?
ANYWAY, ENOUGH SMALL TALK.
JUST THIS ONCE, SORRY TO SAY, I HAVEN'T COME TO PUT THE SQUEEZE ON OR EVEN TO SLAP CUFFS ON LAUGHING BOY HERE.
YOU SEE, WE'VE GOT OURSELVES A SITUATION.
A "SITUATION"?
IT'S SOME FUCKED-UP WEIRD BUG SHIT. SO WHO DO I THINK OF BUT MY OLD EXTERMINATING BUDDIES DOWN AT BUG BEE?
DON'T YOU HAVE OVER-FUNDED GOVERNMENT BUREAUCRACIES FOR THESE "SITUATIONS"?
AND HAVE A BUNCH OF PIMPLY COLLEGE GRADUATES IN FBI BASEBALL HATS CRAWLING ALL OVER MY BACK YARD, TURNING OVER ROCKS AND PISSING IN THE SHRUBBERY?
FUCK THAT. THIS PLACE IS A SHITHOLE, BUT AT LEAST IT'S MY SHITHOLE.
RESIST
RESIST
SO IT'S JUST BETWEEN US, ON THE DOWN-LOW YOU MIGHT SAY.
AND ANY ONGOING INVESTIGATIONS YOU MAY HAVE INTO ANY OF MY EMPLOYEES?
PERSONALLY MISPLACED THE FILES BEHIND A FILING CABINET ABOUT AN HOUR AGO. THIS GOES SMOOTH LIKE EX-LAX AND THE CABINET STAYS PUT.
OKAY, SO WHERE'S THE "SITUATION"?
ELECTRICAL SUBSTATION #4.
JESUS CHRIST, YOU CATCHING THIS?

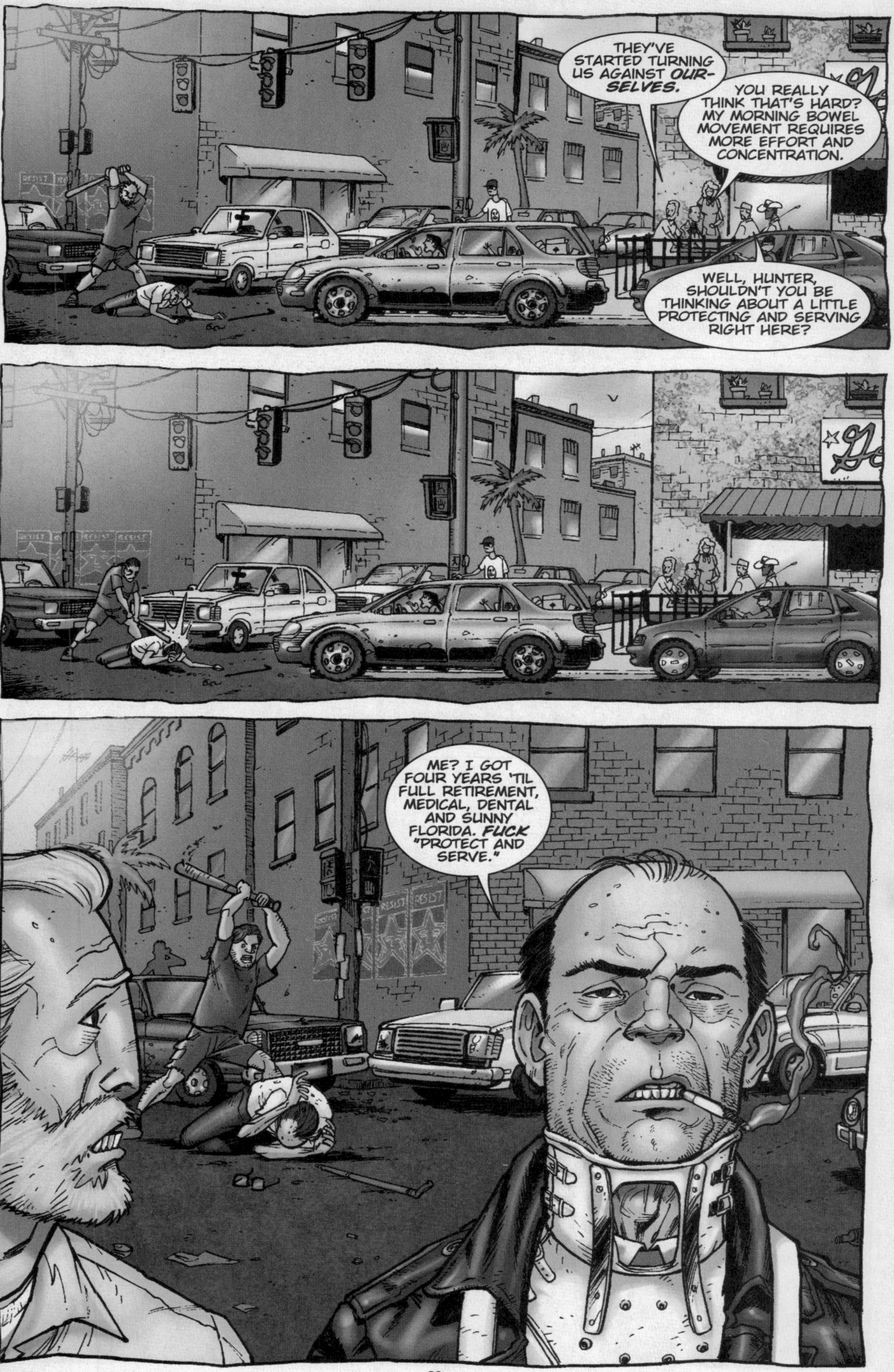

THEY'VE STARTED TURNING US AGAINST OUR-SELVES.
YOU REALLY THINK THAT'S HARD? MY MORNING BOWEL MOVEMENT REQUIRES MORE EFFORT AND CONCENTRATION.
WELL, HUNTER, SHOULDN'T YOU BE THINKING ABOUT A LITTLE PROTECTING AND SERVING RIGHT HERE?
RESIST
ME? I GOT FOUR YEARS 'TIL FULL RETIREMENT, MEDICAL, DENTAL AND SUNNY FLORIDA. FUCK "PROTECT AND SERVE."

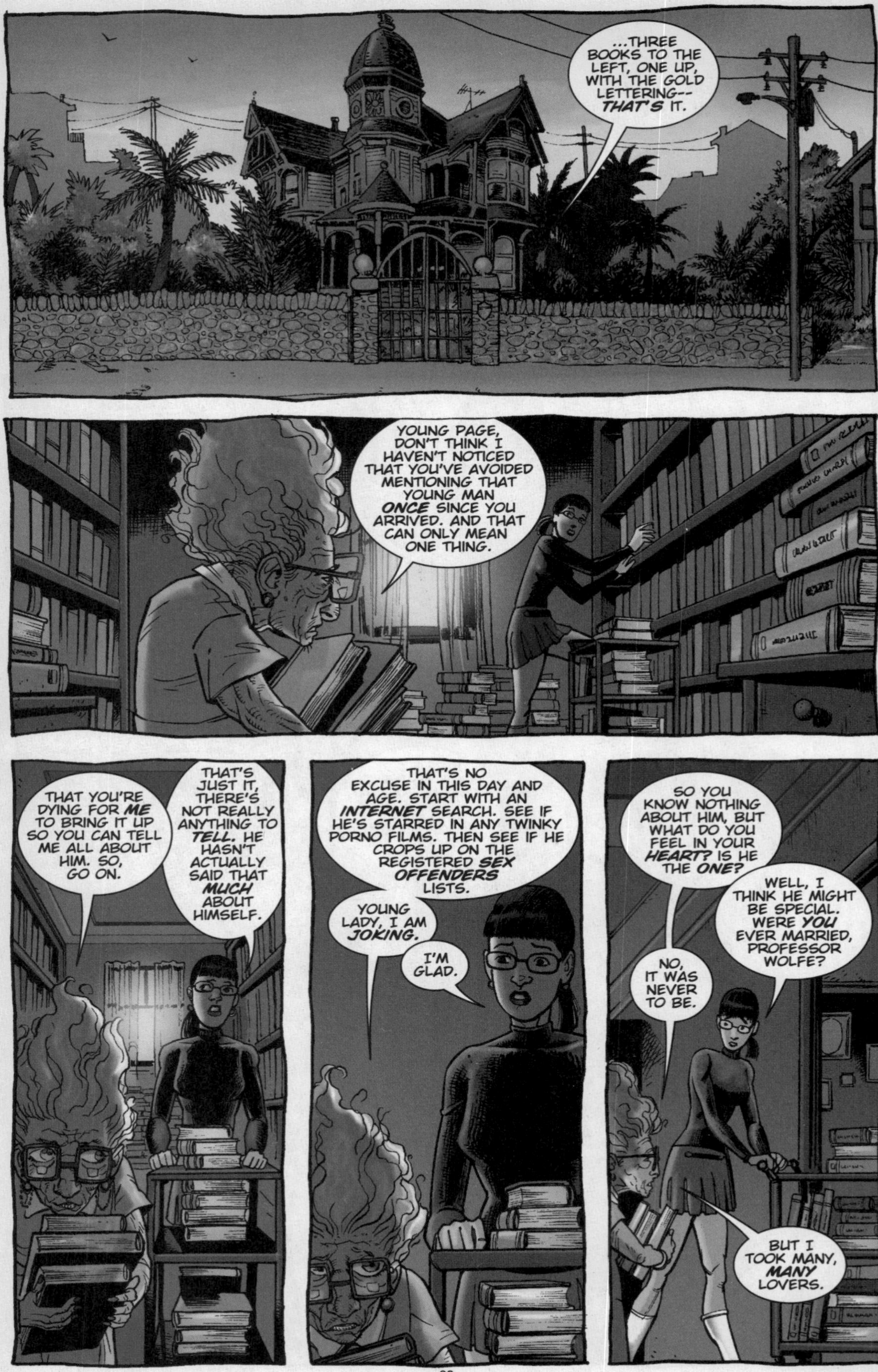
...THREE BOOKS TO THE LEFT, ONE UP, WITH THE GOLD LETTERING-- THAT'S IT.
YOUNG PAGE, DON'T THINK I HAVEN'T NOTICED THAT YOU'VE AVOIDED MENTIONING THAT YOUNG MAN ONCE SINCE YOU ARRIVED. AND THAT CAN ONLY MEAN ONE THING.
THAT YOU'RE DYING FOR ME TO BRING IT UP SO YOU CAN TELL ME ALL ABOUT HIM. SO, GO ON.
THAT'S JUST IT, THERE'S NOT REALLY ANYTHING TO TELL. HE HASN'T ACTUALLY SAID THAT MUCH ABOUT HIMSELF.
THAT'S NO EXCUSE IN THIS DAY AND AGE. START WITH AN INTERNET SEARCH. SEE IF HE'S STARRED IN ANY TWINKY PORNO FILMS. THEN SEE IF HE CROPS UP ON THE REGISTERED SEX OFFENDERS LISTS.
YOUNG LADY, I AM JOKING.
I'M GLAD.
SO YOU KNOW NOTHING ABOUT HIM, BUT WHAT DO YOU FEEL IN YOUR HEART? IS HE THE ONE?
WELL, I THINK HE MIGHT BE SPECIAL. WERE YOU EVER MARRIED, PROFESSOR WOLFE?
NO, IT WAS NEVER TO BE.
BUT I TOOK MANY, MANY LOVERS.

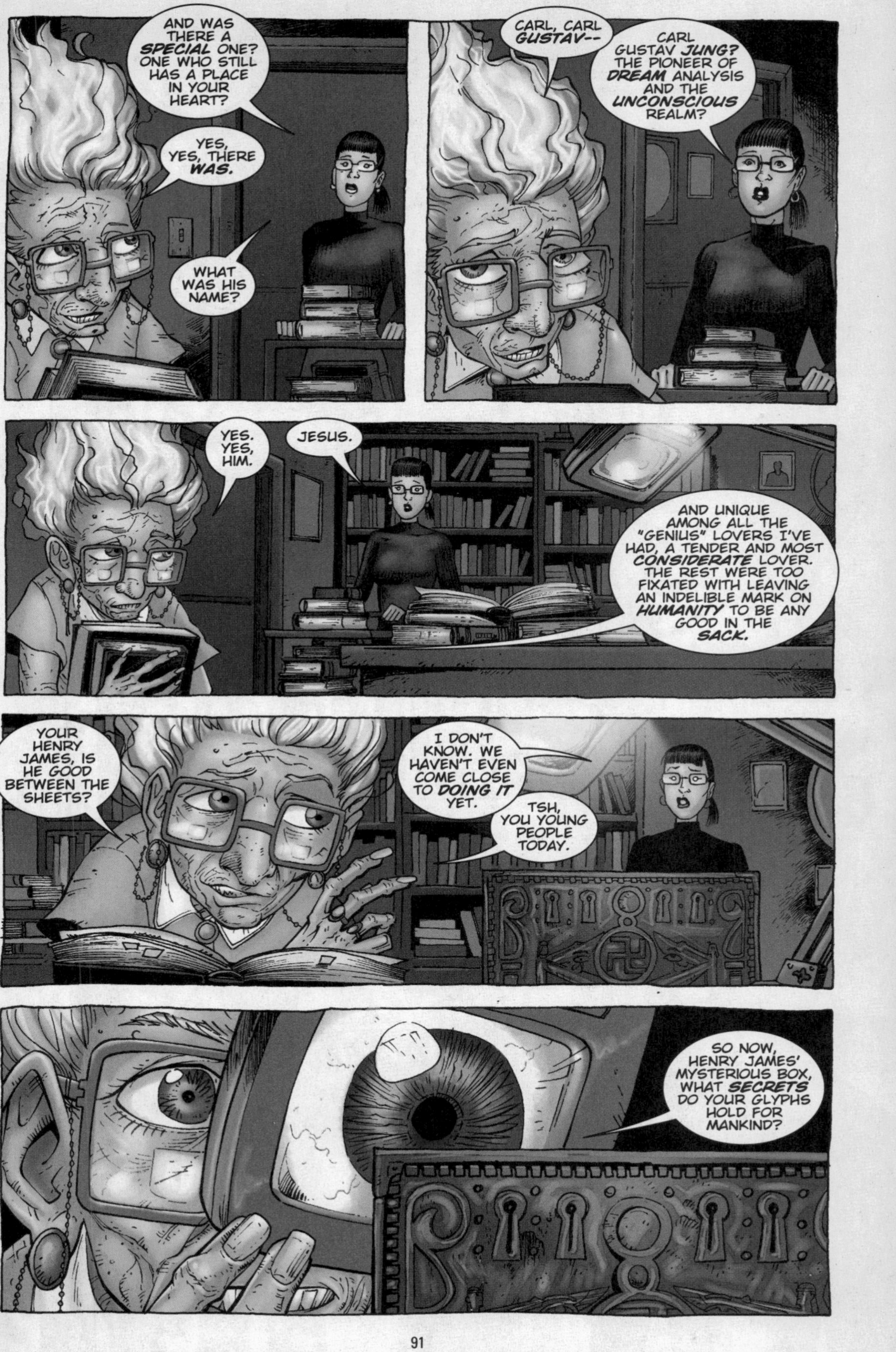
AND WAS THERE A SPECIAL ONE? ONE WHO STILL HAS A PLACE IN YOUR HEART?
YES, YES, THERE WAS.
WHAT WAS HIS NAME?
CARL, CARL GUSTAV--
CARL GUSTAV JUNG? THE PIONEER OF DREAM ANALYSIS AND THE UNCONSCIOUS REALM?
YES. YES, HIM.
JESUS.
AND UNIQUE AMONG ALL THE "GENIUS" LOVERS I'VE HAD, A TENDER AND MOST CONSIDERATE LOVER. THE REST WERE TOO FIXATED WITH LEAVING AN INDELIBLE MARK ON HUMANITY TO BE ANY GOOD IN THE SACK.
YOUR HENRY JAMES, IS HE GOOD BETWEEN THE SHEETS?
I DON'T KNOW. WE HAVEN'T EVEN COME CLOSE TO DOING IT YET.
TSH, YOU YOUNG PEOPLE TODAY.
SO NOW, HENRY JAMES' MYSTERIOUS BOX, WHAT SECRETS DO YOUR GLYPHS HOLD FOR MANKIND?

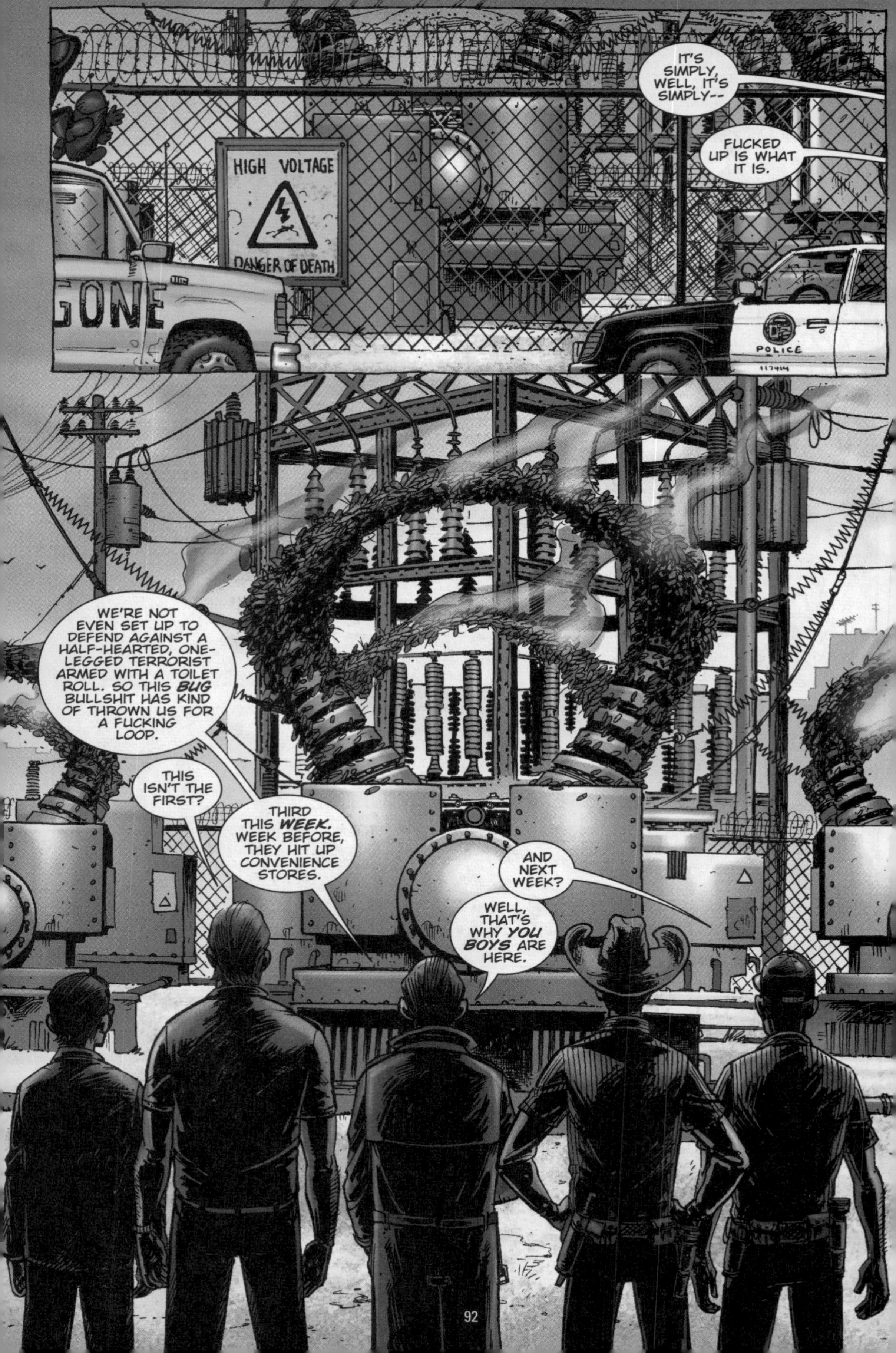
HIGH VOLTAGE
DANGER OF DEATH
GONE
POLICE
IT'S SIMPLY, WELL, IT'S SIMPLY--
FUCKED UP IS WHAT IT IS.
WE'RE NOT EVEN SET UP TO DEFEND AGAINST A HALF-HEARTED, ONE-LEGGED TERRORIST ARMED WITH A TOILET ROLL. SO THIS *BUG* BULLSHIT HAS KIND OF THROWN US FOR A FUCKING LOOP.
THIS ISN'T THE FIRST?
THIRD THIS *WEEK.* WEEK BEFORE, THEY HIT UP CONVENIENCE STORES.
AND NEXT WEEK?
WELL, THAT'S WHY *YOU BOYS* ARE HERE.

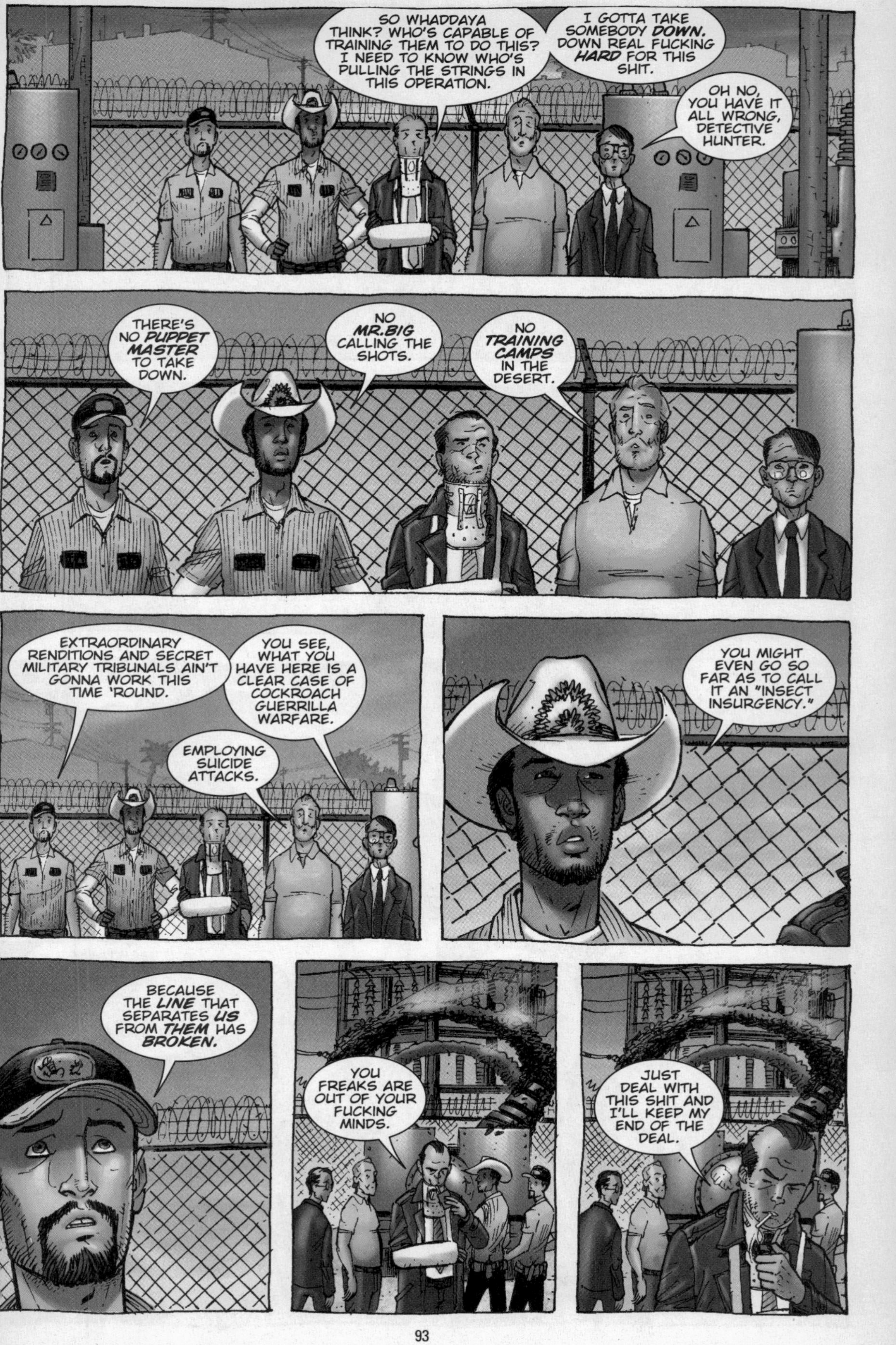
SO WHADDAYA THINK? WHO'S CAPABLE OF TRAINING THEM TO DO THIS? I NEED TO KNOW WHO'S PULLING THE STRINGS IN THIS OPERATION.
I GOTTA TAKE SOMEBODY DOWN. DOWN REAL FUCKING HARD FOR THIS SHIT.
OH NO, YOU HAVE IT ALL WRONG, DETECTIVE HUNTER.
THERE'S NO PUPPET MASTER TO TAKE DOWN.
NO MR.BIG CALLING THE SHOTS.
NO TRAINING CAMPS IN THE DESERT.
EXTRAORDINARY RENDITIONS AND SECRET MILITARY TRIBUNALS AIN'T GONNA WORK THIS TIME 'ROUND.
YOU SEE, WHAT YOU HAVE HERE IS A CLEAR CASE OF COCKROACH GUERRILLA WARFARE.
EMPLOYING SUICIDE ATTACKS.
YOU MIGHT EVEN GO SO FAR AS TO CALL IT AN "INSECT INSURGENCY."
BECAUSE THE LINE THAT SEPARATES US FROM THEM HAS BROKEN.
YOU FREAKS ARE OUT OF YOUR FUCKING MINDS.
JUST DEAL WITH THIS SHIT AND I'LL KEEP MY END OF THE DEAL.

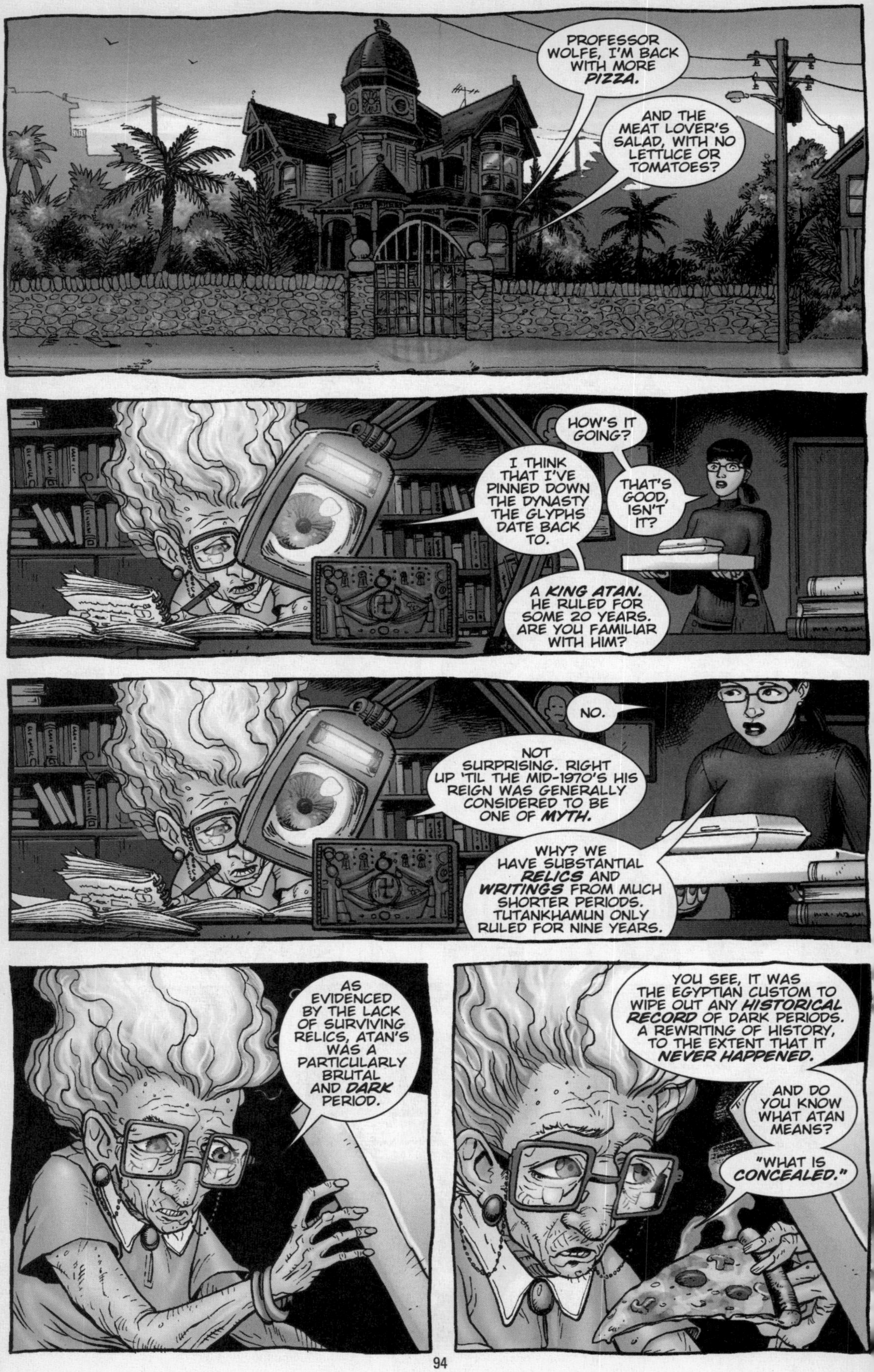
PROFESSOR WOLFE, I'M BACK WITH MORE PIZZA.
AND THE MEAT LOVER'S SALAD, WITH NO LETTUCE OR TOMATOES?
HOW'S IT GOING?
I THINK THAT I'VE PINNED DOWN THE DYNASTY THE GLYPHS DATE BACK TO.
THAT'S GOOD, ISN'T IT?
A KING ATAN. HE RULED FOR SOME 20 YEARS. ARE YOU FAMILIAR WITH HIM?
NO.
NOT SURPRISING. RIGHT UP 'TIL THE MID-1970'S HIS REIGN WAS GENERALLY CONSIDERED TO BE ONE OF MYTH.
WHY? WE HAVE SUBSTANTIAL RELICS AND WRITINGS FROM MUCH SHORTER PERIODS. TUTANKHAMUN ONLY RULED FOR NINE YEARS.
AS EVIDENCED BY THE LACK OF SURVIVING RELICS, ATAN'S WAS A PARTICULARLY BRUTAL AND DARK PERIOD.
YOU SEE, IT WAS THE EGYPTIAN CUSTOM TO WIPE OUT ANY HISTORICAL RECORD OF DARK PERIODS. A REWRITING OF HISTORY, TO THE EXTENT THAT IT NEVER HAPPENED.
AND DO YOU KNOW WHAT ATAN MEANS?
"WHAT IS CONCEALED."

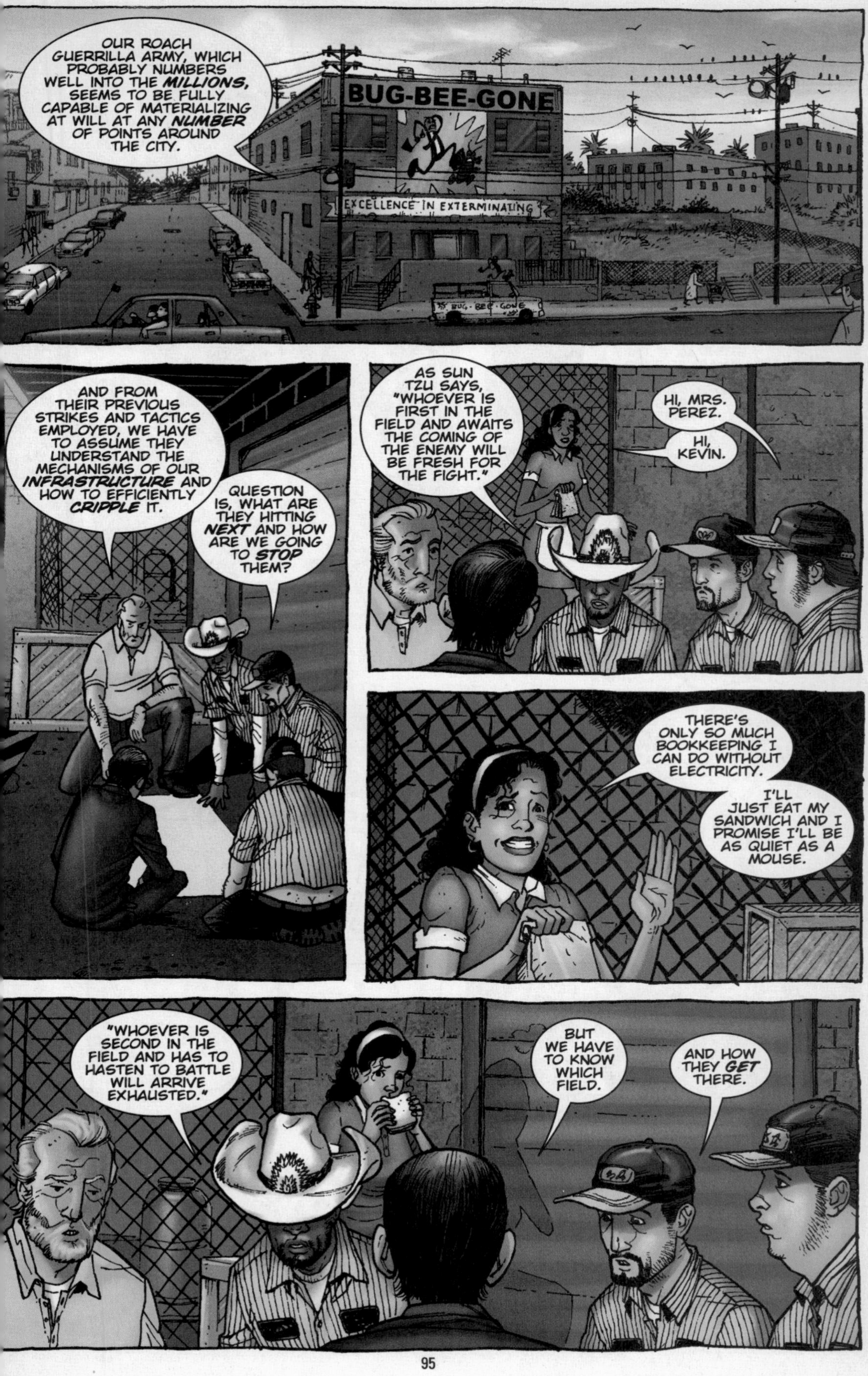
OUR ROACH GUERRILLA ARMY, WHICH PROBABLY NUMBERS WELL INTO THE *MILLIONS,* SEEMS TO BE FULLY CAPABLE OF MATERIALIZING AT WILL AT ANY *NUMBER* OF POINTS AROUND THE CITY.
BUG-BEE-GONE
EXCELLENCE IN EXTERMINATING
BUG-BEE-GONE
AND FROM THEIR PREVIOUS STRIKES AND TACTICS EMPLOYED, WE HAVE TO ASSUME THEY UNDERSTAND THE MECHANISMS OF OUR *INFRASTRUCTURE* AND HOW TO EFFICIENTLY *CRIPPLE* IT.
QUESTION IS, WHAT ARE THEY HITTING *NEXT* AND HOW ARE WE GOING TO *STOP* THEM?
AS SUN TZU SAYS, "WHOEVER IS FIRST IN THE FIELD AND AWAITS THE COMING OF THE ENEMY WILL BE FRESH FOR THE FIGHT."
HI, MRS. PEREZ.
HI, KEVIN.
THERE'S ONLY SO MUCH BOOKKEEPING I CAN DO WITHOUT ELECTRICITY.
I'LL JUST EAT MY SANDWICH AND I PROMISE I'LL BE AS QUIET AS A MOUSE.
"WHOEVER IS SECOND IN THE FIELD AND HAS TO HASTEN TO BATTLE WILL ARRIVE EXHAUSTED."
BUT WE HAVE TO KNOW WHICH FIELD.
AND HOW THEY *GET* THERE.

ARE THEY GOING TO CONTINUE THE CAMPAIGN AGAINST THE POWER SYSTEM, OR MAYBE MOVE ONTO PUBLIC TRANSPORT, OR...?
BUT I DON'T UNDER-STAND HOW THEY MOVE AROUND THE CITY WITH NOBODY EVER SEEING THEM?
KOFF!
I GUESS YOU GUYS DON'T SPEND MANY SATURDAY NIGHTS STAYING IN WATCHING LATE-NIGHT B HORROR MOVIES?
UHHHH?
THEY'RE TRAVELING IN THE SEWER SYSTEM.
GOD DAMN! SHE'S RIGHT.
Loomita
Harbor City
Hawthorne Blvd
Wilmington
Coast Hwy
Signal Hill
Long Beach
Pedro Hills
San Pedro
Friendship
21
47
101
41
WELL, DON'T SOUND SO SURPRISED.
HEY NILS, YOU NEED TO TAKE A LOOK AT THIS.
THE MAIN SEWER LINE TO THE VALLEY CONNECTS UP ALL THE PREVIOUS ATTACKS--
--AND ENDS AT THE LARGEST SEWAGE TREATMENT FACILITY IN SOUTHERN CALIFORNIA.
Pilchard St
Main Sewer & Interceptor Units

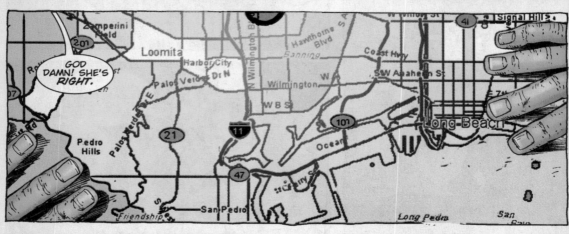

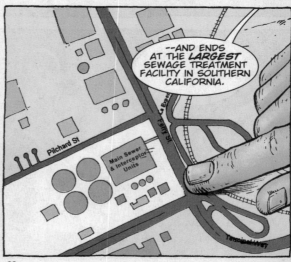

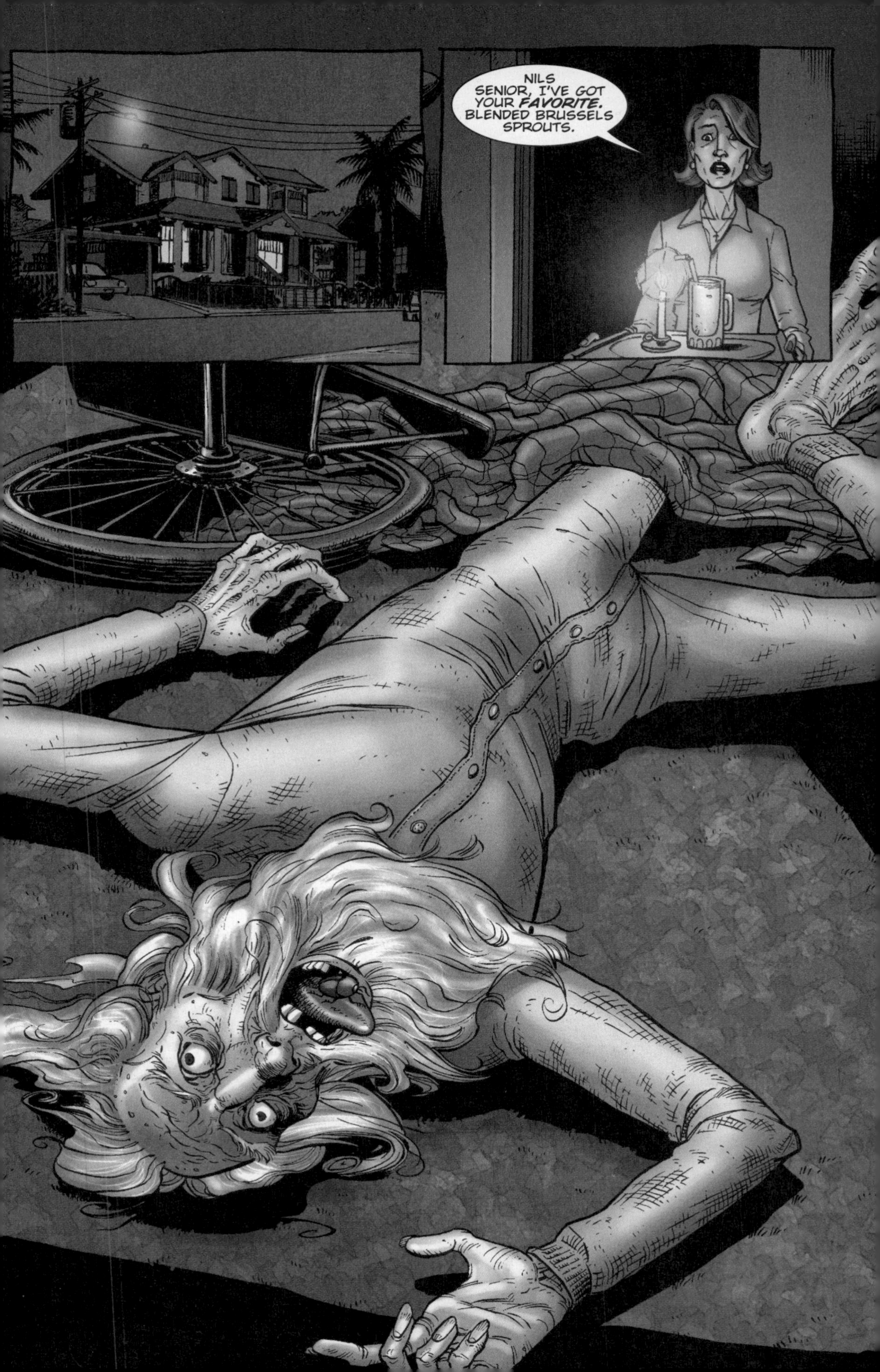
NILS SENIOR, I'VE GOT YOUR *FAVORITE.* BLENDED BRUSSELS SPROUTS.

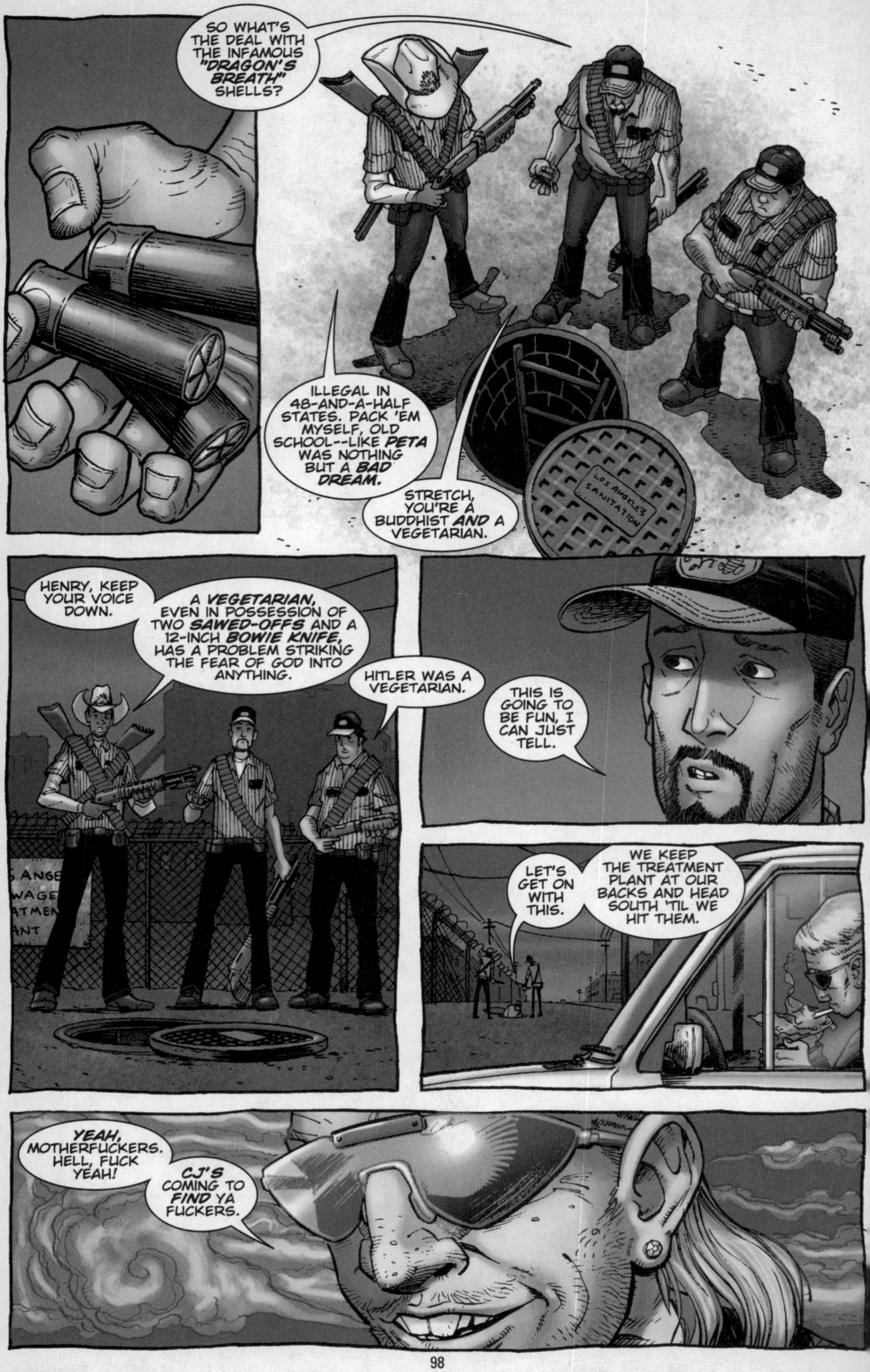

SO WHAT'S THE DEAL WITH THE INFAMOUS "DRAGON'S BREATH" SHELLS?
ILLEGAL IN 48-AND-A-HALF STATES. PACK 'EM MYSELF, OLD SCHOOL--LIKE PETA WAS NOTHING BUT A BAD DREAM.
STRETCH, YOU'RE A BUDDHIST AND A VEGETARIAN.
LOS ANGELES SANITATION
HENRY, KEEP YOUR VOICE DOWN.
A VEGETARIAN, EVEN IN POSSESSION OF TWO SAWED-OFFS AND A 12-INCH BOWIE KNIFE, HAS A PROBLEM STRIKING THE FEAR OF GOD INTO ANYTHING.
HITLER WAS A VEGETARIAN.
THIS IS GOING TO BE FUN, I CAN JUST TELL.
LET'S GET ON WITH THIS.
WE KEEP THE TREATMENT PLANT AT OUR BACKS AND HEAD SOUTH 'TIL WE HIT THEM.
YEAH, MOTHERFUCKERS. HELL, FUCK YEAH!
CJ'S COMING TO FIND YA FUCKERS.

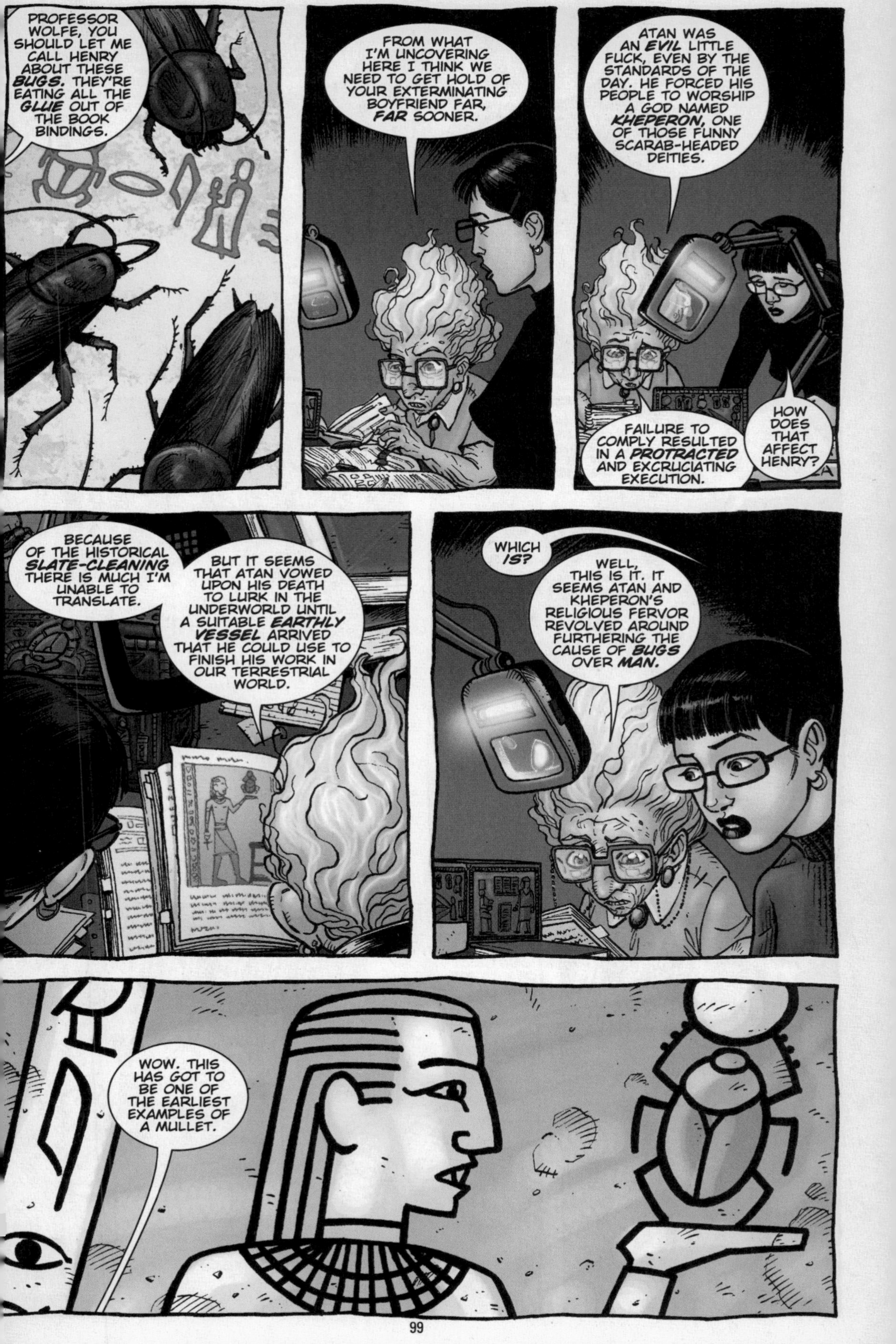

PROFESSOR WOLFE, YOU SHOULD LET ME CALL HENRY ABOUT THESE BUGS. THEY'RE EATING ALL THE GLUE OUT OF THE BOOK BINDINGS.
FROM WHAT I'M UNCOVERING HERE I THINK WE NEED TO GET HOLD OF YOUR EXTERMINATING BOYFRIEND FAR, FAR SOONER.
ATAN WAS AN EVIL LITTLE FUCK, EVEN BY THE STANDARDS OF THE DAY. HE FORCED HIS PEOPLE TO WORSHIP A GOD NAMED KHEPERON, ONE OF THOSE FUNNY SCARAB-HEADED DEITIES.
FAILURE TO COMPLY RESULTED IN A PROTRACTED AND EXCRUCIATING EXECUTION.
HOW DOES THAT AFFECT HENRY?
BECAUSE OF THE HISTORICAL SLATE-CLEANING THERE IS MUCH I'M UNABLE TO TRANSLATE.
BUT IT SEEMS THAT ATAN VOWED UPON HIS DEATH TO LURK IN THE UNDERWORLD UNTIL A SUITABLE EARTHLY VESSEL ARRIVED THAT HE COULD USE TO FINISH HIS WORK IN OUR TERRESTRIAL WORLD.
WHICH IS?
WELL, THIS IS IT. IT SEEMS ATAN AND KHEPERON'S RELIGIOUS FERVOR REVOLVED AROUND FURTHERING THE CAUSE OF BUGS OVER MAN.
WOW. THIS HAS GOT TO BE ONE OF THE EARLIEST EXAMPLES OF A MULLET.

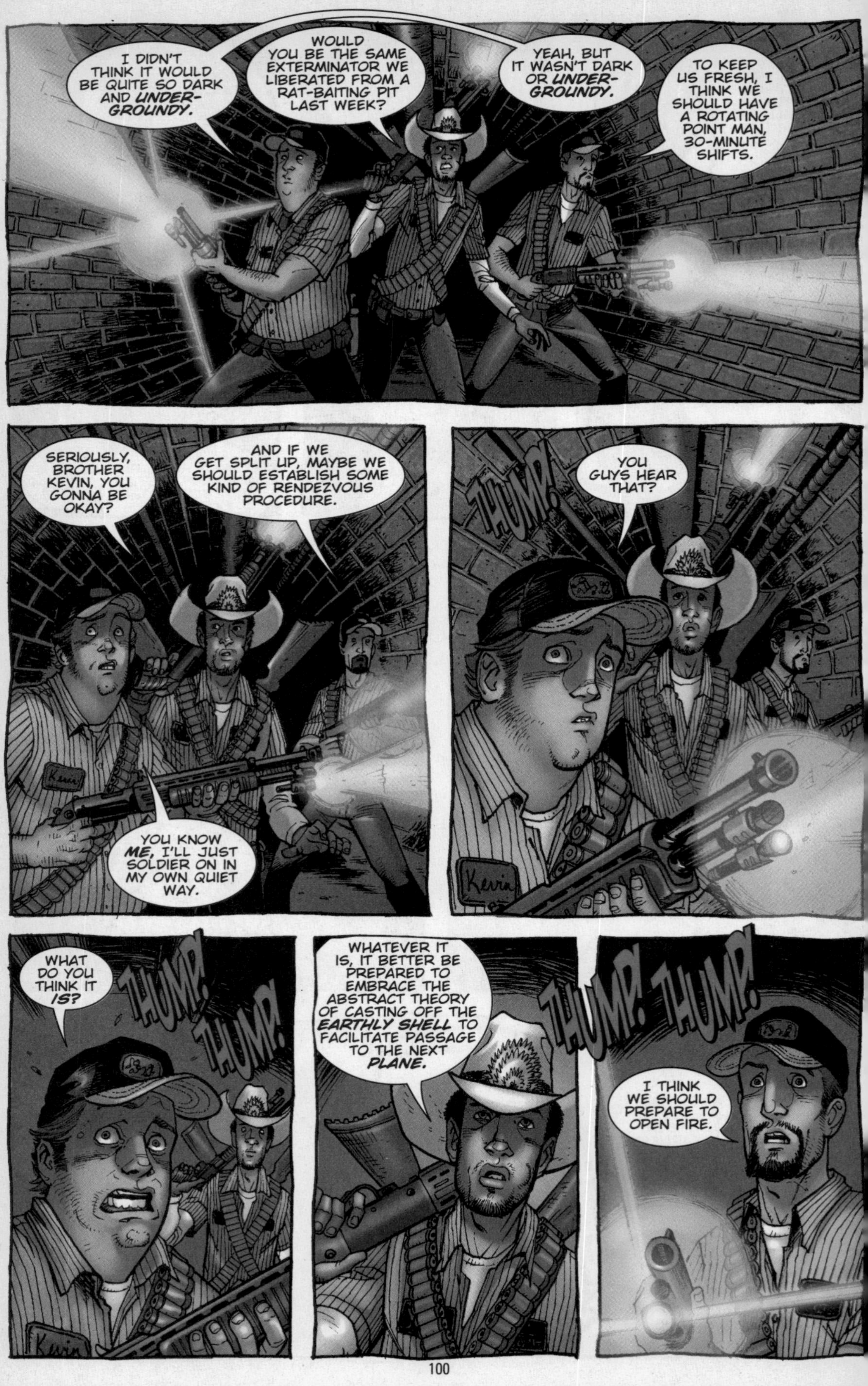
I DIDN'T THINK IT WOULD BE QUITE SO DARK AND *UNDER-GROUNDY.*
WOULD YOU BE THE SAME EXTERMINATOR WE LIBERATED FROM A RAT-BAITING PIT LAST WEEK?
YEAH, BUT IT WASN'T DARK OR *UNDER-GROUNDY.*
TO KEEP US FRESH, I THINK WE SHOULD HAVE A ROTATING POINT MAN, 30-MINUTE SHIFTS.
SERIOUSLY, BROTHER KEVIN, YOU GONNA BE OKAY?
AND IF WE GET SPLIT UP, MAYBE WE SHOULD ESTABLISH SOME KIND OF RENDEZVOUS PROCEDURE.
YOU KNOW *ME,* I'LL JUST SOLDIER ON IN MY OWN QUIET WAY.
Kevin
THUMP!
YOU GUYS HEAR THAT?
Kevin
WHAT DO YOU THINK IT *IS?*
THUMP! THUMP!
Kevin
WHATEVER IT IS, IT BETTER BE PREPARED TO EMBRACE THE ABSTRACT THEORY OF CASTING OFF THE *EARTHLY SHELL* TO FACILITATE PASSAGE TO THE NEXT *PLANE.*
THUMP! THUMP!
I THINK WE SHOULD PREPARE TO OPEN FIRE.

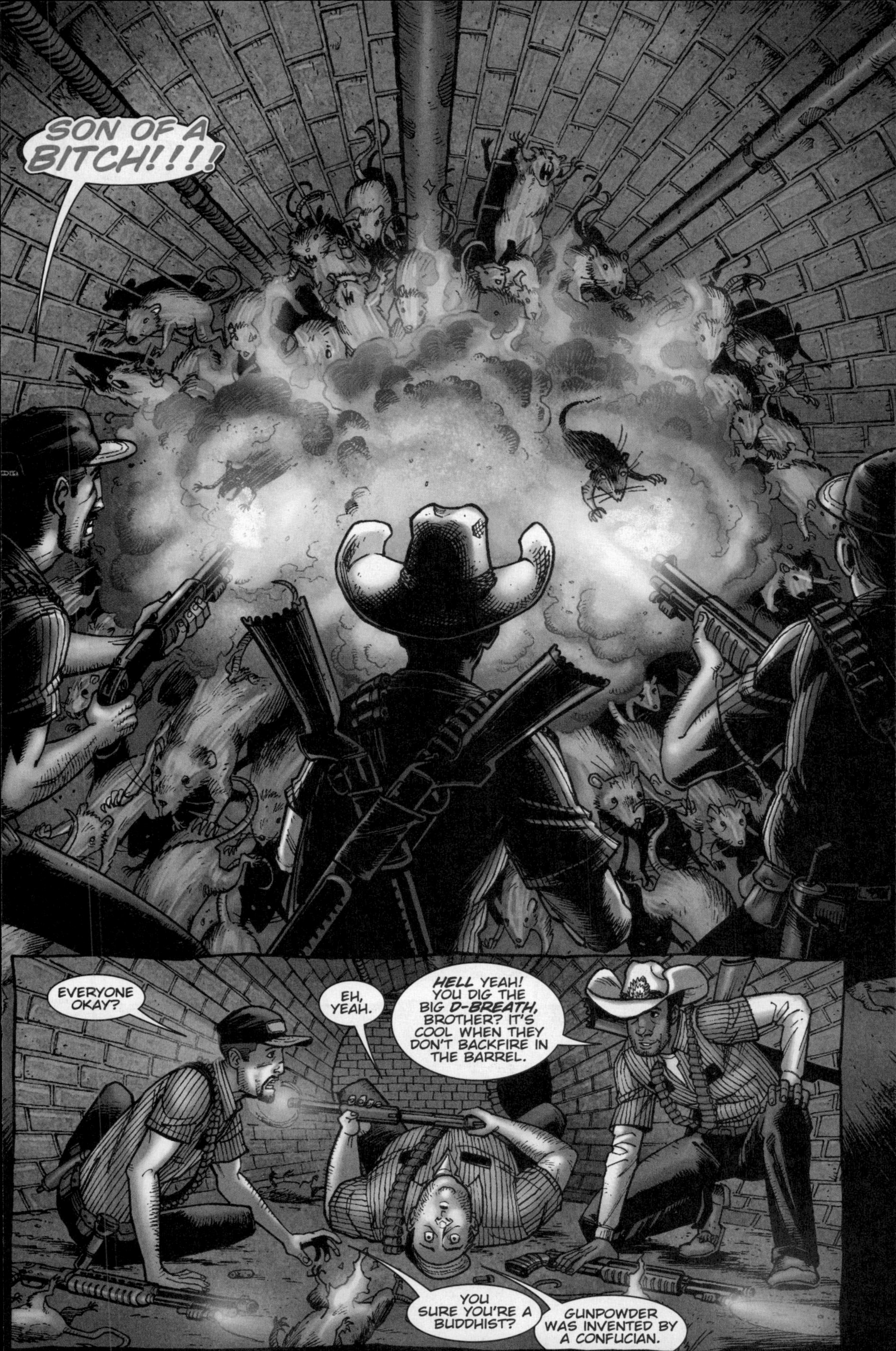
SON OF A BITCH!!!!
EVERYONE OKAY?
EH, YEAH.
HELL YEAH! YOU DIG THE BIG D-BREATH, BROTHER? IT'S COOL WHEN THEY DON'T BACKFIRE IN THE BARREL.
YOU SURE YOU'RE A BUDDHIST?
GUNPOWDER WAS INVENTED BY A CONFUCIAN.

MAYBE WE SCARED THEM OFF.

I DON'T BELIEVE THEY EVER INTENDED TO ATTACK US.

I THINK FREAKBOY HERE'S CORRECT. THOSE RATS WERE *RUNNING.*

RUNNING *SCARED.*

WHAT THE FUCK IS A 20-POUND SEWER RAT *AFRAID* OF?

YEAH, MOTHER-FUCKERS.

IT'S FUCKING *HOME-COMING* DAY.

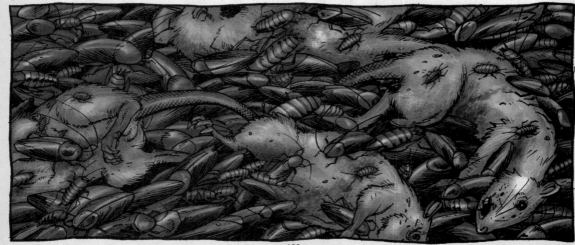

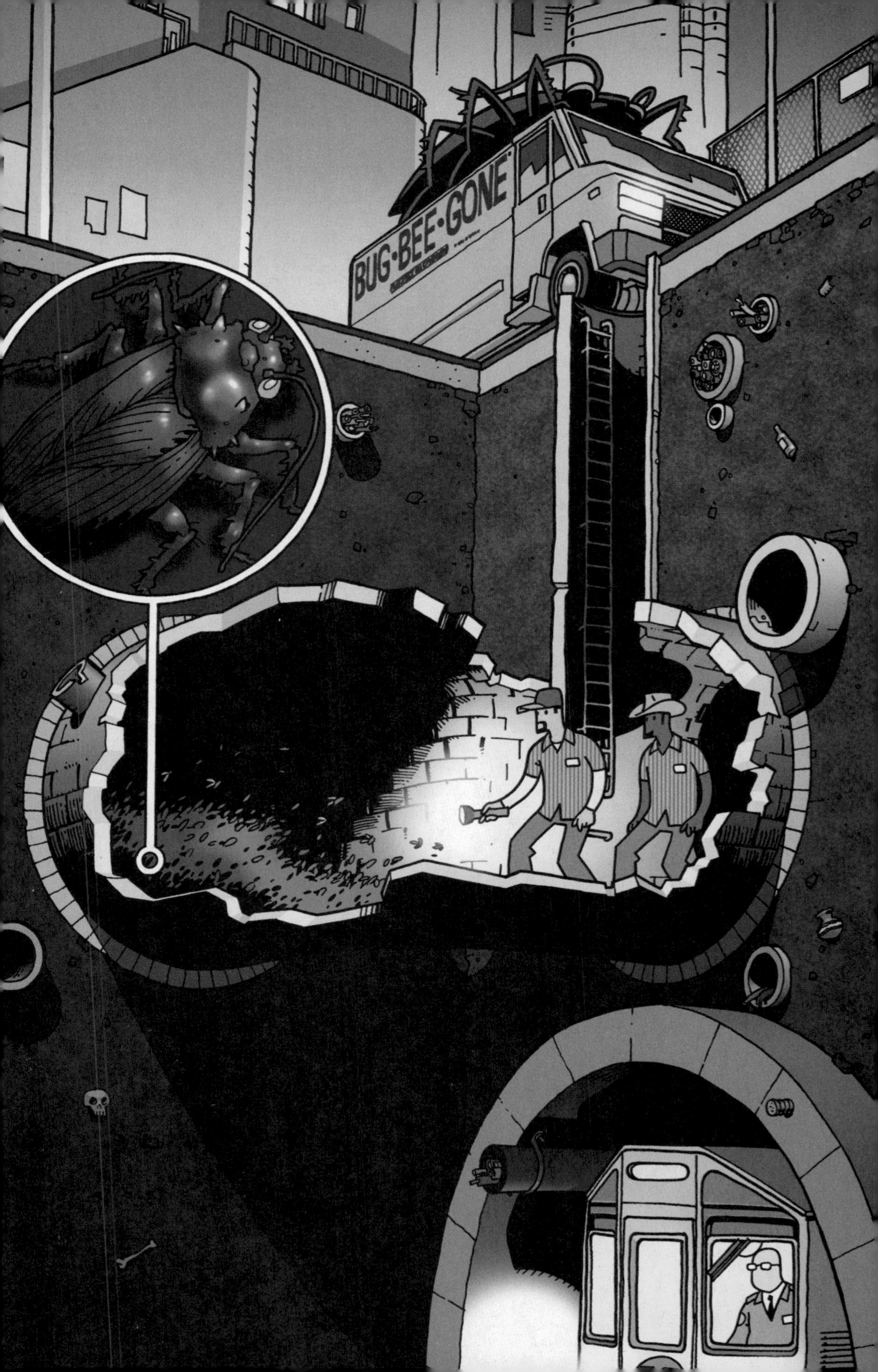
BUG·BEE·GONE

CHAPTER FOUR

TONY MOORE
PENCILLER

ANDE PARKS
INKER

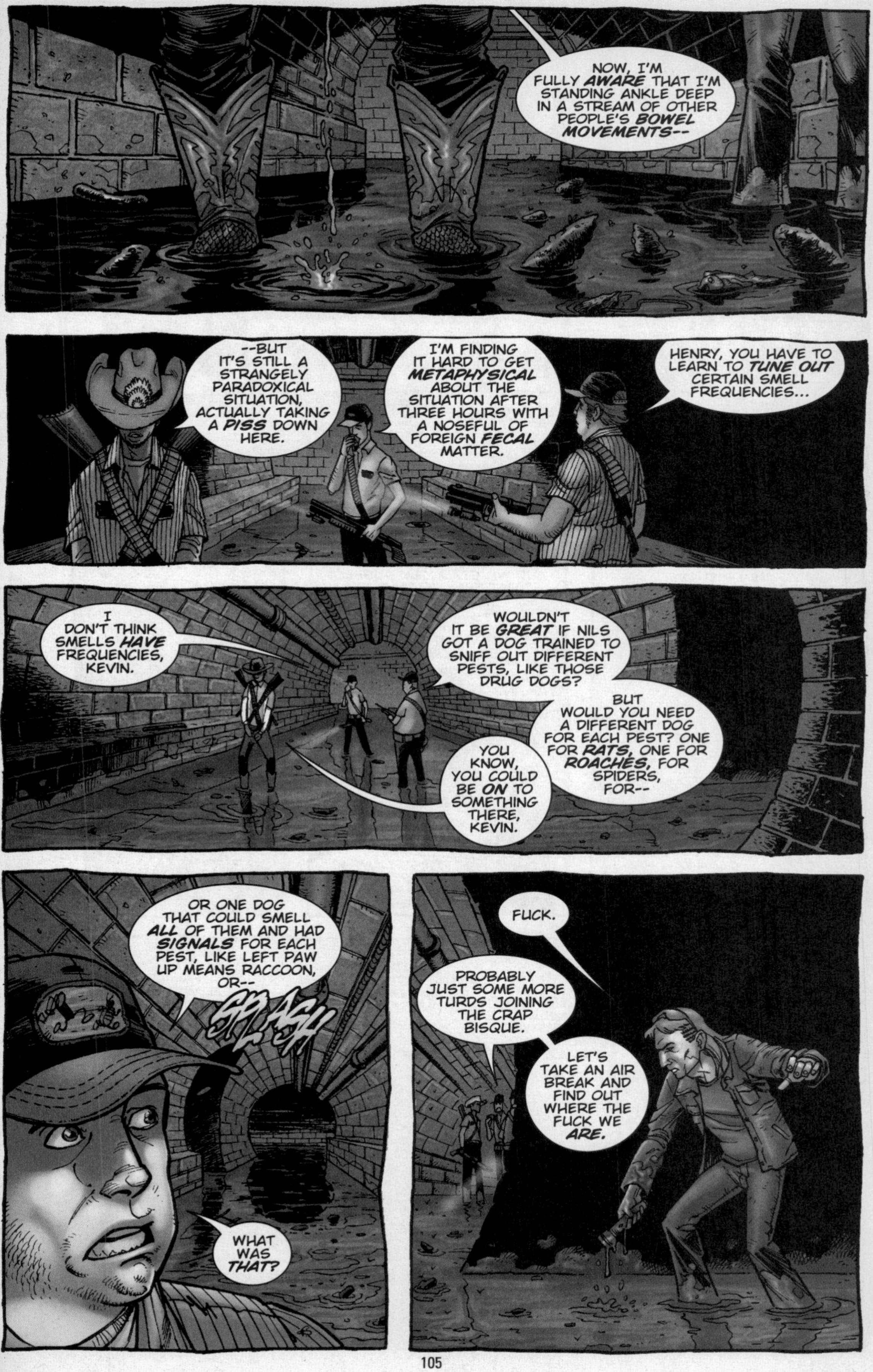
NOW, I'M FULLY AWARE THAT I'M STANDING ANKLE DEEP IN A STREAM OF OTHER PEOPLE'S BOWEL MOVEMENTS--
--BUT IT'S STILL A STRANGELY PARADOXICAL SITUATION, ACTUALLY TAKING A PISS DOWN HERE.
I'M FINDING IT HARD TO GET METAPHYSICAL ABOUT THE SITUATION AFTER THREE HOURS WITH A NOSEFUL OF FOREIGN FECAL MATTER.
HENRY, YOU HAVE TO LEARN TO TUNE OUT CERTAIN SMELL FREQUENCIES...
I DON'T THINK SMELLS HAVE FREQUENCIES, KEVIN.
WOULDN'T IT BE GREAT IF NILS GOT A DOG TRAINED TO SNIFF OUT DIFFERENT PESTS, LIKE THOSE DRUG DOGS?
YOU KNOW, YOU COULD BE ON TO SOMETHING THERE, KEVIN.
BUT WOULD YOU NEED A DIFFERENT DOG FOR EACH PEST? ONE FOR RATS, ONE FOR ROACHES, FOR SPIDERS, FOR--
OR ONE DOG THAT COULD SMELL ALL OF THEM AND HAD SIGNALS FOR EACH PEST, LIKE LEFT PAW UP MEANS RACCOON, OR--
SPLASH
WHAT WAS THAT?
FUCK.
PROBABLY JUST SOME MORE TURDS JOINING THE CRAP BISQUE.
LET'S TAKE AN AIR BREAK AND FIND OUT WHERE THE FUCK WE ARE.

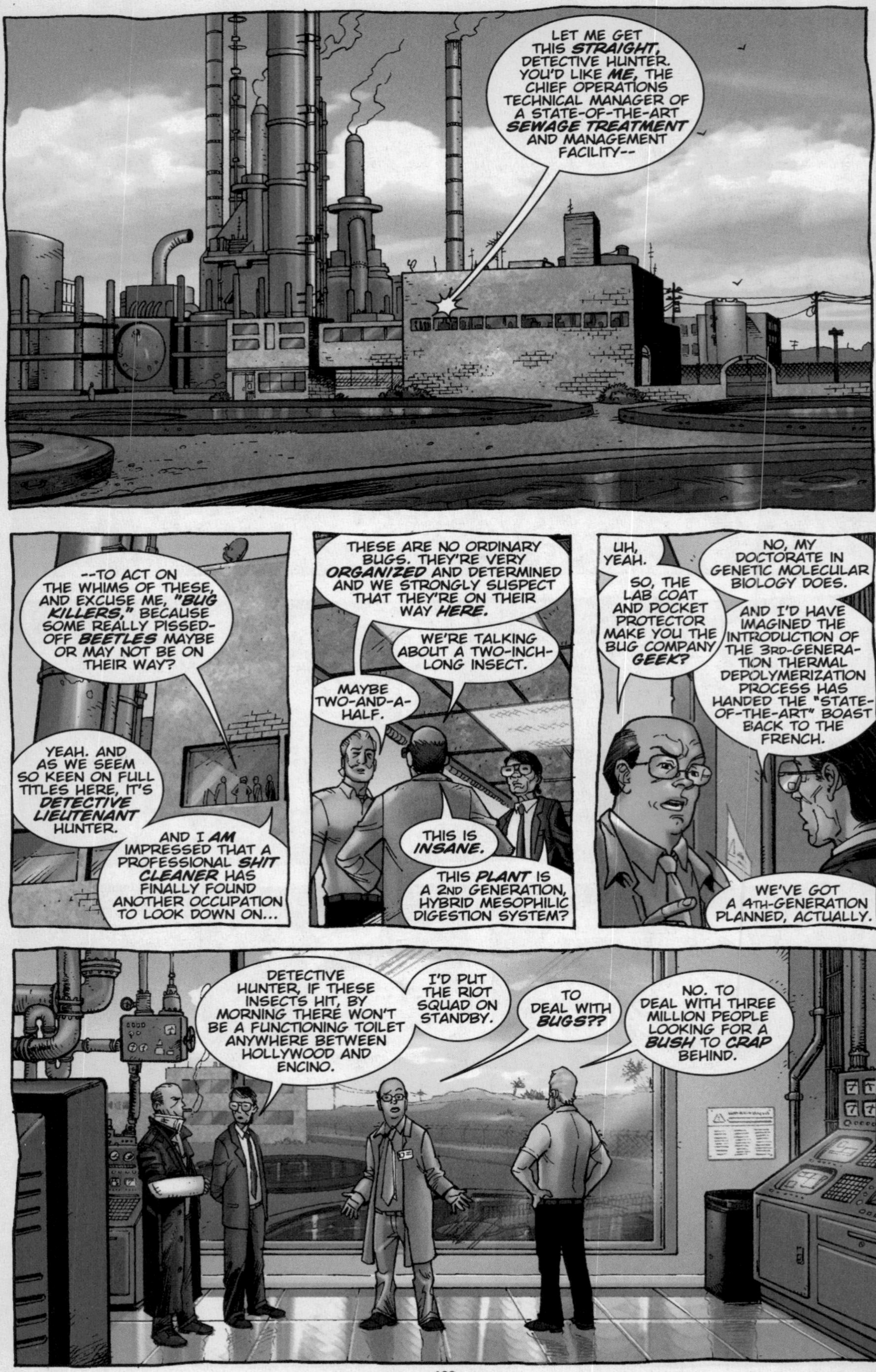
LET ME GET THIS STRAIGHT, DETECTIVE HUNTER. YOU'D LIKE ME, THE CHIEF OPERATIONS TECHNICAL MANAGER OF A STATE-OF-THE-ART SEWAGE TREATMENT AND MANAGEMENT FACILITY--
--TO ACT ON THE WHIMS OF THESE, AND EXCUSE ME, "BUG KILLERS," BECAUSE SOME REALLY PISSED-OFF BEETLES MAYBE OR MAY NOT BE ON THEIR WAY?
YEAH. AND AS WE SEEM SO KEEN ON FULL TITLES HERE, IT'S DETECTIVE LIEUTENANT HUNTER.
AND I AM IMPRESSED THAT A PROFESSIONAL SHIT CLEANER HAS FINALLY FOUND ANOTHER OCCUPATION TO LOOK DOWN ON...
THESE ARE NO ORDINARY BUGS. THEY'RE VERY ORGANIZED AND DETERMINED AND WE STRONGLY SUSPECT THAT THEY'RE ON THEIR WAY HERE.
WE'RE TALKING ABOUT A TWO-INCH-LONG INSECT.
MAYBE TWO-AND-A-HALF.
THIS IS INSANE.
THIS PLANT IS A 2ND GENERATION, HYBRID MESOPHILIC DIGESTION SYSTEM?
UH, YEAH.
SO, THE LAB COAT AND POCKET PROTECTOR MAKE YOU THE BUG COMPANY GEEK?
NO, MY DOCTORATE IN GENETIC MOLECULAR BIOLOGY DOES.
AND I'D HAVE IMAGINED THE INTRODUCTION OF THE 3RD-GENERATION THERMAL DEPOLYMERIZATION PROCESS HAS HANDED THE "STATE-OF-THE-ART" BOAST BACK TO THE FRENCH.
WE'VE GOT A 4TH-GENERATION PLANNED, ACTUALLY.
DETECTIVE HUNTER, IF THESE INSECTS HIT, BY MORNING THERE WON'T BE A FUNCTIONING TOILET ANYWHERE BETWEEN HOLLYWOOD AND ENCINO.
I'D PUT THE RIOT SQUAD ON STANDBY.
TO DEAL WITH BUGS??
NO. TO DEAL WITH THREE MILLION PEOPLE LOOKING FOR A BUSH TO CRAP BEHIND.

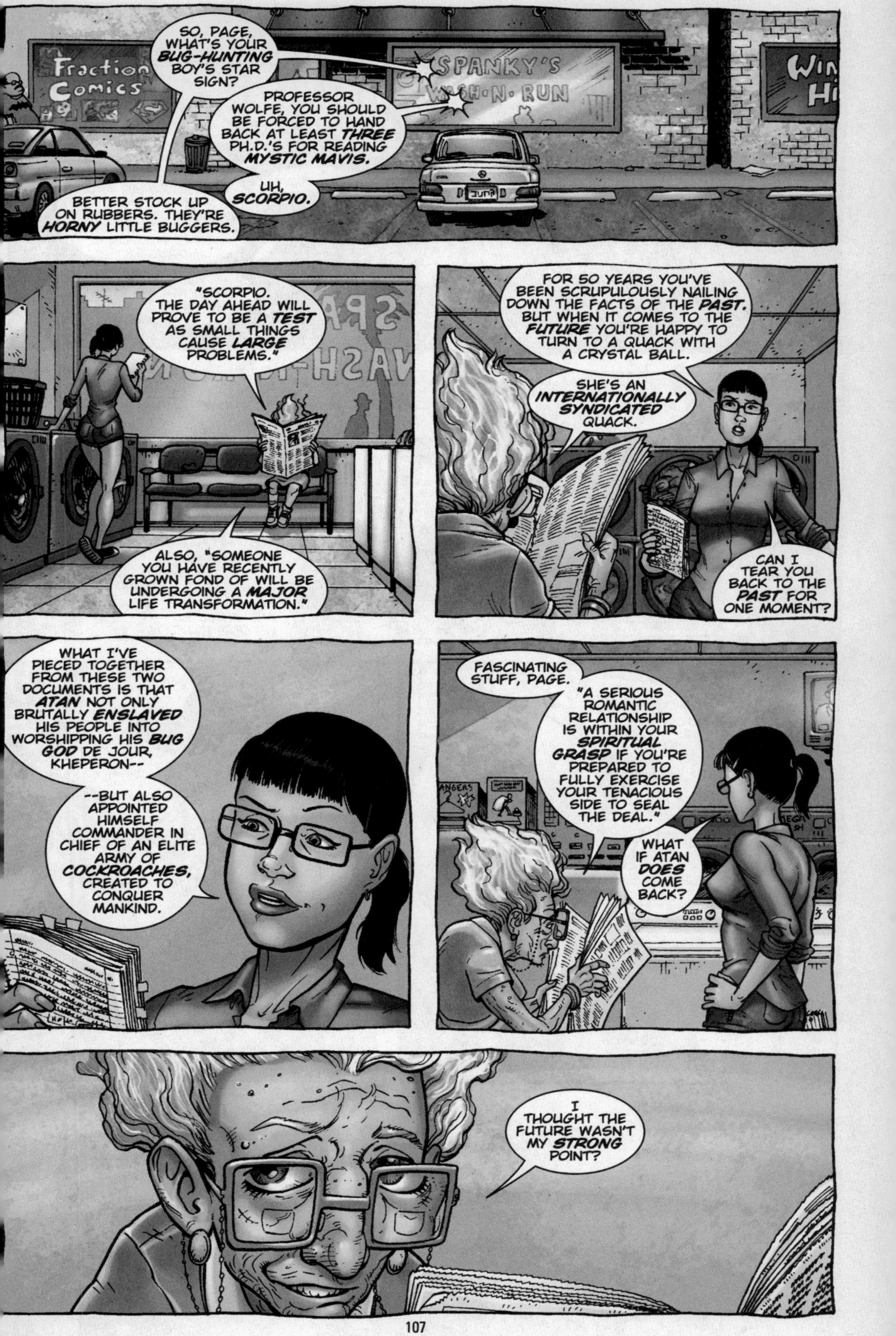
Fraction Comics
SPANKY'S WASH·N·RUN
SO, PAGE, WHAT'S YOUR BUG-HUNTING BOY'S STAR SIGN?
PROFESSOR WOLFE, YOU SHOULD BE FORCED TO HAND BACK AT LEAST THREE PH.D.'S FOR READING MYSTIC MAVIS.
UH, SCORPIO.
BETTER STOCK UP ON RUBBERS. THEY'RE HORNY LITTLE BUGGERS.
"SCORPIO. THE DAY AHEAD WILL PROVE TO BE A TEST AS SMALL THINGS CAUSE LARGE PROBLEMS."
ALSO, "SOMEONE YOU HAVE RECENTLY GROWN FOND OF WILL BE UNDERGOING A MAJOR LIFE TRANSFORMATION."
FOR 50 YEARS YOU'VE BEEN SCRUPULOUSLY NAILING DOWN THE FACTS OF THE PAST. BUT WHEN IT COMES TO THE FUTURE YOU'RE HAPPY TO TURN TO A QUACK WITH A CRYSTAL BALL.
SHE'S AN INTERNATIONALLY SYNDICATED QUACK.
CAN I TEAR YOU BACK TO THE PAST FOR ONE MOMENT?
WHAT I'VE PIECED TOGETHER FROM THESE TWO DOCUMENTS IS THAT ATAN NOT ONLY BRUTALLY ENSLAVED HIS PEOPLE INTO WORSHIPPING HIS BUG GOD DE JOUR, KHEPERON--
--BUT ALSO APPOINTED HIMSELF COMMANDER IN CHIEF OF AN ELITE ARMY OF COCKROACHES, CREATED TO CONQUER MANKIND.
FASCINATING STUFF, PAGE.
"A SERIOUS ROMANTIC RELATIONSHIP IS WITHIN YOUR SPIRITUAL GRASP IF YOU'RE PREPARED TO FULLY EXERCISE YOUR TENACIOUS SIDE TO SEAL THE DEAL."
WHAT IF ATAN DOES COME BACK?
I THOUGHT THE FUTURE WASN'T MY STRONG POINT?

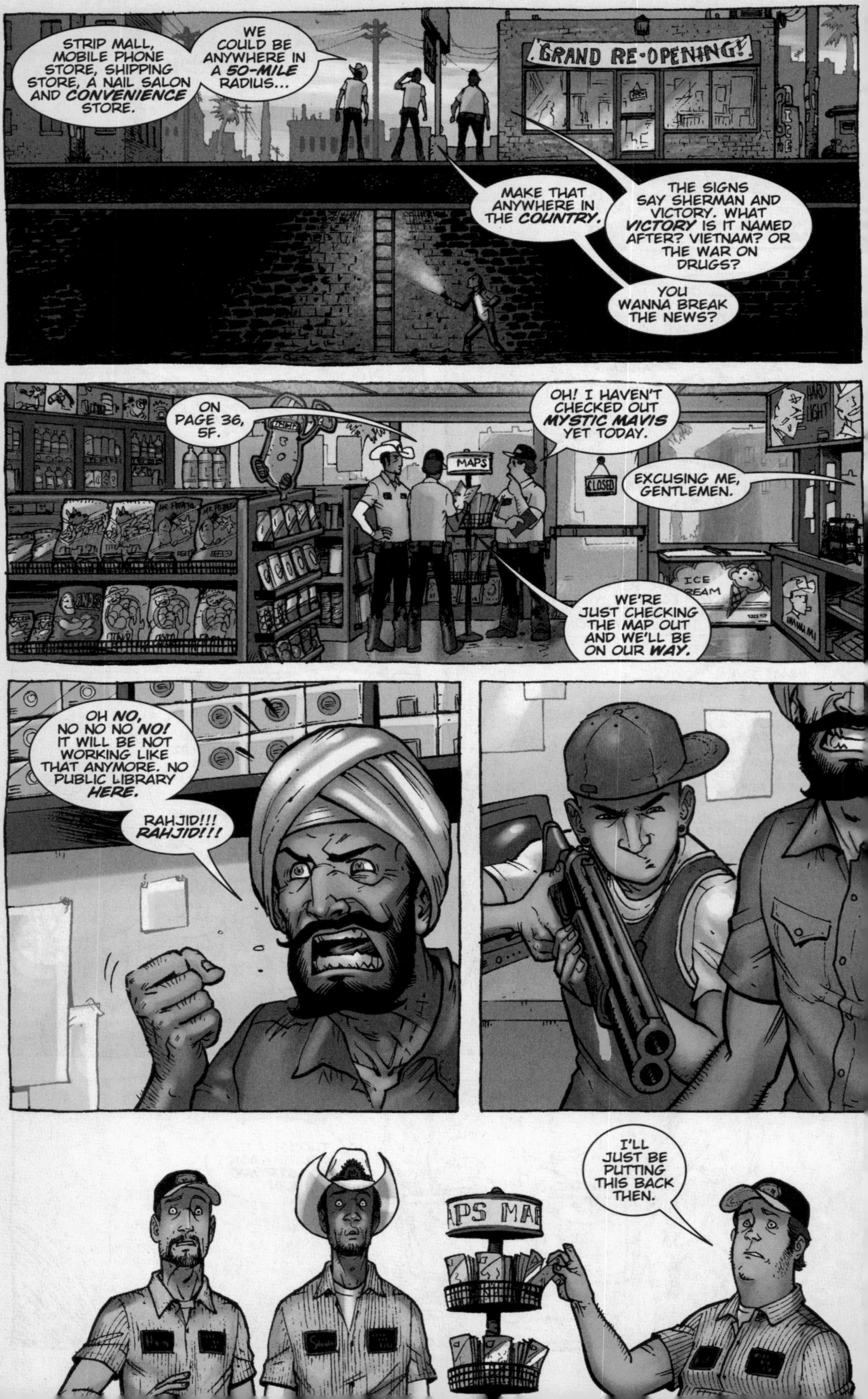

STRIP MALL, MOBILE PHONE STORE, SHIPPING STORE, A NAIL SALON AND CONVENIENCE STORE.
WE COULD BE ANYWHERE IN A 50-MILE RADIUS...
GRAND RE-OPENING!
MAKE THAT ANYWHERE IN THE COUNTRY.
THE SIGNS SAY SHERMAN AND VICTORY. WHAT VICTORY IS IT NAMED AFTER? VIETNAM? OR THE WAR ON DRUGS?
YOU WANNA BREAK THE NEWS?
ON PAGE 36, 5F.
MAPS
OH! I HAVEN'T CHECKED OUT MYSTIC MAVIS YET TODAY.
CLOSED
EXCUSING ME, GENTLEMEN.
ICE CREAM
WE'RE JUST CHECKING THE MAP OUT AND WE'LL BE ON OUR WAY.
OH NO, NO NO NO NO! IT WILL BE NOT WORKING LIKE THAT ANYMORE. NO PUBLIC LIBRARY HERE.
RAHJID!!! RAHJID!!!
I'LL JUST BE PUTTING THIS BACK THEN.
MAPS MAP

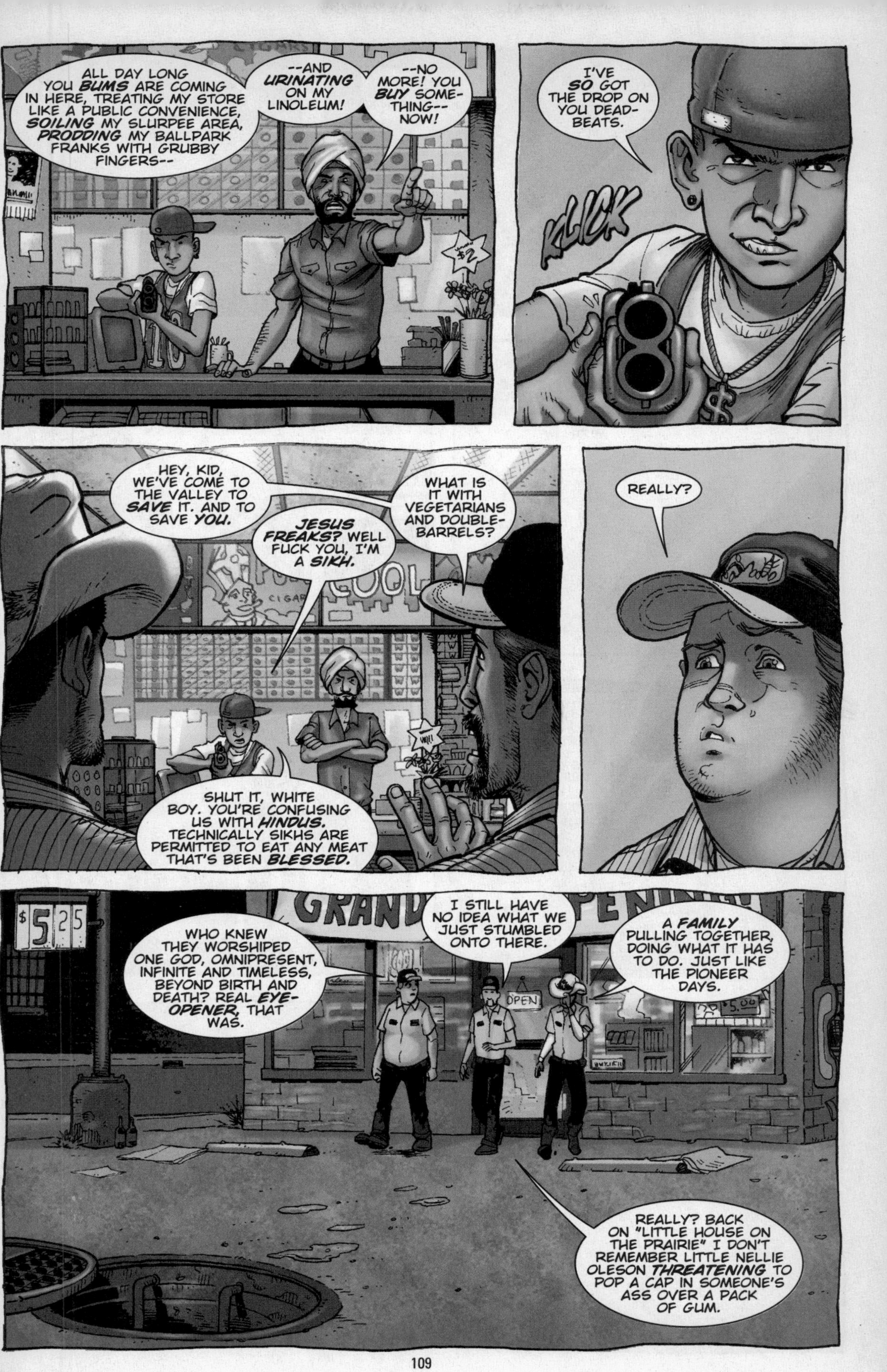
ALL DAY LONG YOU BUMS ARE COMING IN HERE, TREATING MY STORE LIKE A PUBLIC CONVENIENCE, SOILING MY SLURPEE AREA, PRODDING MY BALLPARK FRANKS WITH GRUBBY FINGERS--
--AND URINATING ON MY LINOLEUM!
--NO MORE! YOU BUY SOMETHING--NOW!
$2
I'VE SO GOT THE DROP ON YOU DEADBEATS.
KLICK
HEY, KID, WE'VE COME TO THE VALLEY TO SAVE IT. AND TO SAVE YOU.
JESUS FREAKS? WELL FUCK YOU, I'M A SIKH.
WHAT IS IT WITH VEGETARIANS AND DOUBLE-BARRELS?
SHUT IT, WHITE BOY. YOU'RE CONFUSING US WITH HINDUS. TECHNICALLY SIKHS ARE PERMITTED TO EAT ANY MEAT THAT'S BEEN BLESSED.
REALLY?
$5 25
WHO KNEW THEY WORSHIPED ONE GOD, OMNIPRESENT, INFINITE AND TIMELESS, BEYOND BIRTH AND DEATH? REAL EYE-OPENER, THAT WAS.
I STILL HAVE NO IDEA WHAT WE JUST STUMBLED ONTO THERE.
A FAMILY PULLING TOGETHER, DOING WHAT IT HAS TO DO. JUST LIKE THE PIONEER DAYS.
OPEN
$5.00
REALLY? BACK ON "LITTLE HOUSE ON THE PRAIRIE" I DON'T REMEMBER LITTLE NELLIE OLESON THREATENING TO POP A CAP IN SOMEONE'S ASS OVER A PACK OF GUM.

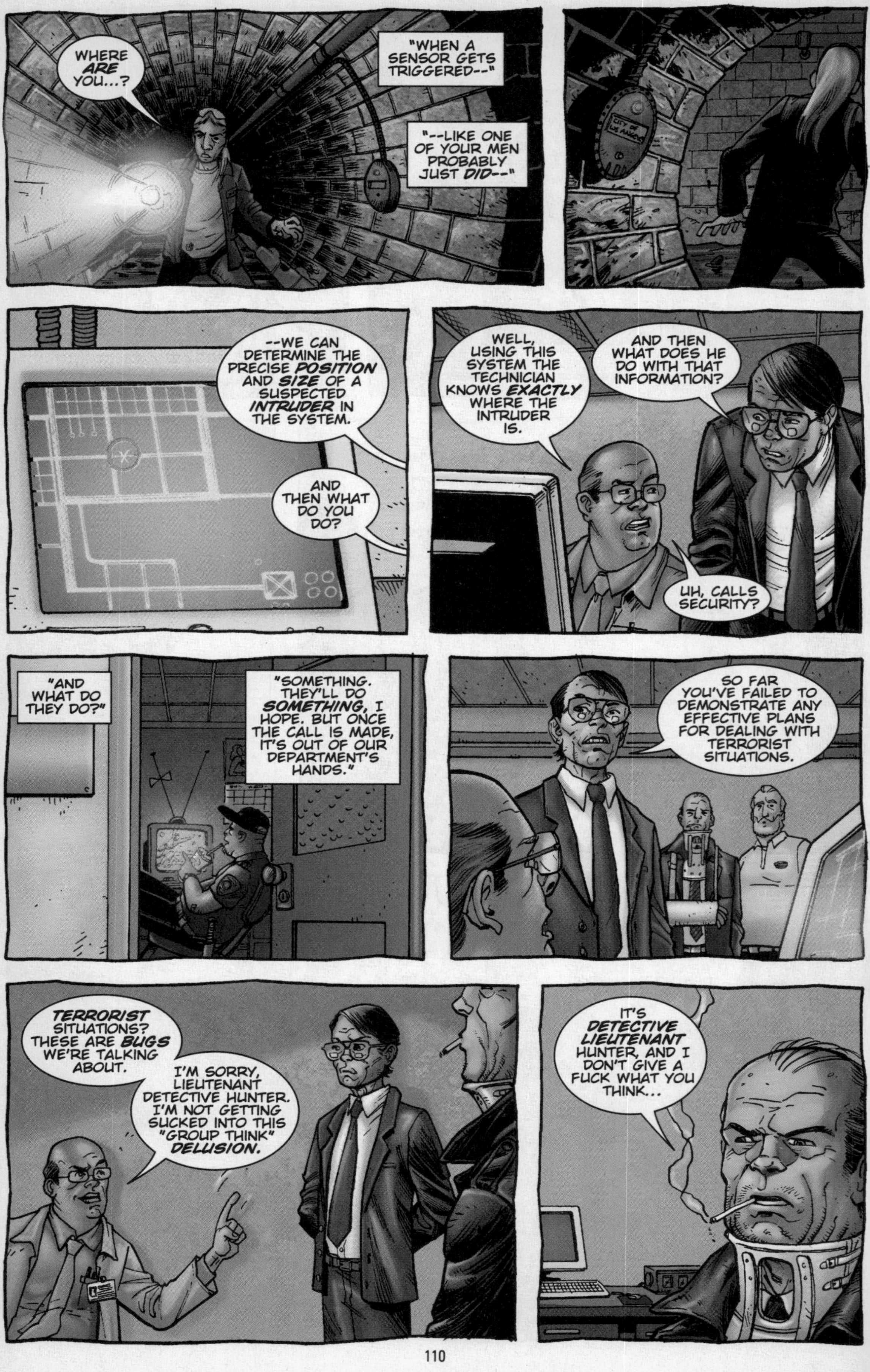
WHERE ARE YOU...?
"WHEN A SENSOR GETS TRIGGERED--"
"--LIKE ONE OF YOUR MEN PROBABLY JUST DID--"
--WE CAN DETERMINE THE PRECISE POSITION AND SIZE OF A SUSPECTED INTRUDER IN THE SYSTEM.
AND THEN WHAT DO YOU DO?
WELL, USING THIS SYSTEM THE TECHNICIAN KNOWS EXACTLY WHERE THE INTRUDER IS.
AND THEN WHAT DOES HE DO WITH THAT INFORMATION?
UH, CALLS SECURITY?
"AND WHAT DO THEY DO?"
"SOMETHING. THEY'LL DO SOMETHING, I HOPE. BUT ONCE THE CALL IS MADE, IT'S OUT OF OUR DEPARTMENT'S HANDS."
SO FAR YOU'VE FAILED TO DEMONSTRATE ANY EFFECTIVE PLANS FOR DEALING WITH TERRORIST SITUATIONS.
TERRORIST SITUATIONS? THESE ARE BUGS WE'RE TALKING ABOUT.
I'M SORRY, LIEUTENANT DETECTIVE HUNTER. I'M NOT GETTING SUCKED INTO THIS "GROUP THINK" DELUSION.
IT'S DETECTIVE LIEUTENANT HUNTER, AND I DON'T GIVE A FUCK WHAT YOU THINK...

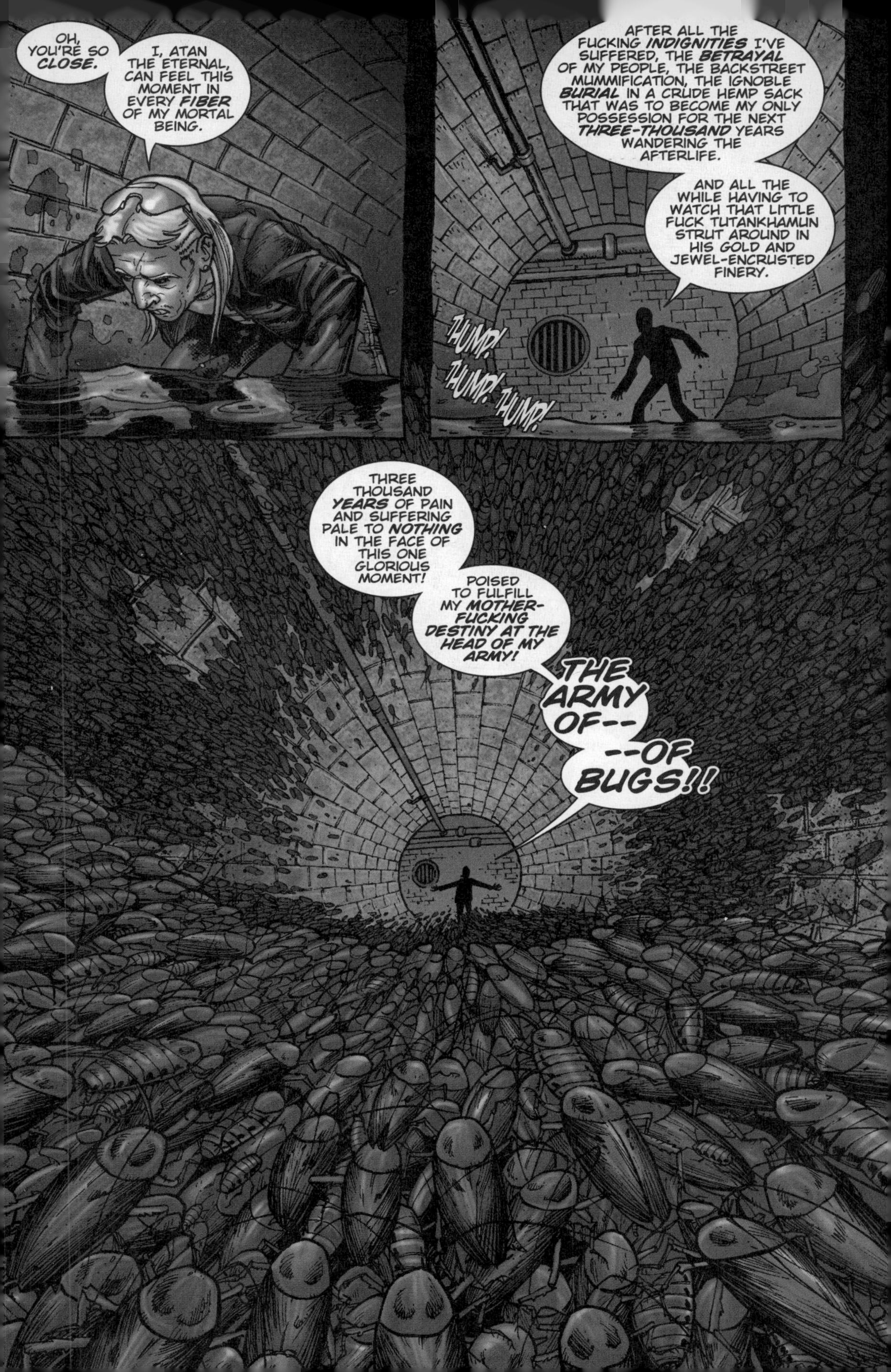
OH, YOU'RE SO CLOSE.
I, ATAN THE ETERNAL, CAN FEEL THIS MOMENT IN EVERY FIBER OF MY MORTAL BEING.
AFTER ALL THE FUCKING INDIGNITIES I'VE SUFFERED, THE BETRAYAL OF MY PEOPLE, THE BACKSTREET MUMMIFICATION, THE IGNOBLE BURIAL IN A CRUDE HEMP SACK THAT WAS TO BECOME MY ONLY POSSESSION FOR THE NEXT THREE-THOUSAND YEARS WANDERING THE AFTERLIFE.
AND ALL THE WHILE HAVING TO WATCH THAT LITTLE FUCK TUTANKHAMUN STRUT AROUND IN HIS GOLD AND JEWEL-ENCRUSTED FINERY.
THUMP! THUMP! THUMP!
THREE THOUSAND YEARS OF PAIN AND SUFFERING PALE TO NOTHING IN THE FACE OF THIS ONE GLORIOUS MOMENT!
POISED TO FULFILL MY MOTHER-FUCKING DESTINY AT THE HEAD OF MY ARMY!
THE ARMY OF--
--OF BUGS!!

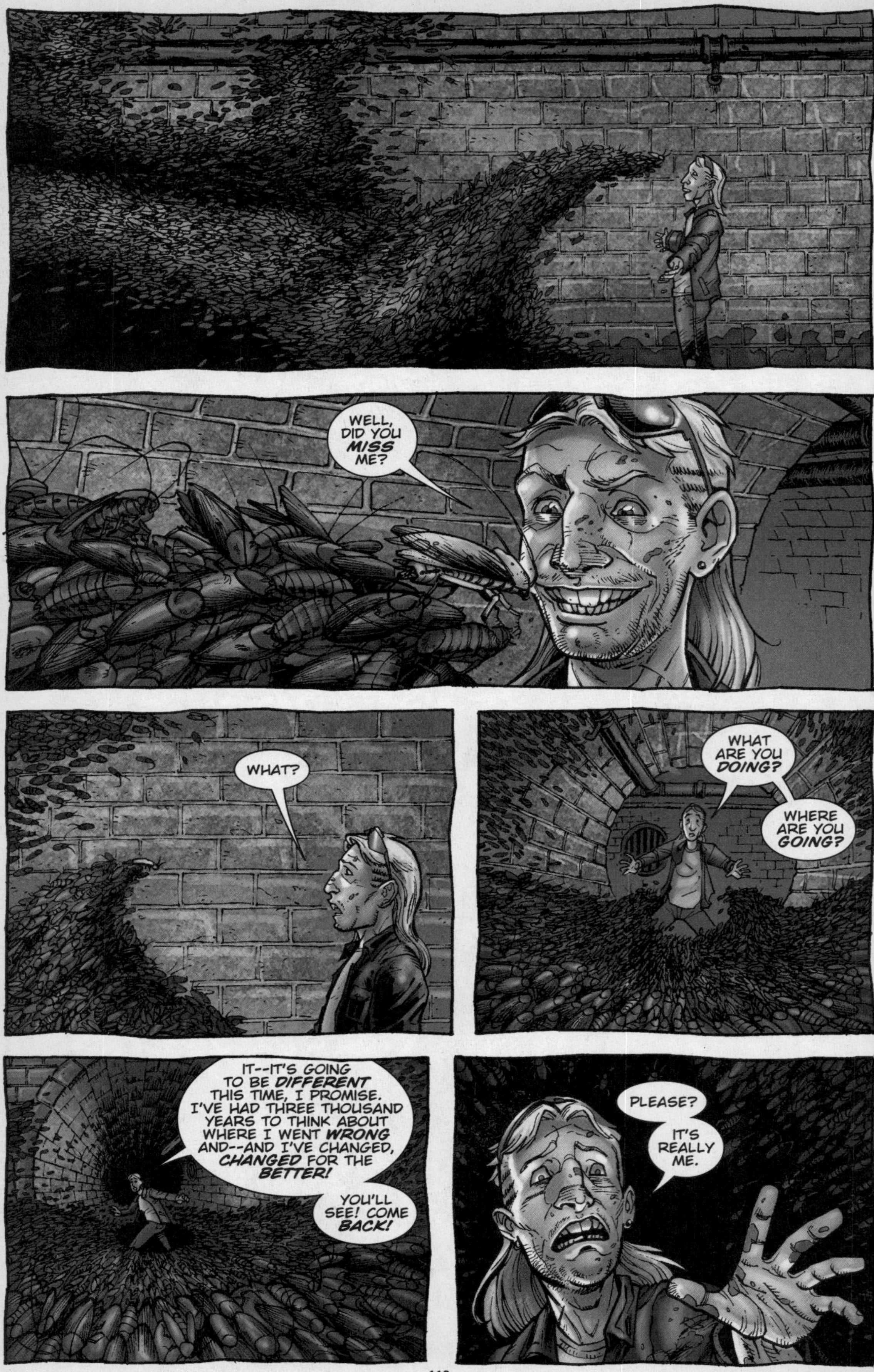
WELL, DID YOU MISS ME?
WHAT?
WHAT ARE YOU DOING?
WHERE ARE YOU GOING?
IT--IT'S GOING TO BE DIFFERENT THIS TIME, I PROMISE. I'VE HAD THREE THOUSAND YEARS TO THINK ABOUT WHERE I WENT WRONG AND--AND I'VE CHANGED, CHANGED FOR THE BETTER!
YOU'LL SEE! COME BACK!
PLEASE?
IT'S REALLY ME.

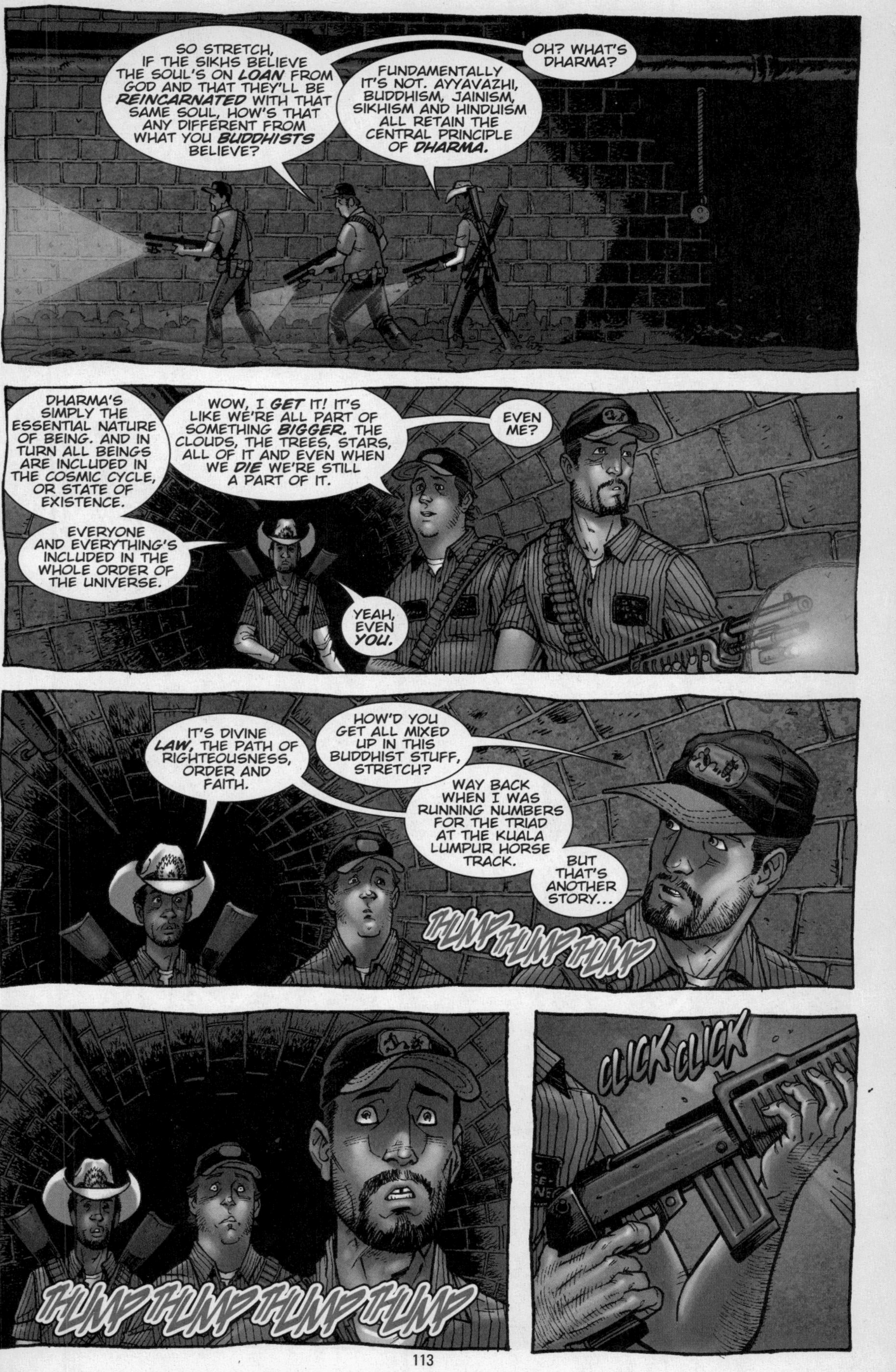
SO STRETCH, IF THE SIKHS BELIEVE THE SOUL'S ON LOAN FROM GOD AND THAT THEY'LL BE REINCARNATED WITH THAT SAME SOUL, HOW'S THAT ANY DIFFERENT FROM WHAT YOU BUDDHISTS BELIEVE?
FUNDAMENTALLY IT'S NOT. AYYAVAZHI, BUDDHISM, JAINISM, SIKHISM AND HINDUISM ALL RETAIN THE CENTRAL PRINCIPLE OF DHARMA.
OH? WHAT'S DHARMA?
DHARMA'S SIMPLY THE ESSENTIAL NATURE OF BEING. AND IN TURN ALL BEINGS ARE INCLUDED IN THE COSMIC CYCLE, OR STATE OF EXISTENCE.
EVERYONE AND EVERYTHING'S INCLUDED IN THE WHOLE ORDER OF THE UNIVERSE.
WOW, I GET IT! IT'S LIKE WE'RE ALL PART OF SOMETHING BIGGER. THE CLOUDS, THE TREES, STARS, ALL OF IT AND EVEN WHEN WE DIE WE'RE STILL A PART OF IT.
EVEN ME?
YEAH, EVEN YOU.
IT'S DIVINE LAW, THE PATH OF RIGHTEOUSNESS, ORDER AND FAITH.
HOW'D YOU GET ALL MIXED UP IN THIS BUDDHIST STUFF, STRETCH?
WAY BACK WHEN I WAS RUNNING NUMBERS FOR THE TRIAD AT THE KUALA LUMPUR HORSE TRACK.
BUT THAT'S ANOTHER STORY...
THUMP THUMP THUMP
THUMP THUMP THUMP THUMP
CLICK CLICK

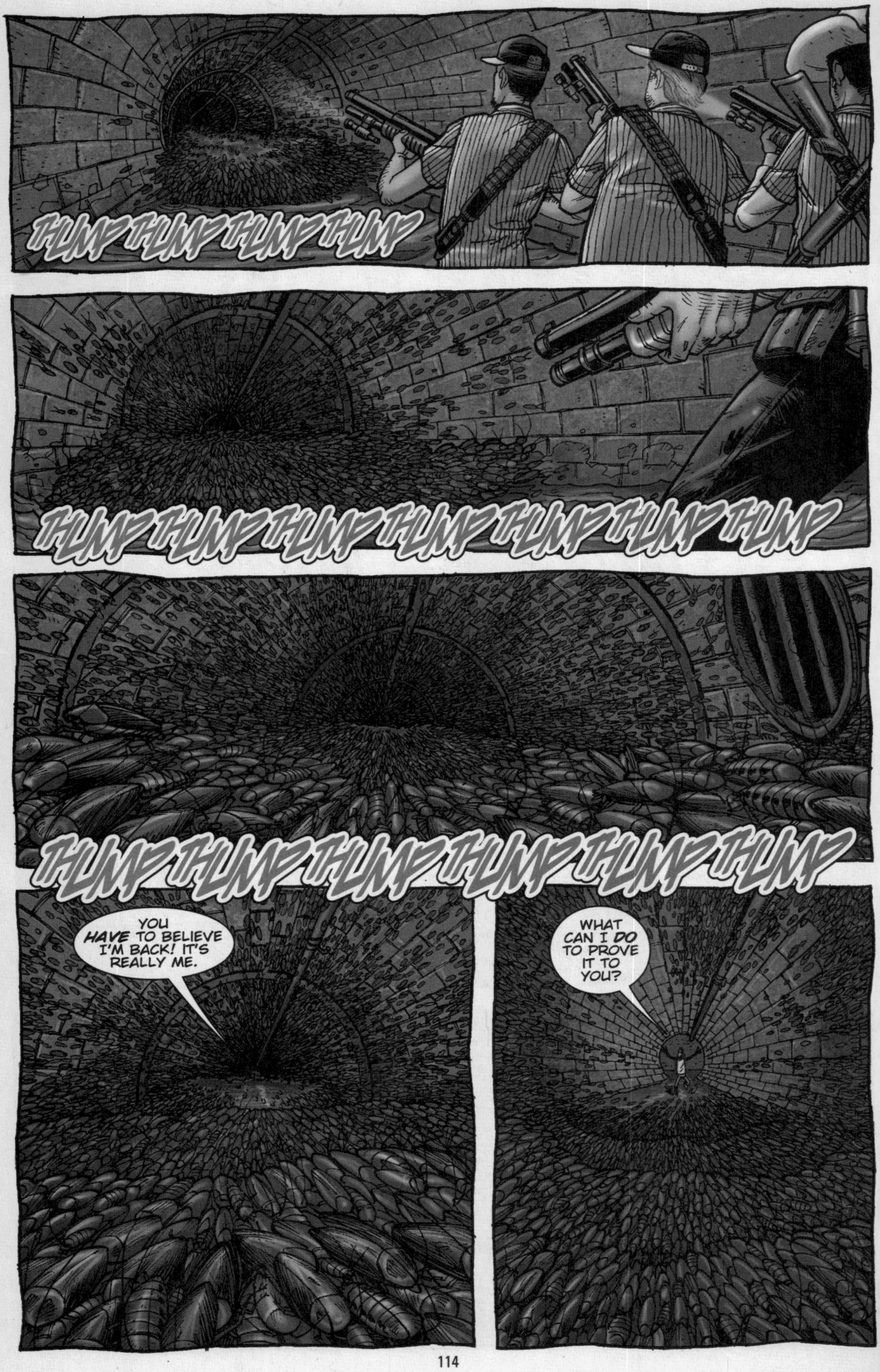
THUMP THUMP THUMP THUMP
THUMP THUMP THUMP THUMP THUMP THUMP THUMP
THUMP THUMP THUMP THUMP THUMP THUMP THUMP
YOU HAVE TO BELIEVE I'M BACK! IT'S REALLY ME.
WHAT CAN I DO TO PROVE IT TO YOU?

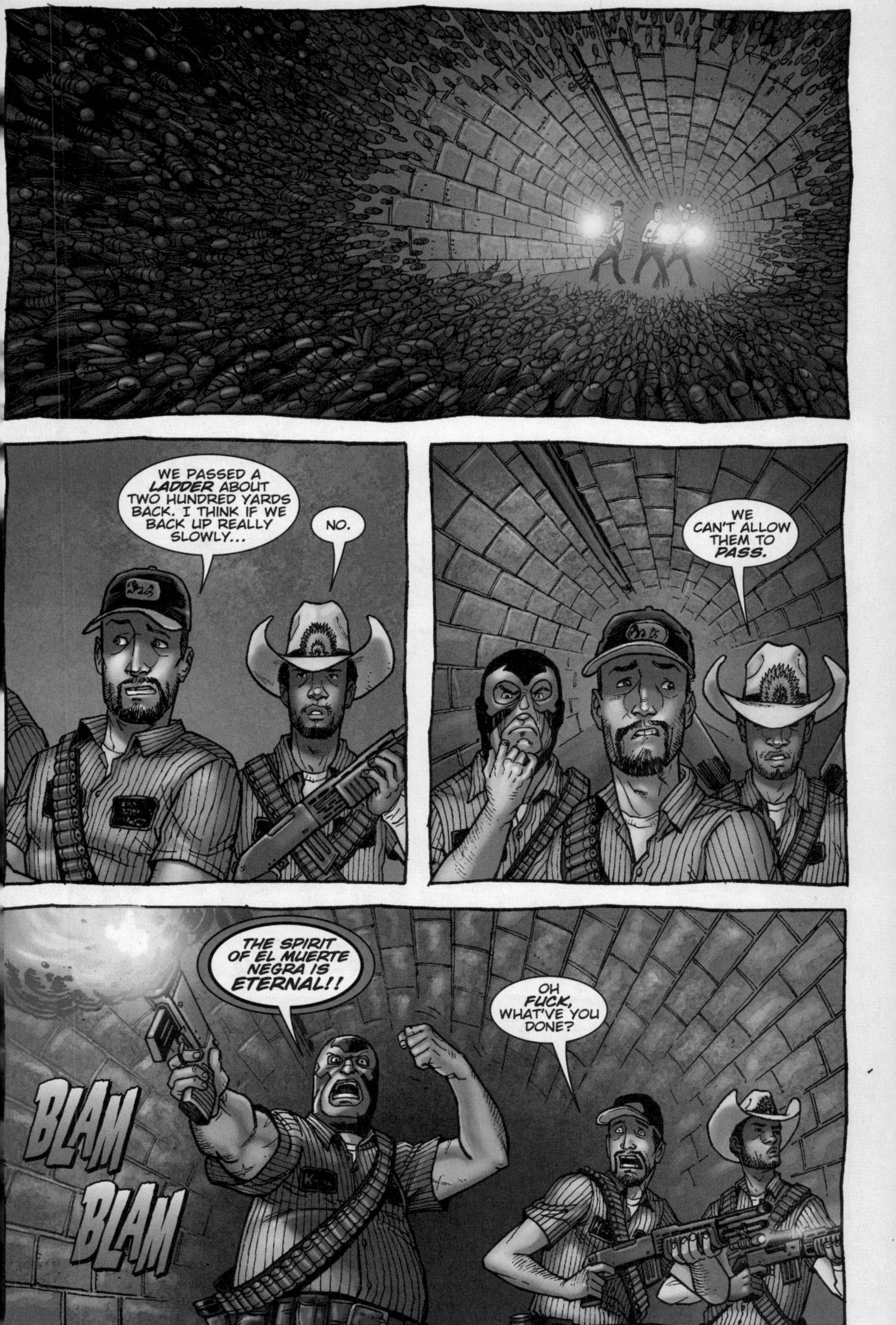
WE PASSED A LADDER ABOUT TWO HUNDRED YARDS BACK. I THINK IF WE BACK UP REALLY SLOWLY...
NO.
WE CAN'T ALLOW THEM TO PASS.
THE SPIRIT OF EL MUERTE NEGRA IS ETERNAL!!
OH FUCK, WHAT'VE YOU DONE?
BLAM
BLAM

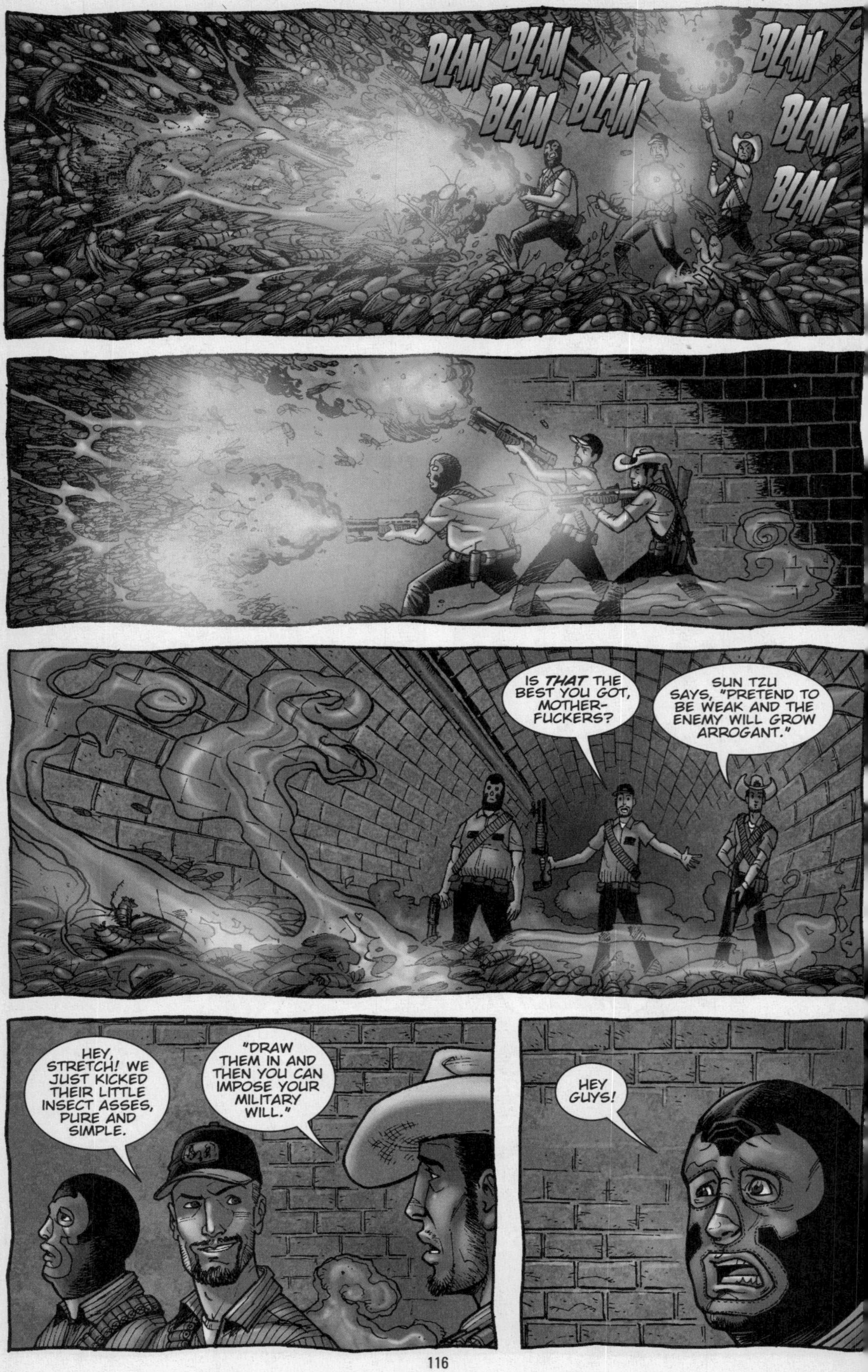
BLAM BLAM BLAM BLAM BLAM BLAM BLAM BLAM
IS THAT THE BEST YOU GOT, MOTHER-FUCKERS?
SUN TZU SAYS, "PRETEND TO BE WEAK AND THE ENEMY WILL GROW ARROGANT."
HEY, STRETCH! WE JUST KICKED THEIR LITTLE INSECT ASSES, PURE AND SIMPLE.
"DRAW THEM IN AND THEN YOU CAN IMPOSE YOUR MILITARY WILL."
HEY GUYS!

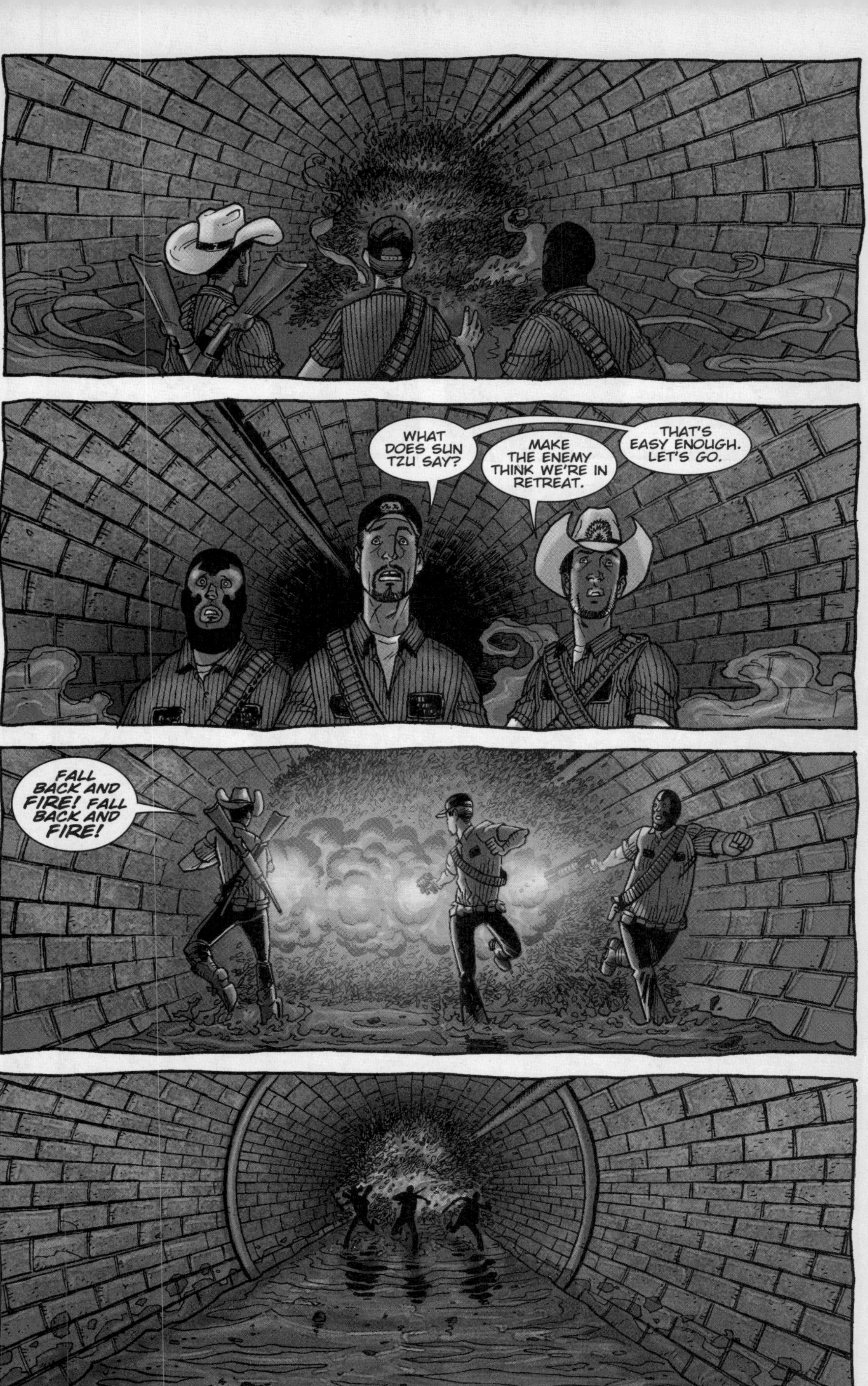
WHAT DOES SUN TZU SAY?
MAKE THE ENEMY THINK WE'RE IN RETREAT.
THAT'S EASY ENOUGH. LET'S GO.
FALL BACK AND FIRE! FALL BACK AND FIRE!

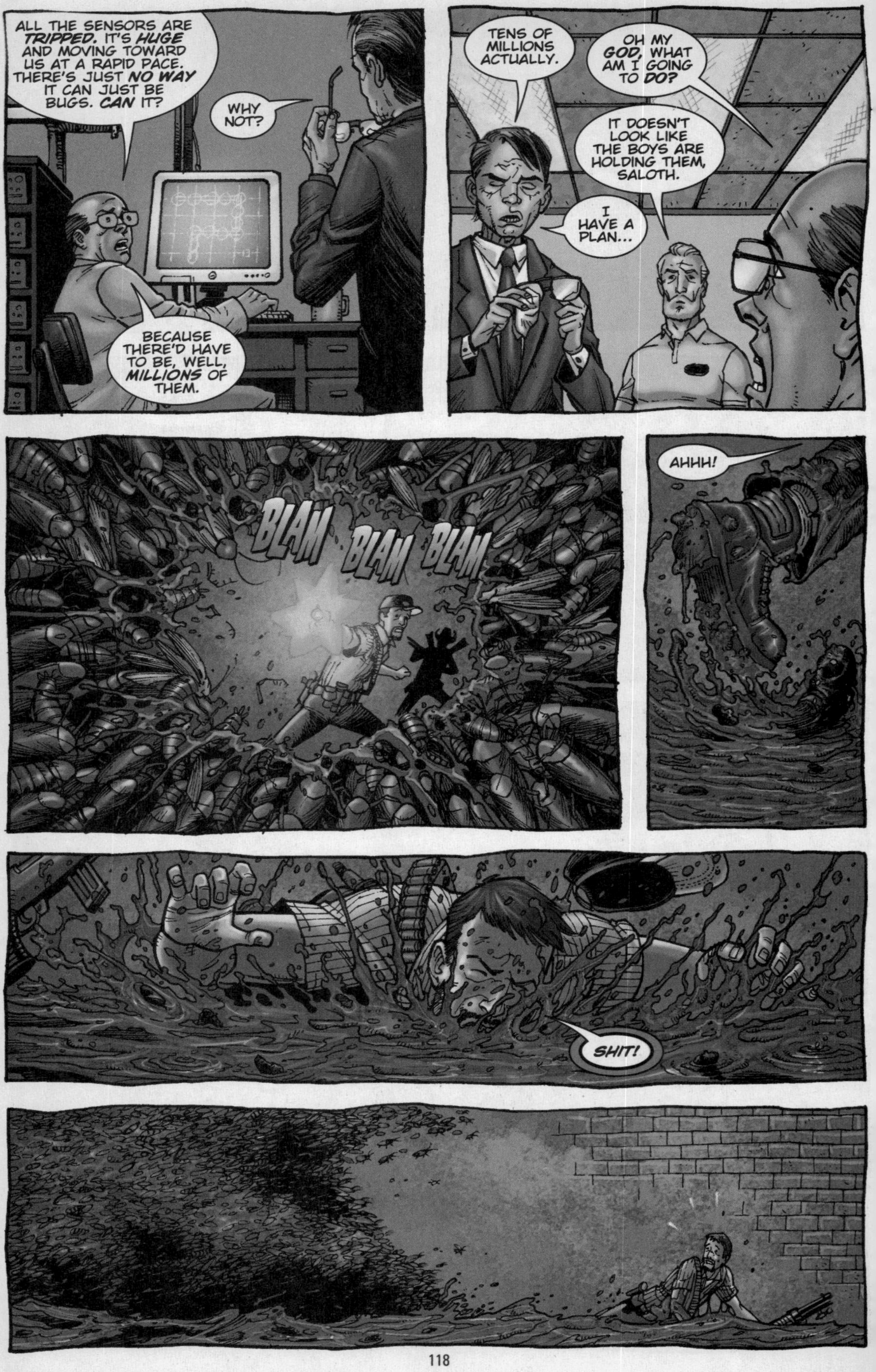
ALL THE SENSORS ARE TRIPPED. IT'S HUGE AND MOVING TOWARD US AT A RAPID PACE. THERE'S JUST NO WAY IT CAN JUST BE BUGS. CAN IT?
WHY NOT?
BECAUSE THERE'D HAVE TO BE, WELL, MILLIONS OF THEM.
TENS OF MILLIONS ACTUALLY.
OH MY GOD, WHAT AM I GOING TO DO?
IT DOESN'T LOOK LIKE THE BOYS ARE HOLDING THEM, SALOTH.
I HAVE A PLAN...
BLAM BLAM BLAM
AHHH!
SHIT!

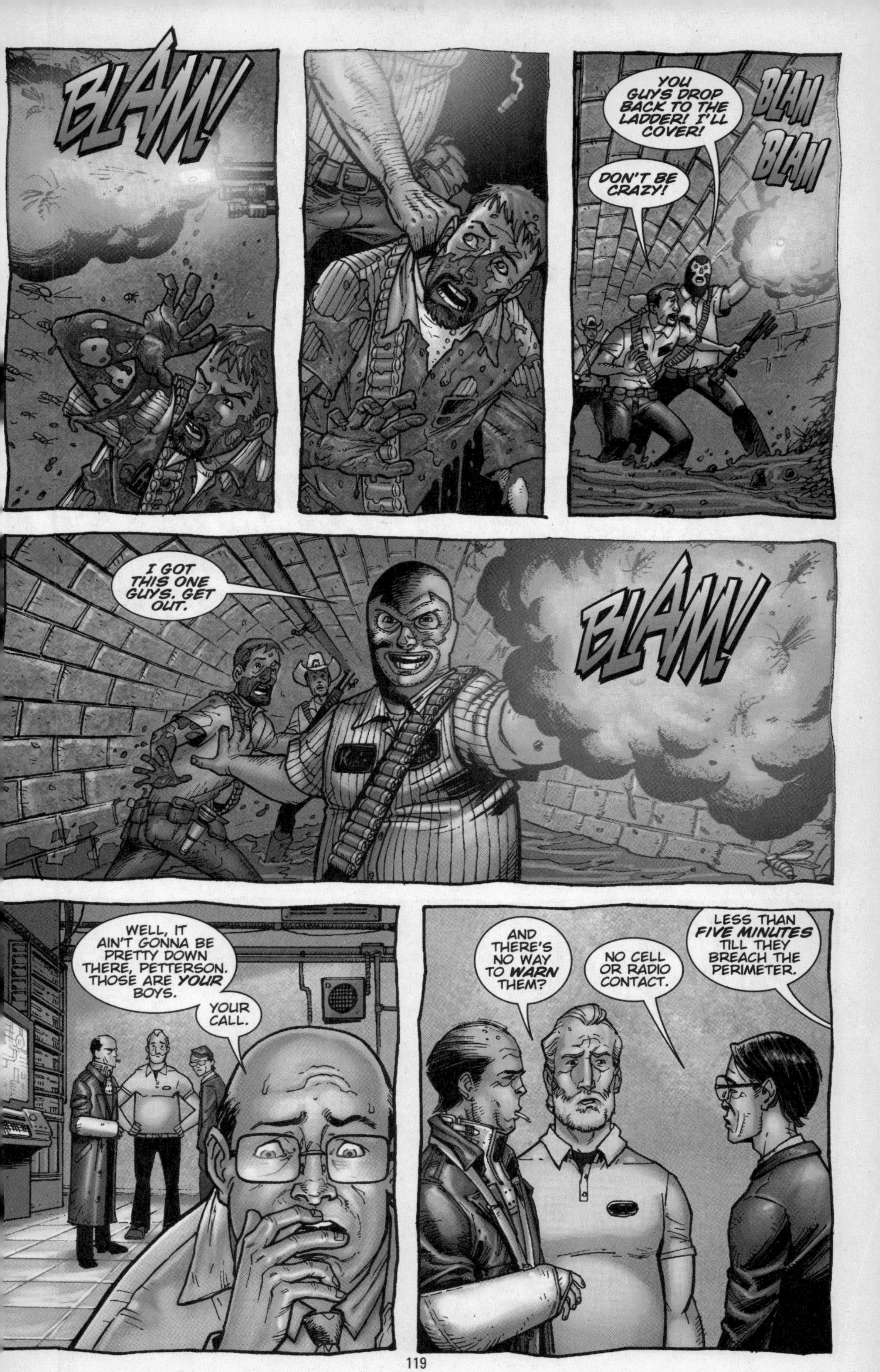
BLAM!
YOU GUYS DROP BACK TO THE LADDER! I'LL COVER!
BLAM BLAM
DON'T BE CRAZY!
I GOT THIS ONE GUYS. GET OUT.
BLAM!
WELL, IT AIN'T GONNA BE PRETTY DOWN THERE, PETTERSON. THOSE ARE *YOUR* BOYS.
YOUR CALL.
AND THERE'S NO WAY TO *WARN* THEM?
NO CELL OR RADIO CONTACT.
LESS THAN *FIVE MINUTES* TILL THEY BREACH THE PERIMETER.

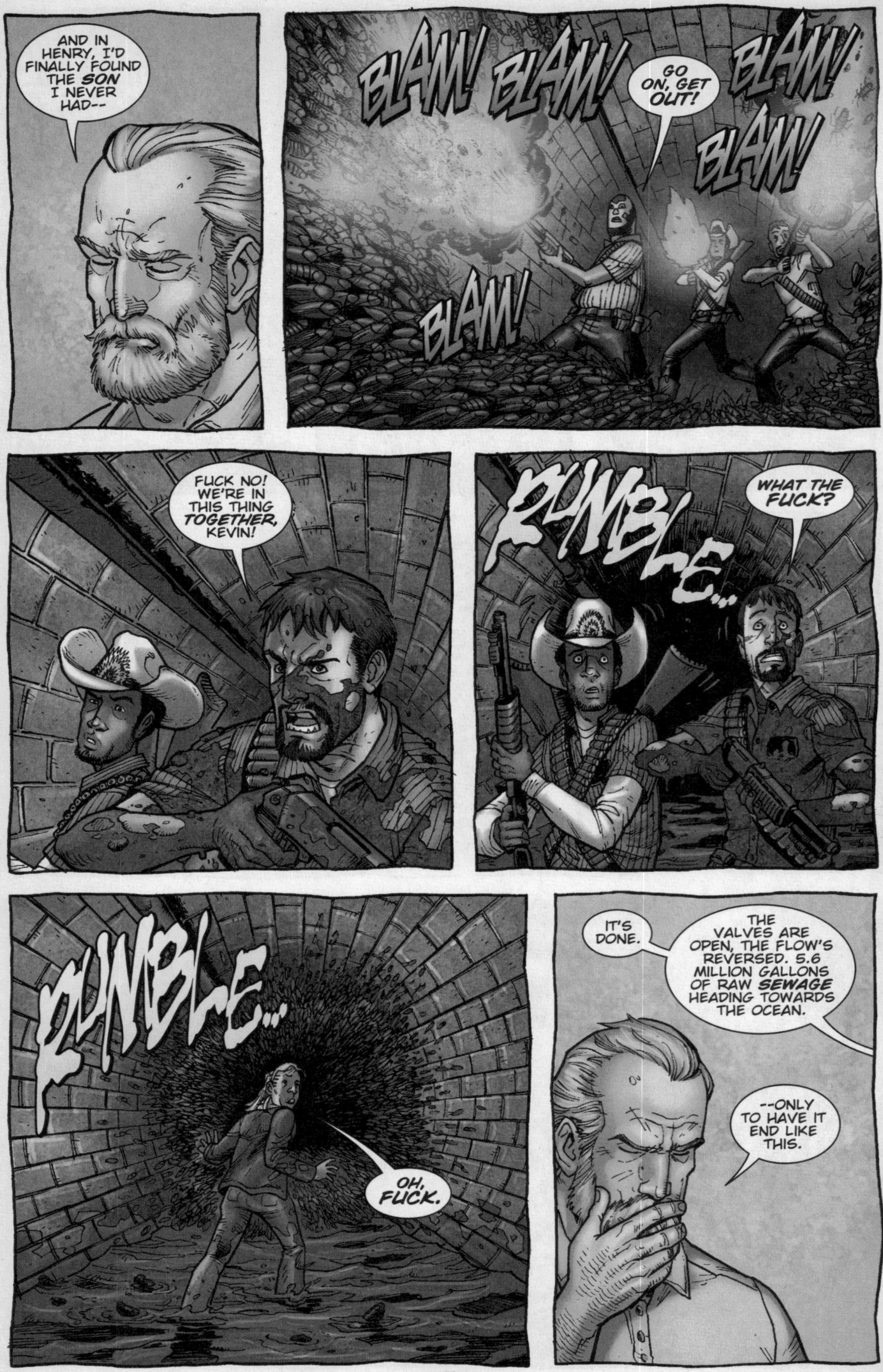

AND IN HENRY, I'D FINALLY FOUND THE SON I NEVER HAD--
BLAM! BLAM!
GO ON, GET OUT!
BLAM! BLAM!
BLAM!
FUCK NO! WE'RE IN THIS THING TOGETHER, KEVIN!
RUMBLE...
WHAT THE FUCK?
RUMBLE...
OH, FUCK.
IT'S DONE.
THE VALVES ARE OPEN, THE FLOW'S REVERSED. 5.6 MILLION GALLONS OF RAW SEWAGE HEADING TOWARDS THE OCEAN.
--ONLY TO HAVE IT END LIKE THIS.

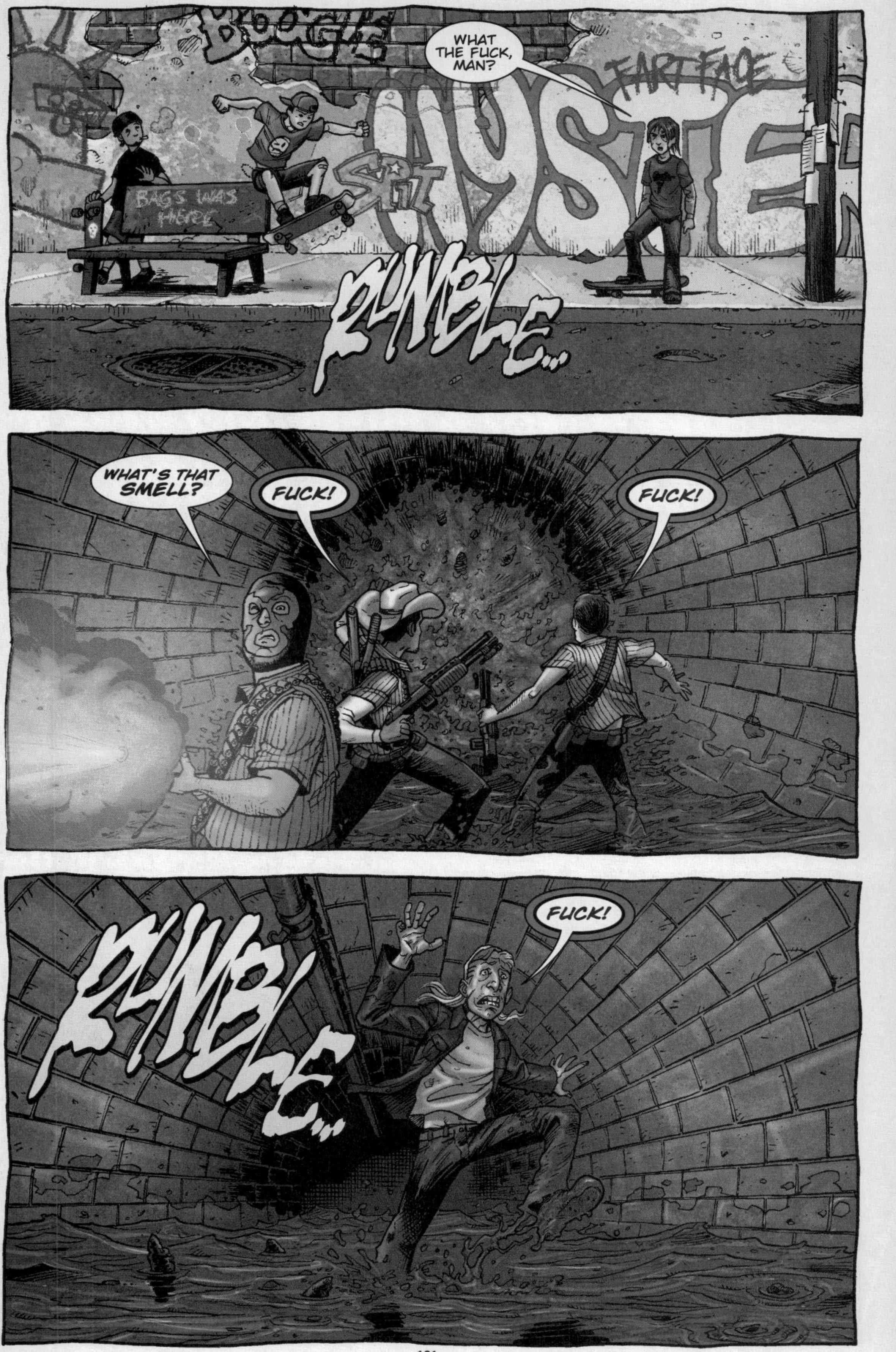
FART FACE
BAGS WAS HERE
WHAT THE FUCK, MAN?
RUMBLE...
WHAT'S THAT SMELL?
FUCK!
FUCK!
RUMBLE...
FUCK!

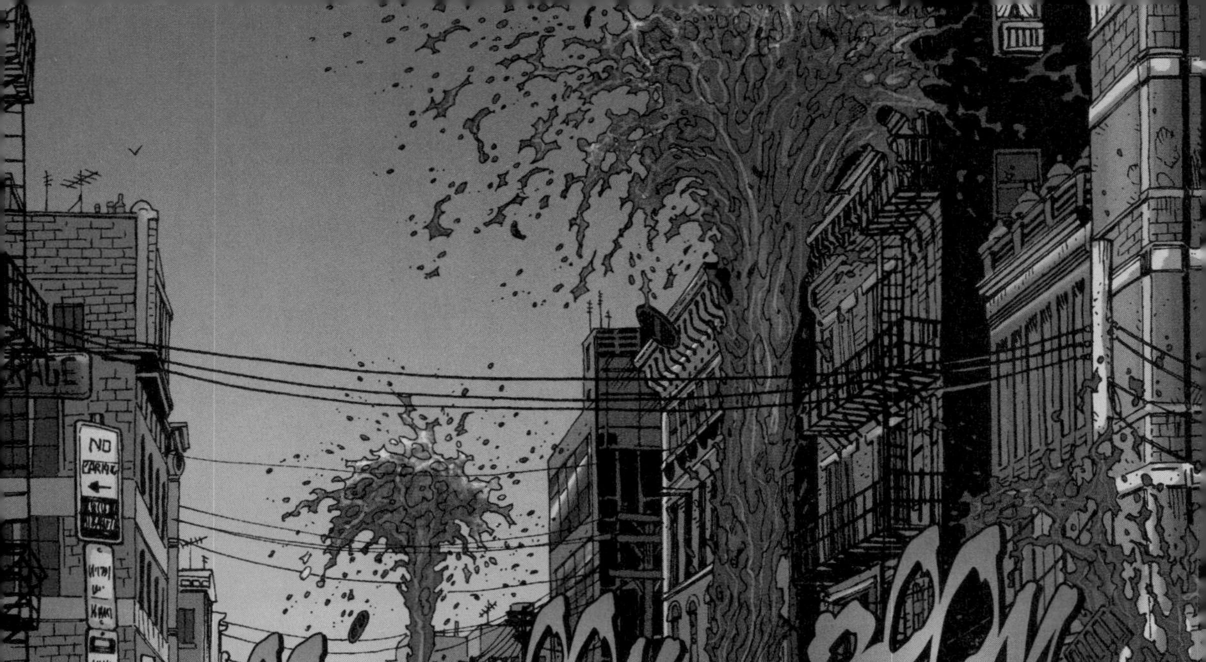
BOOM
BOOM
BOOM
NO PARKING
I ♥ L.A.
FRAGNT

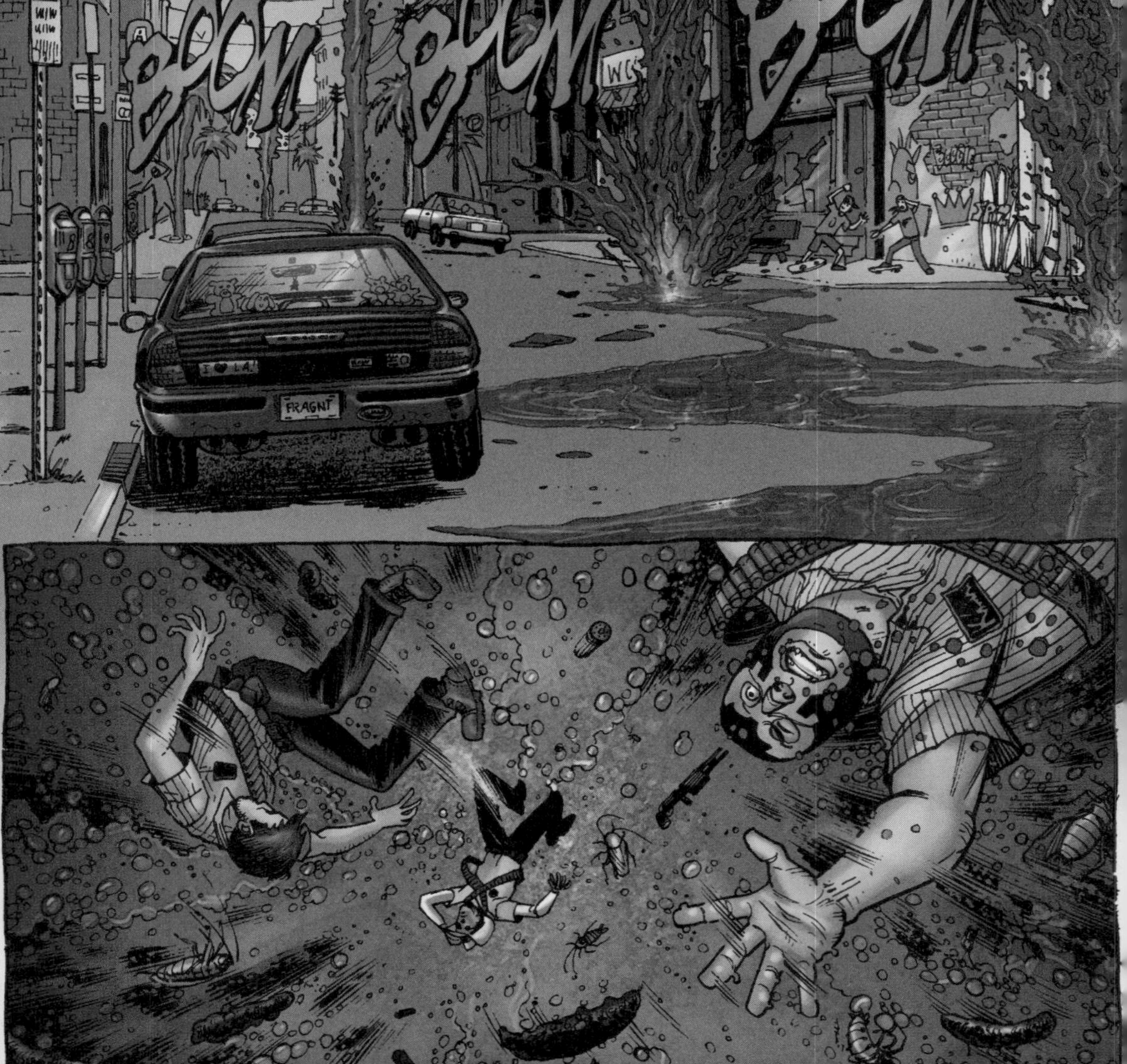

GOT TO GET *AIR*...

GOT TO FIND THE *SURFACE*...

WHICH WAY? IT'S A TOSS OF THE COIN.

BUT UP ISN'T *UP*, IT'S *DOWN*.

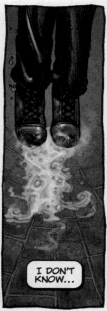

I DON'T KNOW...

...IF I CAN *MAKE* IT.

AND...?

ANYTHING THAT WAS IN THAT SEWER TUNNEL, WELL, IT'S FAST ON *IT'S* WAY TO A FULL *FLUSH* OUT TO SEA.

WELL, JOB'S *DONE.* I'LL ARRANGE YOUR PAYMENT FROM THE SLUSH FUND. AND HENRY'S FILE, WELL, I GUESS *THAT'S* A MOOT POINT.

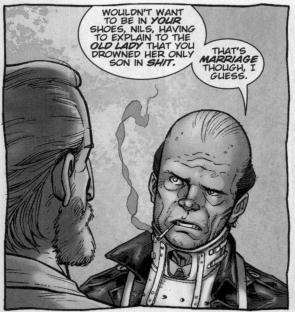

WOULDN'T WANT TO BE IN *YOUR* SHOES, NILS, HAVING TO EXPLAIN TO THE *OLD LADY* THAT YOU DROWNED HER ONLY SON IN *SHIT.*

THAT'S *MARRIAGE* THOUGH, I GUESS.

YOU MADE THE RIGHT DECISION, NILS. IT WAS FOR THE GREATER GOOD.

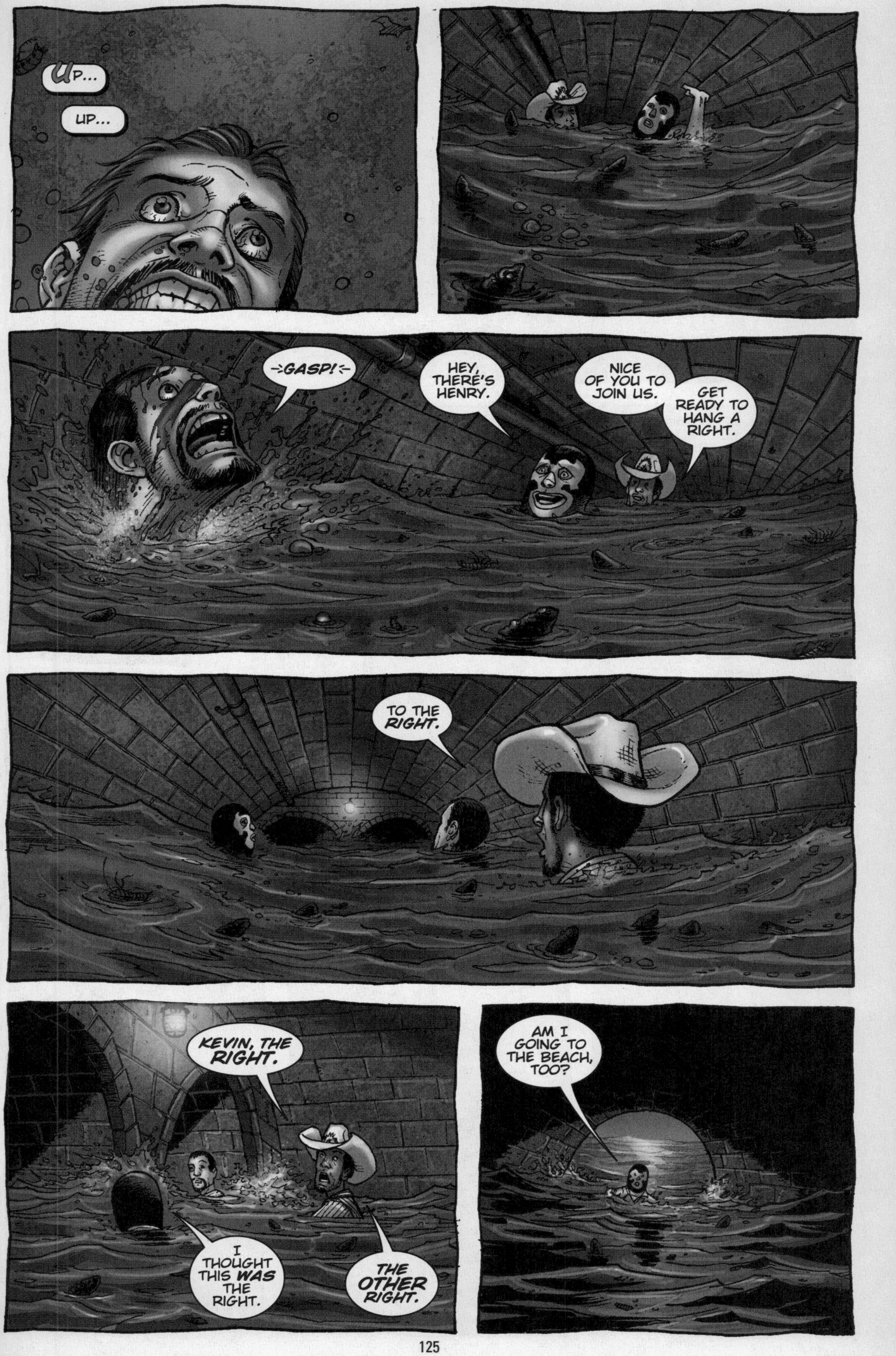
UP...
UP...
-GASP!-
HEY, THERE'S HENRY.
NICE OF YOU TO JOIN US.
GET READY TO HANG A RIGHT.
TO THE RIGHT.
KEVIN, THE RIGHT.
I THOUGHT THIS WAS THE RIGHT.
THE OTHER RIGHT.
AM I GOING TO THE BEACH, TOO?

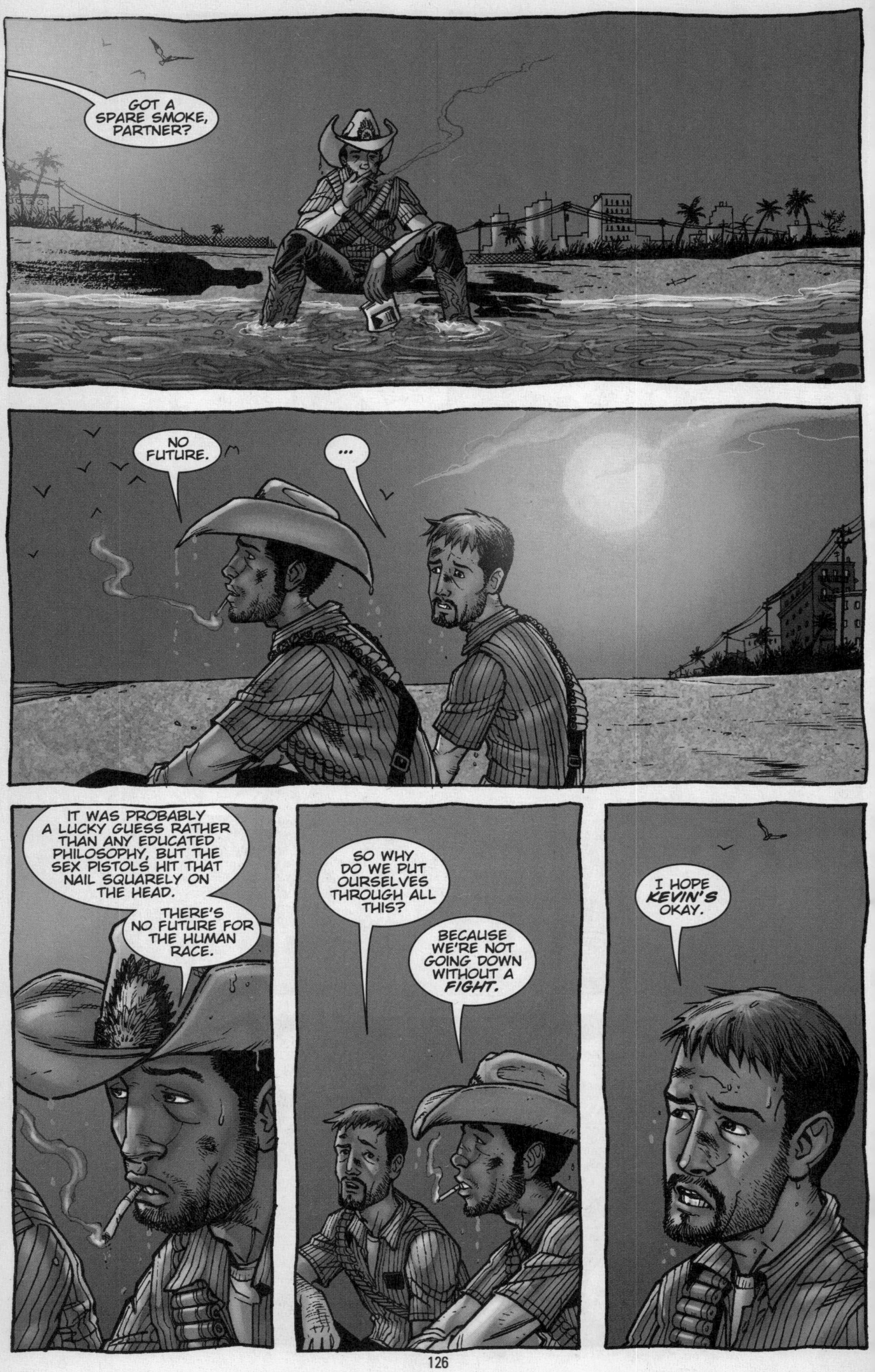
GOT A SPARE SMOKE, PARTNER?
NO FUTURE.
...
IT WAS PROBABLY A LUCKY GUESS RATHER THAN ANY EDUCATED PHILOSOPHY, BUT THE SEX PISTOLS HIT THAT NAIL SQUARELY ON THE HEAD.
THERE'S NO FUTURE FOR THE HUMAN RACE.
SO WHY DO WE PUT OURSELVES THROUGH ALL THIS?
BECAUSE WE'RE NOT GOING DOWN WITHOUT A *FIGHT.*
I HOPE *KEVIN'S* OKAY.

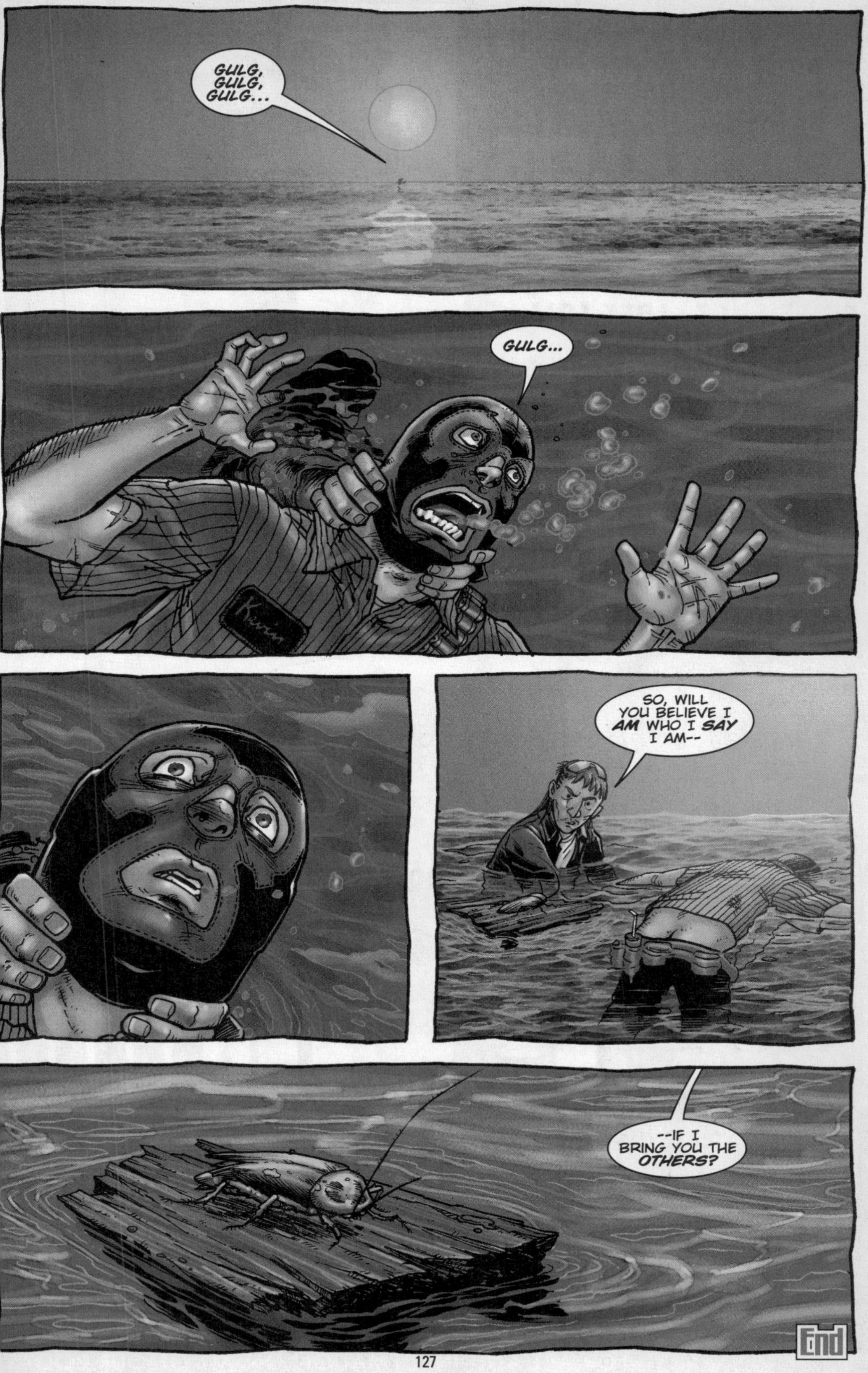
GULG, GULG, GULG...
GULG...
SO, WILL YOU BELIEVE I AM WHO I SAY I AM--
--IF I BRING YOU THE OTHERS?
End

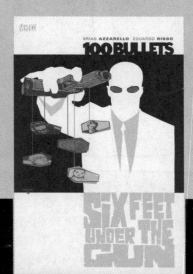